Pasolini, Chaucer and Boccaccio

Pasolini, Chaucer and Boccaccio

*Two Medieval Texts and
Their Translation to Film*

AGNÈS BLANDEAU

McFarland & Company, Inc., Publishers
Jefferson, North Carolina, and London

LIBRARY OF CONGRESS CATALOGUING-IN-PUBLICATION DATA

Blandeau, Agnès, 1966–
    Pasolini, Chaucer and Boccaccio : two medieval texts and their translation to film / Agnès Blandeau.
    p.   cm.
    Includes bibliographical references and index.

    ISBN-13: 978-0-7864-2247-0
    softcover : 50# alkaline paper ∞

    1. Pasolini, Pier Paolo, 1922–1975 — Criticism and interpretation. 2. Decameron (Motion picture)   3. Racconti di Canterbury (Motion picture)   4. Chaucer, Geoffrey, d. 1400. Canterbury tales. 5. Boccaccio, Giovanni, 1313–1375. Decamerone.   I. Title.
PN1998.3.P367B53 2006
791.43'75–dc22   2006009591

British Library cataloguing data are available

©2006 Agnès Blandeau. All rights reserved

No part of this book may be reproduced or transmitted in any form or by any means, electronic or mechanical, including photocopying or recording, or by any information storage and retrieval system, without permission in writing from the publisher.

Cover photograph ©2006 Photodisc

Manufactured in the United States of America

McFarland & Company, Inc., Publishers
  Box 611, Jefferson, North Carolina 28640
    www.mcfarlandpub.com

To Jean-Luc, Marie, and Anna

Table of Contents

Preface   1
Introduction   5

I. THE FILM: AN ALTERNATIVE FORM OF TELLING, ANOTHER TEXTUAL ARCHITECTURE, AND DIFFERENT MEANINGS

1. *I Racconti di Canterbury*: The Film Text of *The Canterbury Tales*   11
2. Placing *I Racconti di Canterbury* in Perspective with *The Decameron*   49
3. *Il Fiore delle mille e una notte:* The Last Panel of the Triptych   86

II. THE ADAPTATION: A CLOSE ENCOUNTER OF THE THIRD KIND

4. The Shock of Pasolini's Trilogy   89
5. A Trans-semiotization: The Subversive Intention in *I Racconti di Canterbury*   97
6. Eloquent Pictures   111
7. A Defense of Adaptation   140

Conclusion   155
Appendix 1: Chart Showing Narrative Structure of I Racconti di Canterbury *in Text and Film*   165

Appendix 2: Chart Showing Narrative Structure of
    The Decameron *in Text and Film*   167

Appendix 3: Chart Showing Echoes and Correspondences
    Between I Racconti di Canterbury *and* The Decameron   170

Notes   175
Bibliography   191
Index   205

Preface

Chaucer's *Canterbury Tales* introduced major innovations in late medieval narrative poetry. This loose, eclectic composition embracing all genres and styles actually signals the act of telling. As the implied author and narrator of what is said and done during the pilgrims' physical and verbal peregrinations, Chaucer brings to the fore his hesitations and doubts as a poet laboring at a work in progress. He does so by drawing our attention to creation and the subtle working of a heterogenuous form of writing. The author's poetics bespeak an acute awareness of the literariness of the text.

The disconcerting multiplicity of the voices and semantic directions taken by the astutely self-reflexive *Canterbury Tales* distinguishes them from Boccaccio's *Decameron,* a harmoniously designed, textual construction consisting of one hundred stories contained within a solidly and clearly delineated frame. Nevertheless, some common denominators at the structural and thematic levels justify an approach that places *The Tales* in perspective with the *Centovelle*. This is exactly what Italian filmmaker and poet Pier Paolo Pasolini does six centuries later in the early 1970s. In a totally different cultural and intellectual context, through the mediation of cinema, two masterpieces of 14th century literature inspire a certain reflection of themselves in images, some kind of refraction as in a dream. Our study focuses on the first two panels of the *Trilogy of Life,* Pasolini's famous and controversial cinematic triptych, composed of *Il Decameron* (1971), *I Racconti di Canterbury* (1972), and *Il Fiore delle mille e una notte* (1974), to which we will devote but a few pages.

In Part I, I attempt to show that, through the prism of a different semiotic system, the film reading of *The Canterbury Tales* can create a new aesthetic being of its own. Still, the screening of Chaucer's eight tales cannot be fully appreciated if not considered in its close relation to that of *The Decameron* one year earlier. Similar attention will be paid to the narrative metaporphoses entailed by the trans-semiotization of Boccaccio's work into film. The first part closes with brief scrutiny of *Il Fiore* that confirms Pasolini's aesthetic and ideological intentions. The exhibition of bodies and especially genitals expresses the desire to oppose to the normative discourse a marginal counter-discourse, as far as narration, sexuality or painting are concerned.

Part II, titled after a 1977 film by Steven Spielberg, attempts to highlight the distinctiveness of two original "imag(e)inings" of the literary sources, which turn out to be everything but film adaptations strictly speaking. I do not seek to establish a comparison between text and film, as it is too often done with a view to bringing into light the shortcomings of the cinematic version, inevitably reproached with altering and even betraying the original, which Chaucer sholars view as the reference. Pasolini's mutants, characterized by a defamiliarizing degree of poetic expressiveness, somewhat baffle the spectator, however familiar with Chaucer and Boccaccio.

What with their undeniable bawdiness, both movies were branded as obscene and pornographic when released, and consequently suffered the blow of censorship. Nonetheless, a close look at the treatment of characters and the scarce use of dialogues, that sets off the strange "imageity" of the film shot strongly contaminated by painting, will reveal that Pasolini's *Canterbury Tales* and *Decameron* constitute extraordinarily innovative works of art, existing independently from their sources. Besides, they can be delightfully subversive and unexpectedly creative at the same time.

My defense of what I call a visualization, rather than a mere vision of *The Canterbury Tales*— upon which we focus given our special interest in Chaucer's text — has no other ambition than to demonstrate that, though polemical and phantasmatic, this cinematic re-writing opens the way to a new possibility of interpretation of the text. Even a specialist in English medieval literature is likely to take it into account as a (re)creative re-creation, existing beside the authoritative text.

Precisely because it is a highly personal, visual perception of the *Tales*, *I Racconti di Canterbury*, freely inspired by them, sheds new light on one of the most widely studied literary works, whose meanings are sometimes blurred by the multifarious readings that tend to hinder its reception. Surprisingly, although the Italian film author fails to offer a proper medievalist's look on his sources, he succeeds through the filter of his artist's gaze in visually restoring a certain Middle Ages, endowed with a strikingly poetic radiance. Perhaps it is this absence of a learned approach to the texts that saves their cinematic renderings from the weighty rigidity of academic film adaptation.

The reason I have chosen to devote a whole book to a work so disparaged by so many Chaucerians was the desire to rehabilitate Pasolini's *I Racconti* in particular, for it has so often been looked down upon as the most imperfect episode of the *Trilogy of Life*. The year 2005 was the thirtieth anniversary of the death of Pasolini, a filmmaker who not only gave a larger audience access to a literary masterpiece through the universal language of cinema — "the written language of reality," as he described it — but also used his source to project a specific vision of artistic creation in a cleverly meta-cinematic work, just as Chaucer's composition is actually about poetic writing. The distorting distance, like a phantasm between *The Canterbury Tales* and their modern "translatio" (in the medieval sense of rendering, passing on to, and betraying), allows Pasolini to give shape to an aesthetic "form" as such, a form that both subverts and celebrates the original. Interested in Chaucer's text as much as in cinema, I could not resist the temptation to draw attention to an alternative reading of the *Tales*.

Introduction

At the end of the 14th century, *The Canterbury Tales* definitely broke new ground in the realm of medieval narrative poetry. This huge poem makes the act of telling the very subject of fiction by means of the frame story technique, which provides the author with the appropriate device for staging narration. The Parson's stern didactic sermon that closes the series of tales actually highlights by contrast the bewildering stylistic variety of the 23 preceding stories. Basically oral and borrowing from the conversational mode, telling in *The Canterbury Tales* is intimately linked to a poetics of the work in progress. The reader is invited both to react and to cooperate in the writing process. The implied author, who is also the witness relating the events on the way to Canterbury, brings into light his hesitations and doubts as a poet grappling with his material. The text indirectly points to a new concern with authorship. What matters most is not so much the topic of the poem as the act of creating and the effects produced on the readers/audience. The latter are also faced with the stunning diversity of styles and strategies to represent reality. In other words, Chaucer's writing indicates an unusual awareness of the literariness of the text.

Yet, this vast composition bringing together all sorts of genres seems to lack some kind of principle of hierarchical arrangement. At first, the reader may feel that there is no real immutable unity to the work like, for instance the preestablished order devised in the *cornice* at the beginning of *Il Decameron*.[1] Chaucer seems to be going through a miscellany of poetic genres, altered into various forms, distorted or subverted. It is as if he were aiming at giving the impression that it is a random juxtaposition of modes of writing, intended to render the multifariousness and unpredictability of human experiences and the countless fashions of putting them into words. Its puzzling polyphony adds to the interest of such an astutely self-reflexive text. Consequently, it raises the question of the reception of the work. Failing to lie upon a perfect mathematical textual structure, *The Canterbury Tales* still share some common points with the *Centovelle*[2] at the formal, stylistic and thematic levels. This justifies a parallel with *Il Decameron*, a look at the English poem through the filter of the Italian work that Chaucer knew. Boccaccio's text rests upon a poetics of narration, which attains various degrees of complexity, as shown in the astounding yet rigid mise en abyme of the narrative. The author's frequent extradiegetic voice breaks particularly into the *cornice*,[3] betraying his intention to underline a form of writing that claims its emancipation from tradition. In this regard, we can legitimately liken the novelty introduced by *Il Decameron* to that brought and experienced even further by *The Canterbury Tales*.

Six centuries later in a totally different cultural and intellectual situation, the medieval text inspires a certain reflection of itself—though distorted as in a dream—by means of another artistic medium. Specialists in literature have recently developed a growing interest in film adaptations of literary works. This can be accounted for by the fact that both literature and cinema tell stories, and deal with the art of narration. A film is conceived as a "large unit" that relates a story. So cinema appears as the most adequate mode of reception of literature. In addition, this particular medium sheds new light on essential literary notions such as enunciation, point of view, and authorship. Examining film semiotics cannot but enrich and renew the expert reader's approach of a work, the words of which are translated into images—embodied so as to come to life on the screen. What I am pointing at is the "corporeality" that Pasolini successfully instills into Chaucer's descriptions and portraits. The filmmaker's visualization of *The Canterbury Tales* deserves scrutiny inasmuch as his is a "cinema of poetry," resulting from an extraordinarily rich, stimulating and marginal vision. Therefore, the Italian poet and film auteur's artistic sensitivity gives shape to an innovative version of his source. In the early 1970s *The Decameron*, followed by *I Racconti di Canterbury* one year later, came as a real aesthetic shock for an audience unexpectedly faced with the oddness of two cinematographic meteors. Not only was this kind of cinema somewhat unconventional at the time, it was also the result of a very personal semiotic transmutation of a text. A mutant: this would be the adequate term to describe Pasolini's film practice (and theory). What he achieves in *The Decameron* and *I Racconti di Canterbury* is an extremely unexpected yet inventive vision of Boccaccio's and Chaucer's works. In fact, instead of a film adaptation in the strict sense of the word, we are faced with an original visual figuration of the texts, bearing the personal mark of an author keen to explore the limits of representation. This is why the *Trilogy of Life* is articulated on a poetics (and politics) of the contamination of discourse by non-narrative intrusions, a de-familiarizing editing of the diegetic sequences, and the presence of non-professional performers acting in a very artificial way. Furthermore, what makes the two films so unlike any classical adaptation is their remoteness from period pieces, as well as their emphasis on the vitality of physical bodies in their instinctive animal-like aspects. *Il Fiore delle mille e una notte* (1974) confirms the artist's ideological and aesthetic orientation. By staging naked bodies and sexual organs, he expresses his determination to oppose a marginal counter-discourse to the established narrative vision of the majority.

I have avoided undertaking a strictly comparative study of *I Racconti di Canterbury* with Chaucer's poem. So narrow a perspective would inevitably lead to the conclusion that the film version falls short of the original owing to all the alterations committed regarding both form and meaning. Pasolini offers a visual reading of *The Canterbury Tales*, which should not be restricted to its mere bawdy, carnival-like dimension. Despite the scandal caused by the display of nudity on the screen, the film never sinks into pornography, though it verges on it — an indirect way of denouncing it. If one takes a close look at the treatment of characters and dialogues, one becomes aware of the creativity, the clever artistry of visual equivalents of a well-known text, looked upon as the reference which cannot possibly be equaled. Now, *I Racconti di Canterbury* is not intended to be the scrupulous screening of its literary source. On the contrary, it seems to assert itself as what André Bazin called "a new aesthetic being."[4] My defense for Pasolini's film "imag(e)-ination" of *The Canterbury Tales* aims at pointing that, however distant from its source, dreamlike and polemical it may be, this cinematic rendering calls for a new interpretation of the text. It is entitled to careful consideration as a distinct work that claims an artistic existence of its own, despite its debt to the original. The reading of a work such as *The Canterbury Tales* should not be reserved to the happy few specialists in English medieval literature. It belongs to all, and the universal language of cinema precisely helps to make it more widely accessible. *I Racconti di Canterbury* can be viewed as an unusual yet fascinating artistic comment upon Chaucer's poem. Although Pasolini is not a medievalist with advanced knowledge of the text, he simultaneously pictures and dreams a "certain" Middle Ages suffused with a compelling poetic radiance.

From a basically medieval perspective, I suggest we compare Pasolini to an imitator who, paradoxically enough, adapts a material belonging to the poetic tradition in a quite original fashion. Equating a controversial film auteur with Chaucer, who is considered as the forerunner of English vernacular poetry, can be justified, however preposterous this may sound at first. The filmmaker "follows" his source, as the implied author of *Troilus and Criseyde* (II, 49) means: "Myn auctour shal I folwen if I konne." This term should be grasped in a double sense. On the one hand, it refers to the notion of imitation ("taking after"). On the other hand, it points to the posteriority of the reception of the original from a diachronic point of view ("coming after").[5] "Folwen," which according to the definition is synonymous to "being guided by (an authority),"[6] raises the problem of examining a poetic canon and consequently running the risk of failing in the perilous entreprise of its rewriting. Inheriting a masterpiece of the past might turn out to be a hindrance for the adaptor. Nevertheless, the status of literary reference of the imitated work suffices to legitimize its appropriation. "Folwen" also means "to translate (a book)." A translation is likely to offer a whole range of variations of the notion of faithfulness to the original. Either it closely sticks to it or, freely, almost irreverently, drifts away from it. Then the source is subject to some manipulations that transpose it into a quite different ideological, sociological and aesthetic context. "Translating" or mediating *The Canterbury Tales* through a different medium, Pasolini submits a reading of the work, which falls into the "coming after" category. He has the benefit of the posteriority of his artistic project, what Hanning calls "the fruit of belatedness" (Hanning, 37). "Taking after" appears all the more delicate as over six centuries the context and language evolved from middle English to modern Italian, mainly Neapolitan. In addition, *I Racconti di Canterbury* results from the transmutation of a semiotic system into another one. As a consequence, Pasolini actually makes his source his own in a personal way with sufficient distance that frees him from the stressful responsibility of adapting a text. The *auctor* ceases to look like an awesome shadow in the background. The filmmaker aims to narrate again, from a new perspective, in a different manner. Although he runs the risk of inviting disapproval on the part of the Chaucer specialists, he deems the experiment worthwhile and reveals the existence of an alternative to flat imitation.

Still, in spite of the tribute paid to Chaucer, the film mediation of the work is neither neutral nor atonal. The author of the trilogy insinuates alternative meanings linked to the situation of the last quarter of the 20th century. Should this alteration be viewed as an act of vandalism or an appropriate counterfeit (a fecund rewriting that avails *The Canterbury Tales*)? Their "lapsarian poetic," Hanning points out, betrays a form of dissent with John Gower's normative poetry imbued with the Christian doctrine. In *I Racconti di Canterbury* we can discern a similar heretical resistance against the ideology of the neo-capitalist world of mass consumption. To the normative discourse the film opposes a counter-discourse, expressed through a personal conception of a cinema that values subversion and human nature in its coarsest and earthliest aspects. This is why the light tales appeal to Pasolini, whereas the morally edifying serious stories are dismissed. From Chaucer's "bibliography," in the Retraction, he retains nothing but the literary sins, the reproved secular writings—"many a song and many a leccherous lay, that Crist for his grete mercy foryeve me the synne" (1087)—as opposed to "...other bookes of legendes of seintes, and omelies, and moralitee, and devocioun" (1088) / "that thanke I oure Lord..." (1089). These point to the penitential devotional literature held as the standard, in reference to which the aesthetic criteria of the Middle Ages situate the intermediary and low poetry at an inferior ethical level. Pasolini's poetic actually seeks to transcend or "dissolve disapproval in laughter."[7] The bias in favor of the ribald farcical stories cannot be accounted for by a shameful partiality for the vulgar and the scandalous. As Chaucer conceived it regarding Gower, the filmmaker finds material in *The Canterbury Tales* with a view to attaining

> A richer kind of understanding so that they [*the borrowed stories*] take on meanings different from and sometimes contrary to those which were recognized when they served their original simple moralising and idealising functions. "The effect thus created," as Diekstra (1981, 216) says, "is that of a clash between two modes of apprehending reality, which in Chaucer's [*and Pasolini's*] hands gives rise to a third and richer view, though often ironical and unresolved" [Pearsall, p. xii].

My purpose is to explore the rich resources offered by a modern approach which carries out a "dés-*oeuvre*ment" of Chaucer's work (*œuvre* in French). The film director dismantles and deconstructs his source, and at the same time manages to open it on its visualization. The power of the word as much as that of the film image generates hallucinations in our mind. The text calls for a film which it implicitly projects ahead, just like a hallucination. As in a dream, *I Racconti di Canterbury* was born out of *The Canterbury Tales* more than it literally adapts them. "Perché realizzare un'opera quando è cosi bello sognarla soltanto?"—"Why make a work of art whereas it is so beautiful to content oneself with dreaming it?" This is the conclusion drawn by Giotto's disciple played by Pasolini himself at the end of his *Decameron*. The physical presence of the artist in his film signals the ironic self-reflection of a work put in perspective, and which becomes a personal experiment of mere mystification or game: "*la colpevole mistificazione si rivela come gioco.*"[8]

The film version of *The Canterbury Tales* performs a treatment of the text, which subjects it to a number of alterations—modifications, corruptions or corrections, degenerations or improvements—alternating systolic and less frequent diastolic readings. The distribution of the eight adapted tales hinges upon three thematic axes: The desiring gaze and the blindness it may lead to, the obvious omnipresence of commodified[9] bodies which saturate the film image and, lastly, a sense of a loss of faith in mankind with a grotesque ring to it. However, *Racconti* cannot be fully appreciated if not faced with the first episode of the *Trilogia della vita*. In *The Decameron*, the narrative also undergoes a series of fragmentations, truncations or dilatations. A close scrutiny of the film inspired by Boccaccio's work reveals that it foreshadows *I Racconti di Canterbury*'s ambiguous discourse, under which lie other parallel and marginal discourses. Such ambivalence is made even more palpable by an amazingly pictorial image with an unusual degree of poeticity. In the second part of the book, "Encounter of the third kind," emphasis is laid upon the singularity of a work which, although it emerges from another one, has a unique character to it, and constitutes a whole entity in itself, something both strange and "alien." Again the hint at another famous science fiction movie is meant to draw attention to the mysterious phenomenon of "trans-semiotization," namely the mutation of a written text into a film text. *I Racconti di Canterbury* is a mutant inasmuch as it revives interest in Chaucer's poem and gives rise to questions, criticism and controversy. I will attempt to prove the legitimacy of Pasolini's free rendering of *The Canterbury Tales* and indirectly *The Decameron*. The treatment of the characters and dialogues will serve to enhance the artist's creative and subversive intention. The film not only dreams the text, instead of strictly reproducing it to the letter, but also seeks to figur(at)e representation itself. Far from overshadowing and flouting Velázquez's painting,[10] Picasso's *Meninas* serves the original in a clever, delightful, irreverent homage. So do *I Racconti di Canterbury* and *The Decameron* in regard to *The Canterbury Tales* and *The Centovelle*.

I. The Film: An Alternative Form of Telling, Another Textual Architecture, and Different Meanings

1

I Racconti di Canterbury: The Film Text of *The Canterbury Tales*

Narrative Fragmentation, Contraction, and Expansion

A Puzzling Montage: Various Thematic Directions

In 1972, one year after *The Decameron*, Pasolini made the second part of his Trilogy of Life: *I Racconti di Canterbury*. This film attains the very material substance of cinema. The picture embodies the written word. It becomes its flesh, as implied by the profusion of bodies, the meaning and presence of which I will endeavor to account for by constantly keeping in mind Pasolini's vision of the world and its representation through art. Although they follow one another without any transition or explanation whatsoever — hence the feeling of a discordant brutality in the concatenation of the narrative sequences — the different adapted stories are interrelated by internal motivations. The order of the tales in the text is disrupted. The new arrangement gives a peculiar semantic direction to the string of Chaucerian episodes, the medieval spirit of which is successfully rendered, but on which the author of the film confers a special additional tonality. Despite the numerous contractions and expansions undergone by the stories, each of them is easily identifiable by the reader of *The Canterbury Tales*. Yet one detects a new meaning at work specific to Pasolini's version of his source. What both differs and wanders away from the hypotext are not so much the sundry separate components as the whole set that they make up together. Pasolini states:

> Herein lies the exciting mystery of the film. I would like to devote a study to this question because editing *I Racconti di Canterbury* has been a mad experience. It had gone through countless combinations before I found that which satisfied me as far as rhythm was concerned.[1]

His final intention remains unknown. However, stress is put on an obvious will to fragment the narrative and break the fluidity and the natural sought by classical film telling. More patently than in *The Decameron*, cinematic representation distinguishes itself from conventional realism, which presents facts as self-evident and images as issuing from some impersonal enunciation site. *I Racconti di Canterbury* rests on a subtle network of echoes and resonances that contrive to establish a thematic link between some apparently unrelated sequences. Such thematic connections are retrospectively brought to light by the epilogue, in an oblique way, as the glance, a major motif in the film, strikes by its indirection. For instance, the intervention of the *Friar's Tale*'s summoner in the diegesis is delayed by a long preliminary silent phase, aiming at sketching the spy at his service, as well as the archdeacon whom he tips off. The portrait of the despicable informer is prefigured by being beforehand reflected in those of his accomplices—sneaks and prostitutes—and his employer. Every one of them shares the same ignominious activity, refracted in a mise en abyme of the main character's sinful nature.

Likewise, the viewer's glance is contained in that of the spy at work, itself included in the Devil's messenger's. Our eye merges with that of a wicked being, witnessing acts held as immoral. Later, in anticipation, when the Wife of Bath delights in her future husband's anatomy—which she glimpses through the keyhole at her friend's house—she is depicted in the same voyeuristic position, which introduces another character into the diegetic world. We are kept away from what we are being shown (the fiction) by the "screen" of the bedroom door, a metaphor of the cinema screen. In the three distinct organizations of the eight tales—in the text, in the script, and in the film, *The Wife of Bath's Prologue* is the only one that retains its initial position as the "barycentre."[2] Concerning the film, the self-portrait on the confessional mode is preceded by *The Merchant's Tale*, *The Friar's Tale*, *The Cook's Tale*, then *The Miller's Tale*. It is followed by *The Reeve's Tale*, *The Pardoner's Prologue and Tale* and, finally, *The Summoner's Tale* and its prologue. On either side of this median axis are symmetrically distributed the same number (four) of stories drawn from Chaucer. In addition, the same amount of sequences entirely made up by Pasolini have been fitted in between some of the adapted episodes. I will examine the role and explain the presence of these inserts on the periphery of the diegesis later in my demonstration. The conjugal comedy, a real performance given by the Wife of Bath in the heart of the film, epitomizes both the aesthetics behind the treatment of the text and the thematic contents that take shape as a watermark throughout the work from one story to the next.

In this sequence, Pasolini effects an elliptic fragmentary transposition. Alisoun's experience as a wife starts at the age of 12 as she proudly claims in the fourth line of her seemingly endless introductory speech. On the screen she has already had four husbands. The portrayal of the expert in the art of love is astonishingly synthesized. The character does seem to come to life, though, and we attend the seduction and the subsequent domestication of her fifth prey. Lastly, the Wife of Bath episode combines all the motifs already identifiable in the four preceding tales, which will reappear in the following three. Four main thematic axes run through Pasolini's film text, composing an interpretative reading grid: first, voyeurism or "scopophilia"[3] (the scopic drive[4]) dialectically opposed to blindness; secondly, avidity; thirdly, the merchandizing of bodies as consumer goods; and, lastly, farce, both a mode of treatment and a tonality that suffuses the narrative, which warrants some critical distance from the film, while opening it on a self-reflexive artistic perspective. Let us now consider the alterations made to the text as well as their impact on the reception of the film version.

The Opening Sequence

Pasolini's dream consists of bringing back to life the forgotten sense of human experience by means of the modern form of popular show: cinema. Therefore *I Racconti di Canterbury* seizes our attention because of its uncommon visual radicality, its "spectacularity."[5] The act of looking plays a preeminent part in it. In the script, he defines the introductory sequence in terms of "a large medieval tableau,"[6] the atmosphere and hues of which evoke the Flemish masters. The genre scenes follow one another, mixing a miscellany of servants, merchants, clerics, and members of the emerging middle class—all referred to as "new and homeric" (*Sceneggiature*, 249) as though he meant they had not yet been corrupted by a pre-industrial world motivated by profit. The prologue anchors the film narrative in a theatrical performance. In the Southwark marketplace, the pilgrims, skillfully sketched, make up a sort of popular chorus announcing the show, namely the series of tales to come. Except for the Wife of Bath, they are not narrators, merely actors or witnesses in a performance they are giving. As on the Elizabethan proscenium, they offer us an inaugural comedy separate from the rest of the film, preceding the bulk of the diegesis. The Pardoner is singing passionately, his fellow Summoner whistling along. The wrestling Miller is proudly wielding his trophy (a goat), cheered by the gaping onlookers for getting the upper hand over his opponent. The Wife is prattling on and on, waddling to and fro in a circle, winking lustfully about. The haughty Reeve, out of a holy icon, is meticulously combing his scarce hair in a window frame. All belong to this medieval "folk culture of the marketplace."[7] The laughter and echoes of voices from the busy motley crowd, as well as the snatches of songs heard as early as the credits point to a comedy of the common people in this astoundingly accurate and humorous abridgement of *The General Prologue*.

Through the town gate, Chaucer, played by Pasolini, enters the fiction, bringing the viewer along with him. As a metaphor of the liminal position of the *incipit*, the gate materializes the threshold crossed by the character stepping into the fictitious world. The double figure of the author — the one of the film being assimilated to the one of the text — provides both the movie's "aesthetic key" and a "narrative device," according to Jean Sémolué.[8] Pasolini-Chaucer indeed makes five extradiegetic appearances between some tales and takes up his quill in the final shot. As the renowned poet comes up into the gate frame followed by his horse, the animal pushes him against the Cook, who happens to be there at the same time. The bump against such a big hard nose as that of the humble obliging Cook, who insists upon letting Chaucer go first, makes the latter a laughingstock. Holding his nose in pain, he gets angry and loses the dignity conferred by his authority as a learned man. The film falls into farce. The change of tone is borne out by the Host's remark in *The Cook's Prologue* (4355), here uttered by the Cook as: "Eh, tra scherzi e giochi grandi verità si possono dire!"[9] (*Sceneggiature*, 248). Colorful because of his blue-tattooed face typical of Pasolini's grotesque mugs, the Cook probably embodies the thoroughly frivolous funny spirit and the fresh innocence of the medieval world in the filmmaker's imagination. Thus the film's prologue plunges us into the heart of a vivid, larger-than-life Middle Ages, so vibrant, brimming with colors and events. It also promises to be good fun. Furthermore, the director's presence at the very beginning bespeaks the artist's intention to open his work in an ironical self-allusion. Initializing the frame story, however curtailed it is, the introductory sequence serves to set up a minimal degree of dramatization. It directs our attention towards the enunciation of the narrative. Inside the tavern, in the next scene, the Host suggests that all the pilgrims gathered there should play a storytelling game, so as to enliven their long journey to Canterbury. This is the one and only hint at the pilgrimage. He significantly does not address them as "pilgrims," but instead swears he has never seen "una più lieta brigata riunita tutta insieme in questo albergo" (*Sceneggiature*, 249–50) before. This sounds like a parody of the *Via Crucis*! The ambulatory itinerary taken by the penitents on the road is ignored in the film version. Moreover, no topographical details whatsoever are provided, nor are the various narrators' identities mentioned, so that some pilgrims are not easy to recognize. For instance, we wonder if the young, skinny affected man intently listening to the Wife of Bath is the Clerk or the Nuns' Priest. Adopting the "aesthetics of density" that characterizes the Decameronian novella,[10] the preliminary sequence of *I Racconti di Canterbury* strikes us as being surprisingly brisk and efficient. It fills the semantic (information) gap of the *incipit*, since without even putting names on the protagonists and places, it successfully depicts a quite convincing medieval atmosphere, dark yet brightened up by the beautiful, bright ink-blue and magenta-red hues of the garments. It seduces the spectator and captivates his attention by means of a series of medieval tableaux at the beginning with a view to creating a dominant note of fun. The pilgrims hardly speak, save Alisoun of Bath, but their laughable, if not grotesque, expressions and attitudes tell so much about them. The way the opening sequence roots the film in a specific genre seems to show that a viewer cannot possibly expect a Hollywood recreation of the medieval era, with a classical narrative scheme and a conventional mode of representation. *I Racconti di Canterbury* is devoid of any intention of realism: "If my film is subversive, that is because it is real, and not realistic…," states Pasolini.[11] The lively picture of the pilgrims, whose tales will constitute the very body of the film, suffices to give an idea of the ingredients of the foretold comedy containing derisive bawdy echoes. Furthermore, the Pardoner's favorite motto—*radix malorum est cupiditas*—with which he sprinkles all his lectures betokens the conclusion, in which we are reminded of the fate that awaits unrepenting sinners. The ponderous moralizing sermon seems out of place, for Pasolini's prologue excludes serious and virtuous pilgrims like the Parson.

After this synopsis of *The General Prologue*, one expects to find, if not all of them, at least some pilgrims later, when they start telling their stories. Nevertheless, what follows puzzles the reader of *The Canterbury Tales*. The narrators vanish from the extradiegetic frame; only Chaucer remains as the author at his desk with all his books around him. Then he is presented as a pilgrim, busy taking notes on his bed at night among the other sleeping penitents but never intervening as a narrator. Once all the voices that introduce, develop and conclude the tales have ceased, there remains nothing but a sort of "continuum fabulatio" ("a fictional continuum"), which considerably strips what Pasolini calls "la grande chicchierra di Chaucer" (Canova, 29)—"Chaucer's big cackle." The narrative is rid of the discourse that contains it. The film's rhythm, both at the metadiegetic level (that of the tales themselves in Gérard Genette's terminology) and at the frame-story level, gains in fluidity, as well as rendering the natural fragmentary dimension found in *The Canterbury Tales*. Paradoxically, the film's paratactic construction is emphasized by the eradication of the pauses that focus back on the tellers and audience before and after the tales have been told. By resorting to narrative ellipses, Pasolini deprives narration of any explanatory, illustrative and transitional function, and instead focuses on some particular passages of the text, so as to develop them at will. Of the 24 original tales, the filmmaker selects eight and combines them together in a different order. More staccato than in *The Decameron*, the rhythm on which the "racconti" follow from one another betrays a will to break up the diegetic stream. The order of the tales is completely disrupted at the editing phase of the script. The director of the film stressed the arbitrariness of the montage finally chosen. Yet, a close consideration of *I Racconti di Canterbury* reveals that the very brief scenes of Chaucer writing his work constitute a main thread, which embraces the stories presented in a more systematic fashion. The recurring image of the author provides the viewer with a minimum of landmarks, so that he/she may derive a meaning out of the destabilizing narrative layout — in fact a collection of discordant elements. The extreme reduction of familiar components that usually define narrative in its traditional shape actually offers countless possible interpretations, and gives a glimpse of the inumerable semantic directions likely to stem from a combination of unrelated sequences, forming an apparently random succession to those not having read *The Canterbury Tales*.

Narrative Ellipsis, Condensation, or Dilatation

I suggest that the eight adapted tales should be schematically classified according to the criteria that determined the treatment of the text and, more precisely, the noticeable modifications brought about to the prologues and epilogues. I mean to prove that an aesthetics of both condensation and dilatation of the narrative underlies the screening of *The Canterbury Tales*, whose spirit is miraculously preserved despite a disconcerting fragmentation, a bewildering discontinuity in the whole "montage." *The Miller's Tale* and *The Reeve's Tale* illustrate a transposition technique that suppresses both prologues and short concluding moralities but faithfully sticks to the unfolding of the plot, exempt of portraits, however. In both cases, the narrative's smooth rhythm and light spirit are respected, and push towards a metaphorical and literal fall. *The Miller's Tale* ends on the crash caused by the collapsing kneading trough containing the carpenter. Like the trough hanging on the ceiling at the end of a rope in expectation of the awesome predicted flood, the epilogue is suspended, with neither rumors about the old man's madness nor a lesson drawn from the anecdote. The ending of

The Reeve's Tale is quite as brutal and brutally delivered as the unfortunate punch that knocks the miller senseless by his bed. Pasolini closes the episode by returning to the shot of the two students on their horse, laughing and heartily eating the cake made with the flour Symkyn meant to steal from them. They resume in Latin the prayer they were singing at the beginning.[12] This is a mise en abyme and an echo to Nicholas, who is also a student wearing a red jacket, chanting the same hymn. Not only is the circle completed, but it also brings the two farces together around the common theme of cuckoldry and trickery.

The adaptations of *The Merchant's Tale* and *The Wife of Bath's Prologue* belong to a second category, characterized by a systolic reading of the text. Both the opening and ending of *The Merchant's Tale* more specifically, like the bulk of the narrative, are considerably retracted in such a way that Januarie's introductory speech on the necessity and virtues of marriage sounds funny and ludicrous instead of boring, and does not delay the triggering of the plot. In a parallel, the long argument between Pluto and Proserpina becomes a very brief friendly talk preceding May's final (also abridged) reply to her jealous husband. The plot passes in silence the secret exchange of letters between the lovers, and reduces to one single occurrence Januarie's repeated pathetic sexual deeds. The Wife of Bath episode develops the art of narrative condensation even further. The tale is simply overlooked, and only one-third of the preliminary discourse remains. Pasolini has cleverly transferred part of the self-portrait in anticipation in the opening sequence of the film. As a result, he can focus exclusively on the last third of the Prologue, devoted to the fifth husband. Nevertheless, barely half of the stormy conjugal relationship between Alisoun of Bath and Jankyn is actually exploited, for the interminable enumeration of examples of blameworthy wives read by the clerk is set aside. Lastly, the explanatory detour at the end that exposes the reason why the wife is deaf in one ear is superseded by a tempestuous confrontation, concluded by a comical bite at the husband's nose. The closing of Chaucer's epilogue on the compromise achieved in a couple is "torn off," so to speak, by a virago's castrating teeth. The story ends on an animal cry of pain that recalls the inaugural shot showing the fourth husband breathing his last, exhausted by his wife's insatiable sexual appetite.

The Cook's Tale and *The Friar's Tale* consist of a freer form of adaptation. This unfinished fragment of a tale — the adventures of Perkyn the Revelour — told by the Cook, is nothing but a foreword, which opens up a broad scope of narrative possibilities for the filmmaker. Pasolini indeed retains the very loose inchoative plot, but dilates it so as to introduce therein what could be rendered in French by a play on words "délire / dé-lire" on the burlesque mode, i.e. a "fanciful de-reading" of the text. Perkyn is embodied by Nino Davoli, who facetiously hops about, plays tricks, and takes to his heels in speeded-up motion, as Charles Chaplin did in his silent comedies. This may be construed as a humorous nostalgic quotation of and foray into the early days of cinema. It is also a self-reflexive hint at *The Decameron* and *Uccellacci e uccellini* (1966) in which Davoli's behavior and gait were already reminiscent of Chaplin's happy-go-lucky lightheartedness. In other words, the author of the film appropriates the text to instill a fantastical dimension into it and to heighten its buffoonery, while insinuating a darker shade to the scene through allusions to the commodification of bodies in a repressive system. In short, the by-product is quite remote from its source of inspiration. *The Friar's Tale* does not so much pertain to comedy and play, although it also goes through semantic alterations and is contaminated by Pasolinian motifs. The text is virtually amputated by half. The plot is rid of the horse-drawn cart stuck in the mud (1537–70) and of the numerous questions about Hell that the summonner bombards the Devil's agent with (1447–1522). However, the most striking changes concern the long-drawn-out preliminary exposition of the countless extortions the summoner can boast about. Proportionally speaking, it retains its lengthiness,[13] but the filmmaker chooses to focus on a particular type of exaction in a narrative diastolis. That is, the mysterious comings and goings of the peeping spy, simultaneously being watched by the fiend. What he is actually up to is catching fornicators red-handed in collusion with prostitutes. Pasolini substitutes boys for Chaucer's loose women. In addition to this metamorphosis of the original narrative, he inserts a scene of his own invention: that of the homosexual who burns at the stake, unable to buy the summoner's silence.[14] Here is possibly an indirect denunciation of the Italian bourgeois homophobic society of the early 1970s, intolerant of its minority groups, to which the film auteur belonged. In this most developed prelude in *I Racconti di Canterbury*, the glance theme signals itself insistently. In an ironical contrast, it prefigures the summoner's blindness, since in the epilogue he obstinately persists in not recognizing the fiend in his sworn brother, to whom the actor Franco Citti confers a gentle compassionate look. In the conclusion of the tale, the Friar emphasizes the necessity to repent in a prayer accompanied with a redundant proverb[15]—one more treacherous blow dealt to his enemy. Instead of the sententious words, the camera shows a copper jug, on which the devil's gloomy figure is reflected. This exterior night close-up is very short but successfully suggests the fate that awaits the summoner.

Lastly, a fourth division comprises *The Pardoner's Tale* and *The Summoner's Tale* and their prologues. Pasolini contrives to restrict the body of the text through an ingenious telescoping of both *The Pardoner's Prologue* and *The Pardoner's Tale*. After the exposition of various forms of perverted sex, assimilated to the flesh trade in the opening scene, one of the scoundrels stands upstairs at the railing in the brothel, and starts uttering a parody of a sermon while urinating on the customers below. He epitomizes the narrator of the tale, despicable and immoral like his own character. As he depicts himself in the verbose confession of his duplicity, he addresses his naive audience "as dooth a dowve sittynge on a berne" (*The Pardoner's Tale*, 397). The ironic echo of the text is cinematographically enhanced by the young man's castigating lust, gluttony, betting and drinking. He looks and sounds like a priest in his pulpit, towering above his congregation. Displaced from the Pardoner's mouth into the impenitent rogue's, the sermon delivered in a dingy, dismal setting that foreshadows Hell is altogether subverted. The tears of repentance are replaced by a blasphemous stream of urine. The mock homily is followed by the anecdote itself, faithfully transposed. The plot smoothly progresses toward a short conclusion of only a few lines. Just as expeditious, Pasolini's epilogue strikes by its harshness. One of the three rakes is stabbed and the other two die poisoned. The camera eye bluntly "lets them down," literally among the gold coins, the vomit and excrements in a cold, uneasy silence. Any hope for remission seems lost, as anticipated in the opening shot of the "privee theef Deeth's" victim (*The Pardoner's Tale*, 675), that we recognize as the sinful "preacher!"

In *The Summoner's Tale*, the transformations necessarily implied by the film treatment of the text result in a more obvious deviation from the source. The tale, here preceding its prologue, is reduced to one-eighth of its book length. The mendicant friar's plumpness and simpering, as well as his immediate excitement at the sight of Thomas's chest, skillfully synthesize the detailed illustration of his cupidity, hypocrisy, and love of good food. The unending speech on his vows of poverty, fasting and chastity[16] disappears along with his soporific lecture on wrath containing three examples drawn from the ancients.[17] Considerably shortened, the plot is suddenly suspended on the shot of the friar's screwing up his mouth in disgust for Thomas's breaking wind in his face. The offending wind cuts short the string of indicting abuse showered by the raging "frere" before the lord of the village. There is no mention whatsoever of this extension of the story, which more than a simple epilogue constitutes an additional story in itself.[18] The friar's discomfiture repeated in the arithmetic problem submitted by the squire is rendered quite differently in the film's epilogue. The Franciscan is punished and made fun of again in the infernal vision of Satan, excreting by the thousand the so-called God's servants out of his backside in a thundering flatus. This time, instead of receiving the foul smell to be shared in 12, with his nose on the cartwheel hub, the cleric is condemned to inhale mephitic flatulences forever with the other members of the convent. The dreamed visit of Hell by an awe-stricken John in *The Summoner's Prologue* comes as a conclusion not only of the tale but also obliquely of the whole series of eight sequences that make up the film. Pasolini achieves an ingenious inversion that holds off the morality of the anecdote and replaces it with a phantasmagoria, reaching beyond the anecdotic level to that of the gruesome and outrageous. The friar awakes from his nightmare, just like the spectator that he carries away in his vision, only to be doomed to attend the show of death. Stared at in fright, death in its utmost horridness is being contemplated as if it were a painting, hence the pictorial allusions to Hieronymus Bosch.[19]

Why are we faced with this infernal vision? It occurs right before the final sequence and serves a double purpose. On the one hand, it depicts the logical end of a corrupt churchman. On the other hand, it summarizes the Parson's sanctimonious condemnation of the Seven Deadly Sins leading to the abode of the damned. Although it is not literally adapted, the echo of *The Parson's Tale* can be felt in the background. The representation of the lower world's torments prepares for the revelation of the Celestial Jerusalem announced by the Priest and materialized in the body of Canterbury cathedral, which appears to the pilgrims as they near their goal. Inspired by the spirituality of the holy place, they can be seen in a distance shot kneeling, crossing themselves, and saying amen. Nevertheless, the solemnity of their meditation is ironically counterpoised in the frontal close-up that comes next. It shows Pasolini-Chaucer finishing his text with a smile at the camera. Retrospectively, it can be inferred that the inflated grotesque of the vision of Inferno signifies (with the distance of humor) that despite the unbearable inevitability of death, all this is not to be taken seriously. The originality in Pasolini's epilogue lies in an explosive assimilation between eschatology and scatology. As the author of the film writes, his tales have been told for the mere pleasure of telling: "Here end the Canterbury Tales told only for the pleasure of telling them." The Host's request in *Introduction to The Pardoner's Tale* is granted: "Telle us som myrthe or japes right anon" (VI-C, 319).

Voyeurism and Blindness

The Desiring Gaze

"Cosi riassemblati, *I Racconti di Canterbury* delineano una sorta di parabola sul tema del vedere e del non vedere...."[20] Love literature in Ancient Greece already conceived the look as "the surest vehicle of passion,"[21] and pointed to the danger represented by the light-image-gaze equation. Spying, voyeuristic, or covetous, deceived by appearances or phantasmic, the glance is deliberately made visible throughout *I Racconti di Canterbury*.

First of all, it arouses the irrational lust for flesh or money — to which the medieval thought opposed chastity and temperance. Many an example of characters titillated by another person or an object can be found in the film. In most cases, covetousness is kindled by watching on the sly. Because they are spied on, the longed-for human beings or objects become even more desirable. As early as the beginning of *The Merchant's Tale*, it is impossible to be mistaken about libidinous Januarie's motivations, when he lays eyes on May's pretty backside, unveiled by the innocent hand of a child lifting the girl's skirt while she is on all fours. The elderly, respectable knight, whose protruding eyes light up under his bushy eyebrows, starts quivering with impatience like a clumsy, hairy bear, as he is described in the filmscript.[22] The same lickerishness shines in handsome, impassive Damyan's pale blue eyes. His *mal d'amour* is never put into words, yet it is suggested in several shots of the yearning young man holding his erect penis. Such mutism comically contrasts with the old husband's justificatory tedious discourse on marriage. The *courtois* representation of love confers to the gaze a metaphorical dimension symbolized by Cupid's arrow. However, the lover, whose senses are stimulated at the sight of the beloved, must endure a long, trying wait before being allowed to hold her in his arms. His feelings are put to the test of time, so that such love turns out to be a longing for unsatisfied desire.[23] Damyan embodies a subverted figure of the wooer engrossed in the thought of his lady. The visible swelling of a specific part of his anatomy amounts to a parodic transformation of the poetic motif of the love arrow into a coarse detail. The beau's concupiscence implies fornication and lust. These are the three indissociable notions which served as a basis for a monolithic massive reprobation of sexuality in the Middle Ages.[24] The desire that circulates between the characters in the triangular relationship of *The Merchant's Tale* certainly is the sexual drive, as confirmed in May's animal expression when her eyes meet the squire's for the first time. With her mouth full, she suddenly stops chewing, bewitched by the young man's charm. Pasolini equates her with a gazelle (*Sceneggiature*, 351) or a captive, nimble wild little animal. Oblivious of the rules of etiquette, she eats greedily, just as she greedily eyes her future lover, whom she relishes in anticipation like the fruits in the tree he later hides in with a turgescent penis.

In *The Miller's Tale*, from his window Nicholas watches his landlord setting off. Again his spying betrays his deceitfulness. The spectator infers he has previously set his eyes and mind on the old carpenter's most precious belonging: his pretty young spouse. As soon as the way is clear, the student rushes downstairs into the kitchen, trying to repress an erection. Then he ardently hugs the object of his passion. Later the same physiological transformation affects Absolon, Nicholas's rival. Still, the latter is never shown looking at Alisoun, whom he pretends he is enamored of. He does nothing but talk about her, lasciviously moving his pelvis in a parodic love declaration in his bedroom. He is standing in front of a mirror held upright by a boy, to whom he seems ambiguously close. This has just been implied in the long slow shot of bare-chested Absolon, lying on the bed in a position reminiscent of post-coital exhaustion. The camera languorously lingers over the body of the young man, wearing low-waisted tight-fitting mauve trousers, then almost brushes against his crotch. The viewer is led to wonder about the party to whom the sexual offer is directed. The mirror gives shape to Absolon's desire reflecting itself. It is aimed at a person of his own sex. It is indeed his companion he is eyeing knowingly instead of Alisoun. In a caricature, the Wife of Bath incorporates the lust aroused at the sight of a man's body. After draining her fourth husband of his last strength on the conjugal bed, she calls on her best friend. Through a keyhole, the latter secretly introduces her to her new lodger, who is having a wash. The women start squabbling over the privilege of gazing at the naked man. Beside herself with excitement, the Wife cattily pushes her friend away and physically takes possession of the viewpoint, as if her eye is superimposed on the camera's, putting a filter of lechery over it.

Whereas Alisoun of Bath's new object of desire is described by Chaucer as young and attractive, the actor who plays Jankyn is plain with round dull eyes and a thick mustache. Furthermore, he seems to be middle-aged, like the actress Laura Betti (Alisoun). He lacks Damyan's, Nicholas's or Absolon's charisma. The Wife of Bath's animal sexual appetite[25] is set off comically against the clerk's ridiculous affected manners and stiffness. During their first encounter, the priggish Jankyn feigns interest in his book, but he takes her hand and puts it on his penis. We are reminded that it is the conscience watching that entirely sets the tone of the scene. The Wife of Bath episode, built on her viewpoint, reproduces the comic self-indulgence in Chaucer's confessional portrait by stressing the colorful man-eater's lewdness. Alisoun is characterized through the farcical mode. The actress's play is deliberately overdone so that we are made aware she is acting, putting on a show, as it were. Inside the church, she ostentatiously starts grieving for her late fourth husband — loud enough for the congregation to hear — or stares wide-eyed in alleged astonishment, or else pretends to be breathing her last. Once hit by Jankyn, she gives a double performance: the exuberant, fiery, overbearing actress Laura Betti, plays her true self and plays a shrewd spouse familiar with "the old dance" of the "art of love" (*The General Prologue*, 476). She comes to life only through men's and the spectator's glances, which she constantly attempts to catch. She is nothing but a fictitious being, a set of features that make up a female figure identifiable as the domineering, castrating, garrulous type. Pasolini underlines her grotesque buffoonery, and consequently her mere fictionality. The Peeping Tom at the beginning of *The Friar's Tale* is leaning forward, turning his back on the devil's messenger, who mediates our perception of the scene. In an echo to the preceding *Merchant's Tale*, a rear end is revealed, but this time a man is watching another one in an equivocal position, evoking a form of desire different from that felt by Januarie and Damyan for May. The narrative coherence finds itself momentarily disturbed because of the unexpected interruption of a homosexual scopophilic conscience, which surreptiously diverts the camera from its narrative function. Jill Ricketts speaks of

> the notion of a homosexual *cruising gaze*, exemplified by Pasolini's distinctive, nonnarrative camera work, which commonly rests on enigmatic, tight shots of men looking [Ricketts, 119].

The spectator's feeling is borne out in the next shot when, after the spy has stolen away, the fiend stands at the door and, leaning forward, witnesses the same event on the sly. It is an immoral, contemptible creature's eye that provides us with the viewpoint from which we are secretly beholding an act of sodomy. The fact that the scene occurs in a shady out-of-the-way place, distanced through a twice-mediated glance, makes it even more illicit. Michel Foucault explains that discourse has long submitted sexuality to the economy of reproduction. Until the 18th century, sexual practices were governed by canon law, Christian pastoral law, and civil law that distinguish the lawful from the fraudulent. Carnal relationships, politically and economically useful, are closely watched. In the Middle Ages, married life was saturated with rules, recommendations and prescriptions. Marriage legitimizes sex, tolerated within the bounds of ecclesiastical and matrimonial institutions only. It is subjected to juridical and moral codification. Any offense against the matrimonial order such as adultery breaks the legal match, and therefore appears as condemnable as sodomy. "In both civil and religious orders, what was taken into account was this general illegitimacy."[27] Deemed as an unnatural abomination, homosexuality actually represents only one type of the illegitimate. Yet the sodomite, as a juridical subject merely defined by an act and not by his sexual identity, incurs the stake. Homosexuality is not conceived as a psychological, psychiatric and medical category until the 19th century. "Sodomy" in its medieval sense refers to all practices devoid of any procreative ends, and is not restricted to male homosexuality. "What matters and what is condemned are some acts."[28] Male love-making is not the only form of sex reproved by the Church. Still, it is fiercely censored and prohibited by theologians, who criminalize this sin. Until the mid–12th century, the intellectual and ethical context ensured minimal tolerance of homosexual practices. In the 13th century, deviant acts such as sodomy associated with bestiality became much more severely controlled and punished. In addition, homosexuals were considered as heretics inasmuch as they rejected marriage and procreation and undermined nature, "a normative power, related to God's sovereignty"[29] and which it is criminal to contravene.

> Hence the setting up [in the 14th century], in Italy first because the obsession is more Italian than French..., of commissions responsible for controlling behaviours and morals and repressing sodomites, especially homosexuals [Rossiaud, 43].

Tolerance in sexual matters in the Middle Ages solely issues from male heterosexual authority, and consequently does not apply to women nor male homosexuals. The male relationship in *The Friar's Tale* seems taboo, but paradoxically highlights the transgressive drive of the interdict. At the end of the sequence, the voyeur tracking a victim leaves his hiding place, thrilled about the two acts of sodomy he has just witnessed. He rejoices over the reward he will get from the summoner. Nevertheless, one may wonder if his excitement does not result from some homosexual attraction that he shares with his prey. The unfortunate end of the first sodomite burnt in public for not having the money to pay his blackmailer directs the interpretation of Pasolini's version of *The Friar's Tale* toward an awfully pessimistic political reading of a society that cruelly punishes a form of desire judged abnormal.

The gay gaze is dialectically opposed to the disapproving eye of the moral authority embodied by the church dignitaries. Unconcerned, they are shown attending the tragicomedy of the poor fellow exposed to public condemnation. The almost naked man's desperate yet ludicrous cries and struggle against the guards, feverishly followed by the priest — holding the cross, anxious not to miss a scrap of the show — somewhat de-dramatize the dreadful lot in store for him. In a comic touch, the tense atmosphere is temporarily relieved by a fixed frontal shot showing the clergymen and, in particular, the complacent, indifferent archdeacon in his shimmering purple garment, looking pleased with his summoner — whom we recognize just behind him. Standing still, facing the camera, they pose as if for a painting, as though to remind that death is a mise-en-scène, both morbid and grotesque.

The Reproachful Chastising Look

The yearning gaze supposes an accusatory look, a motif especially developed in *The Cook's Tale*, which follows. For having seduced a bride, disturbed the wedding feast, stolen money from his boss to bet with a bunch of good-for-nothings — one of whom offers him room in his bed with his whore of a wife — Perkyn the Revelour is caught red-handed several times by angry representatives of civil law (the police forces in the market), moral order (his boss), religious authority (the friars doling out soup to the needy standing in a queue) as well as paternal domination (the funny-looking dwarf reproaching him with a casual laziness he ascribes to his real father, an Italian!). In all these situations—in which he bites into a little girl's doughnut, queues up with a huge bowl in hope for a bigger ladleful of soup, or takes delight in knocking an enormous cream-cake over a bridegroom's head—he makes his enemies fly off the handle. They start chasing him, in vain, for he is very agile and crafty like Charles Chaplin (he even sports a bowler hat and walking stick like Chaplin's). Perkyn easily loses his blundering gigantic pursuers. The bridegroom's heavily-built father, with a grim look, bushy eyebrows and beard, is reminiscent of the menacing hulk in *The Gold Rush*.[30] As for Perkyn's father, he is reduced to an irascible dwarf, and the fat friar, who has a strong mind to punish him, has piglike features.

In this sequence, the young reveller's ogling the pretty bride causes her father's frown.[31] Sex and flesh seem to be equated with sin, invented by Christianity, Jacques Le Goff points out, entails referring systematically to the Bible, the ultimate supreme authority, to "justify the repression of most sexual practices."[32] Carnal pleasure loses its positive value and sex is censured and strictly regulated. Monachism represents the new sexual model. It advocates an ideal of purity resting on the foretelling of the impending end of the world. Maybe this is why *The Cook's Tale* closes on a coercive act as the logical outcome of the disapproving eye. Perkyn's mischief and his lust for a bride, then a prostitute—or, more exactly, the latter's husband, since the fact that the two men are in the bed, with the girl in the middle, sows doubts about Perkyn's sexual tastes—lead him to the stocks. A parody of Metro-Goldwyn-Mayer's roaring lion, with his hands and head caught in the wooden collar, the carefree, jeering, challenging Chaplin-like figure snuffles a funny song, a possible insolent reply to the intrusive eye of power.

Right afterward, Pasolini-Chaucer, dozing off, is brutally urged to set to work at once by his imposing formidable wife, glaring at him from above. He bumps his head against the upper part of his chair, for the authoritative voice makes him start! On the semantic level, the film's first three sequences seemingly present punishment as the natural outcome of covetousness, which can emerge from the sight of either a person or a material object. The summoner in *The Friar's Tale* promises his chance fellow traveler an edifying entertainment. He begs him to focus on the skill with which he intends to extort money from a blameless old peasant woman whom he unfairly accuses of adultery and threatens to take her to the ecclesiastical court. It is not so much the insignificant sum of money that motivates the iniquitous blackmailer as the delight in committing such a misdeed, mixed with the ambition to teach Satan a thing or two.

When he sits down facing Thomas in his bed, the plump, obsequious friar in *The Summoner's Tale* notices a chest at his foot. He cautiously lifts the lid, yet instead of the contents we see the clergyman's immediate unambiguous reaction. He opens his eyes wide with greed, but instantly refrains from showing his excitement. All in a flutter at the sight of what is left of Thomas's money, Friar John, who blames the latter for having been too liberal toward his brethren from the convent, starts acting hypocritically with a view to getting one more gift from his host. The sequence begins with a shot of the friar, his face framed in the seat opposite the bed, in an allusion to Perkyn, himself pastiching the MGM lion. It is as though he belonged to the diegetic world of a television fiction, or were an actor about to give us a performance. We are watching a worthless buffoon, whose face expresses alternately self-satisfaction and greed as he surreptitiously bites into a cake, disgust as he drives the cat away to take her place on the chair, then a falsely friendly grin when he hints at the hospitality Thomas and his wife have always offered him so far. The friar's affectedness actually betrays to a further extent his ham acting, which fails to fool Thomas or the spectator. His overemphatic ridiculous behavior shows through his eager crossing himself and swearing to Thomas he will share the gift with the other mendicant friars. Hanging upon the sick man's every word, he rushes to the spot indicated under the blanket, with an avid look in his eyes that he is unable to suppress. He abruptly asks: "Come on, pluck up! Where is it?" Then, just after receiving a gift he did not expect, a frontal close shot reveals the friar in a peaceful sleep, amorously holding tight a huge phallic vegetable marrow in one hand and a wine jug in the other. Next, in a long shot, we find out that his bed is surrounded with victuals, including live chickens cackling about as he awakes to see the angel coming for him. Therefore it seems natural that Hell is the place where he is taken on account of his gluttony and deceitfulness. Moreover, his effeminate manners (he purses his lips and speaks with a lisp) implicitly point to homosexuality, previously linked to the Damned's fire in *The Friar's Tale*.

The same avidity pushes the three rakes in *The Pardoner's Tale* to commit murder. The gold found by the tree, indicated by Death, glistens in the sunshine and leaves them gaping speechlessly as if spellbound. Unlike the parodic sermon in the gloomy, shabby tavern prior to the young men's quest for the mysterious thief, the scene in which they discover the treasure is shot in full daylight. Once the third boy is back with poisoned wine for his so-called sworn brothers ready to stab him in the back, the killing is filmed in a low-angle, overexposed distance shot, suffused with the reflections of bright light. The dazzling effect not only attenuates the scatological crudeness (the victims vomit and excrete) but also, in an ironical inversion, symbolizes the blindness that led the three young rogues to their tragic end.

They were unable to recognize death first in the immortal old man's features, then in the snare of the riches set for them.

The Obscured Vision

It seems that the thirst for taking hold of either a thing or a person deprives the desiring subject of any clearsightedness and plunges him into deserved chastisement. Because he is so confident of playing a trick on his rival, Nicholas does not bother to look out the window before offering his backside to Absolon, who has a painful surprise in store for him. In a comic reversal of situation, Alisoun's wind, which startled the squeamish young clergyman the first time he stood at the window, actually serves his revenge. The sound emitted by his challenger's posterior guides the red iron toward its target. As for *The Friar's Tale*'s summoner, he signs his own damnation warrant for having looked at the devil without proper critical judgment. A character's sightlessness may also be ascribed to darkness, in which finding one's way becomes impossible and thus causes disorder. In Symkyn's bedroom, where it is pitch dark, Aleyn and John seize the opportunity to get even with the dishonest miller by having a good time, one with the daughter, the other with the wife in *The Reeve's Tale*. Still, Aleyn's blowing his own trumpet about his sexual deeds into the wrong man's ear turns the anecdote into a comedy of errors. In the night, the roles are reversed, the trickster tricked, and the lover unmasked! Yet the student manages to escape from the enraged miller, who orders his wife to bludgeon the young man. Once she has leapt out of her bed (forgetting to put her clothes back on), the daughter opens the shutters to let the morning light in. The naked truth then filters in and dispels the confusion caused by the dark. It reveals that the punishment did not fall on the troublemaker. It is also darkness that deceives Absolon and changes his "faire bryd's" lips into a smelly rearend. Whereas in the text the impudent belle just offers "hir nether ye" (*The Miller's Tale,* 3852) for the pretender to kiss so as to cure him of his passion, in the film she proves even more insolent as she delivers him some "(re)sounding" affront. Absolon pays a high price for the pride and lack of sense that made him certain he would win Alisoun's favors.

The blindness that unexpectedly affects Januarie in *The Merchant's Tale* is both literal and metaphorical. Ironically, he recovers his sight just as Damyan, who is having an erection, is about to penetrate his wife up in the tree. May's adultery frees her old husband from his unexplained ailment. Now, though he sees again, the wool is still over his eyes. In other words, he recovers his eyesight, but not his clearsightedness as, with the help of the goddess Proserpina, his dear spouse allays his suspicion with lies and fake tears. The woman's beguiling words contrive to transform reality —

which Januarie should view in a new sagacious light — into illusion, into a fiction made actual through craft, persuasion, and a talent for improvisation. As he opens his eyes to reality, the jealous old man sees a swollen sex belonging to his squire, who takes to his heels for fear of being recognized. Januarie instantaneously identifies Damyan's desire, physically embodied by the latter's organ, while he was utterly unaware of his own "appetyt" (1250) for his pretty wife. He allegedly chose her in expectation of the bliss of married life: "For wedlock is so esy and so clene, / That in this world it is a paradys" (1264–65).

Absolon is quite close to the elderly knight in *The Merchant's Tale*, since both turn out to be victims of the power of illusion or *phantasia*,[33] which they have created of the desired women. It is the disgraceful wind that bluntly puts an end to the clergyman's passion, yet on the contrary, the sight of May's lovely buttocks sets Januarie's mind on fire. His excitement is increased by his blindness, which, teased by fantasy, highlights the girl's erotic aura. "There is a whole technique of illusion to be organized for and against love" (*HS III*, p. 186–87). Furthermore, the irony of the husband's position is underlined by his concern for legitimizing his longing for carnal pleasure within the legal structure of marriage — yet thought of as the model of sexual austerity by the medieval Christian doctrine![34] The darkening of critical judgment due to avidity finds a metaphorical illustration in the epilogue of *The Friar's Tale*. After the old peasant woman, wrongly accused, wishes the summoner and her pitcher to Hell, night falls until the only glow discernable is the one from the copper jug, on which is reflected the figure of the devil, come to fetch what now is his. It is too late when the summoner awakes from his blindness. The only way out (or the only remaining light) is that of eternal damnation: "Thou shalt with me to helle yet tonyght" (*The Friar's Tale*, 1636) — "Tu verrai questa notte stessa conme giù all' Inferno" (*Sceneggiature*, 378) — declares the fiend, with a hand on his dumbfounded prey's shoulder and the other holding the jug. This gloomy ending foreshadows the final vision of the netherworld. The summoner loses his soul, and so does the friar in *The Summoner's Tale* when Chaucer makes him both the witness and mediator of the infernal hallucination, related by Pasolini's fantasy that contaminates the scene with pictorial motifs borrowed from Bosch.

Vision Turning into Fantasy

The adaptation of *The Summoner's Prologue*, put after the tale, provides the opportunity for a phantasmagorical extension of the concept of seeing, which signifies not only looking, spying, taking hold of (under the impulse of desire), but also "dreaming," the most deviate manifestation of vision, in the original sense of "visual perception." In the first extradiegetic interruption, just after *The Cook's Tale*, Pasolini-Chaucer laughs in reading *The Decameron*, which he quickly closes to write down his own stories. He hides it under a high pile of thick reference books and goes back to his desk. But instead of showing the writer take up his quill again, in a slow low angle shot the camera discloses a stern-looking woman standing still, richly dressed in bright red, green, and blue. From above, she watches Chaucer severely as he snoozes in his chair. The viewpoint suggests a commanding, inquiring look. Her imperious, snappish voice awakes him: "Geoffrey Chaucer!!!" The poet wakes up with a start and coweringly resumes work. He has just been roused from a daydream. Maybe his wife embodies a parody of the Muses. This quite unattractive manlike Muse is staring at Chaucer with a menacing look. Moreover, when she appears, the cackle of hens can be heard, first very low, then louder. The cackling confirms the derisive tone, which makes it impossible to take her for the guardian of poetic authorities. In a hieratic pose, she is standing in front of several piles of books, probably representing a most respectable literary heritage, that of the Ancients so remote from the tendentious *Decameron*, which her husband is secretly reading. The artist follows a creative track in his dream from what can be read to what can be seen. Boccaccio's text has unconsciously inspired some images. This is what Pasolini the filmmaker, playing a poet, seems to be saying. Still, the poet, who also happens to be a film auteur, behind the camera lens, stages himself as a writer keen to put his visions into words, taking the opposite path from the *lisible* to the *visible*. In the preceding extradiegetic sequence between *The Friar's Tale* and *The Cook's Tale*, Pasolini-Chaucer writes: "Notes for a book about the pilgrims on the way to Canterbury. The Cook's Tale." Then, all of a sudden, the camera eye propels us into the world of Perkyn's pranks. He is literally kicked in the backside by his angry boss outside both the shot and action frames. The old man's wild shouting abruptly arouses us from our lethargic spectatorial state, in which the silent scene in the dormitory had sent us—Chaucer taking notes for his tales.

The visual translation of text finds its most outstanding illustration in the Hell sequence, picturing the friar frightened by Satan's gigantic posterior defecating dozens of his brethren. Sight, now turned into mental dreamlike vision, is examined at the extradiegetic level of Chaucer-Pasolini visualizing his film-text, but also at the level of some characters in the tales. In his sleep, Perkyn sees pretty young women dancing at the wedding, which he messes up. This time, they wear nothing but bonnets and flowers in their hair, and he prances about excitedly among them. He has the same ribald smile as Andreuccio, also played by Ninetto Davoli, when he first lays eyes on his so-called stepsister in *The Decameron*. Yet Perkyn is the only character whose erotic fantasies are disclosed to the spectator. He is probably taken out of the Chaucerian context to serve as an excuse for a purely cinematic Chaplin-inspired number, which has nothing to do with the text, that the camera eye "de-reads" in a visual and gestural disintegration of the Hollywood musical genre.

Corporeity and Commodified Sex

In *I Racconti di Canterbury* the human body catches the spectator's eye. It is reduced to a consumer good. Deprived of any psychological depth, as they emerge into the fiction (as suddenly as they disappear from it), the characters become alive on the screen thanks more to their corporal presence than their actions and scarce dialogue. They come to life through a corporeity that seems unusual to anyone accustomed to classic cinema, in which the actors' physical presence avoids overshadowing the plot. Pasolini's film, though, shows quite a few characters totally undressed. Still, their bodies more often than not bear a variety of acceptations. Nakedness is first associated with purity and youth, but it soon designates sinfulness that calls for punishment. The body is especially represented through the filter of its commodification a product meant for joyless mechanical consumption. Reified, it is staged in the sexual act as well as satisfying a natural need. The obscenity for which Pasolini was so repeatedly reproached does not so much apply to the display of naked bodies copulating or urinating or breaking wind. In fact, the scatological content of some sequences in *Racconti* indirectly denounces the "petit bourgeois" mentality of profit-making, which views the body as an exchangeable commodity. There lies the real obscenity, according to the author of the film.

The Body in a State of Grace

In the film version of *The Merchant's Tale*, the only undressed bodies are those of May and the two deities that seem to merge harmoniously with the pastoral setting of Januarie's garden. The very first glimpse the old man catches of his future wife is of her charming backside. Such an unexpected revelation delights him and suffices to influence his decision, the validity of which seems to be corroborated a moment later when May turns her pretty face to the camera eye. On the wedding night, we discover her lying nude on the bed, then at her sleeping husband's desk, writing a secret note to her lover. Januarie's ridiculous-looking nightdress, his risible ardor, as well as his clumsy, clownish hops of joy for having accomplished (a poor) sexual deed sharpen the contrast with his spouse's grace and freshness. May's youth, vigor and beauty foreshadow the apparition of Pluto and Proserpina, who saunter about the garden wearing nothing but a wreath of leaves, reminiscent of the pagan antique statues.[1] Because her name recalls the blooming natural forces, May embodies the celebration of a solar Eros, of a sparkling vital spirit that masks the menacing shadow of the Thanatos figure of Januarie, who evokes the cold season. The comely young wife has a sad, indifferent expression like that of a small wild animal in captivity. Yet her face progressively brightens under the effect of lust. Likewise, some characters in *Il Decameron* behave as if exclusively motivated by pleasure and immediate gratifiaction. May seems to emanate from Boccaccio's world of instinctive human beings with a keen appetite for life in its most basic aspect of sensual and especially sexual enjoyment of the present moment, as underscored by Pasolini.

The Fallen Body: A Commodity

Resting on the essential opposition between the flesh and the spirit, Paul's exhortation to virginity and continence, the only salvation for the "tabernacle of the Holy Ghost," accounts for the "diabolization in the Middle Ages of the flesh and the body, assimilated to a place of debauchery, to the centre of the production of sin, (which) will on the contrary deprive the body of all its dignity."[2] As early as the second episode, *The Friar's Tale*, nakedness loses its connotation of innocence synonymous with beauty and the vitality of Eros. The body is treated like a commodity in an economic logic of profit-making and the appropriation of material goods. It is for sale, as confirmed by the two young male prostitutes introduced in the plot by the filmmaker. *The Cook's Tale* also stages a very young woman, Perkyn's chance companion's wife. The mischievous reveler gets acquainted with her in a dim alley in a shady part of London, as she is waiting for a customer. She ends up in the conjugal bed between Perkyn and his new friend. Silent, she smiles at the camera. Her role is purely instrumental, as for a small amount of money she offers her charms to satisfy men's sexual appetites. Furthermore, she fulfills a second function, indirectly referred to this time; that of a mediator between her husband and Perkyn. The three of them indeed stare at the camera with a smirk, as though it were implied that one of them is unwanted. Her intermediary position in the bed may well point out the uselessness of a female presence in a male homosexual relationship.

Let us come back to *The Friar's Tale* which, before *The Pardoner's Tale*, touches on the theme of the domination of the prostituted body by the power of money. While the male prostitute is utterly naked, the second sodomite, rather aged and stout, wears a shirt and interrupts himself for a sip from a jug, without even offering the boy a single drop. The relationship between the two men is one of unambiguous subjection and denotes a social gap between the dominator and the subordinated. Later on, the idea is borne out when the summoner agrees to turn a blind eye on the rich man's shameful secret activity as the latter hands him a purse full of coins. This situation contrasts the preceding one. The first sodomite in the opening sequence of the tale is a frail, skinny fellow, as naked as the prostitute, to whom he offers a bite of his apple. He behaves with the disinterested generosity of one ranking as low on the social ladder as the boy. In both cases, nonetheless, sex is devoid of pleasure and becomes sadly mechanical. Pasolini anticipates the long scene in the brothel that opens the adaptation of *The Pardoner's Tale*.

The film version of *The Pardoner's Tale* endorses that vision of sex which is based on penetration as a mark of male superiority. Man's active role enhances woman's submission. Today's experience of sexuality revolves round the male/female opposition, so that the behaviors that feminize man are perceived as a blow to his sexual function. Yet other attitudes exist regarding the use of pleasures.[3] The viewer of *Racconti* discovers the three rascals in *The Pardoner's Tale*, each in a bedroom with a harlot. They give themselves over to a sin fiercely condemned by Chaucer's Pardoner as well as by Rufo, one of Pasolini's rogues: lust, five variations of which are exposed. In the first brothel room, the girl is seen from behind, kneeling submissively, trying in vain to provide oral pleasure to a somber, impassive-looking youth lying on a bed. His impotence may be ascribable to an undisclosed homosexuality. The following shot shows another young fellow sitting on a chair, taking delight in advance in the sexual gratification he expects from the woman sitting opposite him on the bed. He urges her to go down on bended knee at his feet, as if she were a dog ("cagna," *Sceneggiature*, 389). In other words, it is the debasing of the prostitute, reduced to the condition of an animal, that stimulates his excitement. The third rake, a premature ejaculator, is equated with a rooster in the film script.[4] He consumes his pleasure hurriedly and asks for more, slipping a coin into the very young unresponsive girl's mouth, on top of whom he is lying. She undergoes in utmost apathy the repeated assaults of her customer, whose ridiculous excitement leads to nowhere but the eternal renewal of a convulsive fruitless act. Volume III of *Histoire de la sexualité* brings to mind Galen's precepts. The physician and anatomist's treatise on the use of genitals relates the sexual spasm to a pathology of spasmodic excreta, epilepsy especially. Ejaculation is conceived in terms of loss of vital energy and therefore points to death.[5] It is the other way around in the next passage, wherein the strumpet is given the active role. She has to call herself the queen of a young man lying face down on a bed, whom she whips vigorously. Pleasure is found in pain.

Last but not least, the fifth bedroom, as shabby as the other four, is the scene of a comic mise en abyme of the courtly love relationship, itself the object of a parody in Absolon's wooing of Alisoun in *The Miller's Tale*. The rogue resorts to metaphors, clichés borrowed from the *fin'amor* rhetorics, while fornicating with a girl bending forward. She smiles mockingly on hearing the sweet words addressed to her: "My sweet love, my little pigeon, my sweet little flower."[6] The sexual act again makes the woman a passive subject. The last fille de joie's position reminds us of Gemmata on all fours, taken like a mare by Don Gianni in *The Decameron*. The gullible peasant woman, who expects the promised magic trick to happen, giggles naively, facing the camera, and evokes a gorgeous filly mounted by the shrewd libidinous priest. Such picturings of the human body constitute the opposite extreme of the ideal of chastity dictated by monachism and the contempt of earthly delights. The five situations in the brothel sequence seemingly draw attention to the sexualization by Christianity of human nature, that is, the bringing down of the spiritual sense of the Incarnation (*caro*) to the corruptibility of flesh subject to lust. In Jacques Le Goff's opinion, the crystallization of the flesh/spirit antinomy, the basis for a Christian order that sexualizes the original sin and makes sexuality the root of sin, explains that the notion of unnatural sin developed in the Middle Ages "with the extending concept of sodomy (homosexuality, the sodomization of woman, coitus from behind, or woman on top of man: all will be proscribed)."[7]

The Political Body and the Politics of the Body

These five performances of sex, taking place in dingy bedrooms, look like a show. Different though they may be, this series of representations of fornication has a common denominator. First of all, sex is consumed within a master-and-servant relationship. Only in the fourth situation is the harlot the object of male pleasure, neither down on her knees nor bending forward submissively. On the contrary, she becomes the executor of sensual rapture, which incidentally is never shared. In the initial scene, it is strikingly absent. The girl unambiguously expresses her contempt for her customer's desperately impotent member: "Cut it!," she says—"Tagliatelo!" (*Sceneggiature*, 389). The penis appears as a common instrument meant to be operational in an alienating system governed by the principles of production and consumption. As the object of commercial dealings, the body undergoes a denaturation under the effect of the corruptive potential of money. Consequently, sex is subverted, as it degenerates into the subordination of a slave to a master in a sadomasochistic realtionship. It is so depraved that it is entirely emptied of sensuality and feelings. It becomes a mere excuse for the pathetic display of bored, soulless flesh.

We are a long way from the erotic surge that throws Alisoun into

Nicholas's arms on her bed, where they hasten to take each other's clothes off. The fiery young clerk pulls up the carpenter's wife's dress while she pulls down his trousers. They have scarcely undressed when the camera discloses the reason for their impetuosity. The body is hastily rid of its clothes, just as a manufactured good is rid of its package to be consumed in the next moment. Then follows a still shot of Alisoun and Nicholas, lying side by side the next morning with nothing on. Previously, the young wife is seen in bed with her husband, the covers pulled up to their necks. John and Alisoun, with a night bonnet on, stare at the spectator in a hieratic pose that tells a lot about the scarcity of the amorous embraces a hot-blooded "joly colt" may share with a fat, ugly old husband. As in the preamble to *The Pardoner's Tale*, in which the prostitutes are static and apathetic except for the "queen," who holds a whip, the naked bodies of Alisoun and her lover suggest the morbidity of lifeless flesh, though still young and graceful. The medical prescription concerning the use of pleasures advocates "a submission as strict as possible of the desire of the soul to the bodily needs, an ethics of desire shaped on the model of a physics of excreta."[8] Still, the lovers' souls in *The Miller's Tale* are far from yearning for some ideal goal as they are exclusively bent on "the austere economy of organic evacuations" — "l'économie austère des évacuations organiques" — i.e., the ejaculation of sperm as a natural need described by Galen.

The contrast with the Wife of Bath and her fourth husband is worth considering, since the episode opens with the very act that is deliberately not shown in *The Miller's Tale*. In the conjugal bed, the husband, much older than "hende Nicholas," laboriously pays his marital debt. In this burlesque caricature, sex is presented as a painstaking task, performed mechanically, comically suggested by the stiffness of Alisoun's legs as she urges her husband to step up his efforts to satisfy her. With her arms and legs wide apart and as rigid and taut as those of a puppet, she rolls her eyes desperately, expecting an orgasm that fails to come. She selfishly relishes a pleasure that her exhausted husband wears himself out giving. Yet no sooner is their embrace over than she pushes him away with scant ceremony. She jumps onto the floor without even glancing at him, leaving him behind as though he were a common object of no more use. A heavy consumer of sex, the Wife behaves aggressively like an animal. The idea finds its illustration in the bright red color of the outfit she wears at the beginning of the movie and in the field with Jankyn. During the religious procession in the background, Alisoun of Bath and her fifth husband-to-be are comfortably sitting in the grass behind a hedge, hidden from other people. Also dressed in red from head to toe, Jankyn takes her hand, trying to look as natural as possible. He puts it down on his crotch and feigns to read attentively, as befits a clerk. His silent detachment during Alisoun's relation of her alleged dream ironically points to a hypocritical attempt at concealing the real nature of his intention, betrayed by the color of his clothing. This urge actually echoes the Wife's. Quite aware of it, she relates a dream she pretends to have had so as to justify her lust for him (after having watched him in his bath on the sly). Her so-called vision sounds extremely violent. Jankyn, she claims, tried to kill her and left her lying on her bed covered in blood. Nevertheless, she declares herself under his spell and de-dramatizes the meaning of the scene by interpreting it as a sign of good luck: blood is synonymous to gold. "For blood bitokeneth gold, as me was taught" (*The Wife of Bath's Prologue*, 581)—"...il mio sogno è di buon augurio: perché sangue significa oro" (*Sceneggiature*, 329). In the logic of the shrewd tradeswoman and clothmaker, socially prominent in town, the enchantment of her longing for Jankyn is viewed in terms of a seizure of power or appropriation of his body. Taking possession of the desired body results from a long fierce struggle, the winner of which comes out richer. United by wedlock, Jankyn and Alisoun clinch a deal that enables him to enjoy her personal property, while she is legitimately entitled to use his body.

> This joly clerk, Jankyn, that was so hende, / Hath wedded me with greet solempnytee, / And to hym yaf I al the lond and fee / That evere was me yeven therbifoore. / But afterward repented me ful soore; / He nolde suffre nothyng of my list. / By God, he smoot me ones on the lyst, / For I rente out of his book a leef, / That of the strook myn ere was deef [*The Wife of Bath's Prologue*, 628–36].
>
> "O! hastow slayn me, false theef" I seyde, / "And for my land this hastow mordred me?" [*The Wife of Bath's Prologue*, 800–01].
>
> But atte laste, with muchel care and wo, / We fille acorded by us selven two. / He yaf me al the bridel in myn hond, / To han the governance of hous and lond, / And of his tongue, and of his hond also; / And made hym brenne his book anon right tho [*The Wife of Bath's Prologue*, 811–16].

The Wife sports a flashing red dress and a massive broad-brimmed hat made of the finest and most costly material, just as she openly admits to the worldly nature of her attraction for Jankyn. The intensity of her carnal appetite is matched only by her determination to assert in public the prestige of her privileged social status, which confers her precedence at church over the other women of the rising merchant class:

> In al the parisshe wif ne was ther noon / That to the offrynge bifore hire sholde goon; / And if ther dide, certeyn so wrooth was she / That she was out of all charitee [*The General Prologue*, 449–52].

In offering her body to her new husband, as she puts it herself, Alisoun hands over to him her jewels as well as her estate and money. Foucault emphasizes the interesting analogy between the body and a material good by resorting to etymology. The ancient Greek *soma* refers to both, "hence the possible equivalence between the possession of a body and that of riches."⁹ Sex becomes a transaction made possible by marriage. The matrimonial contract binds the spouses within a system of debts and obligations, shared yet not equal. The temperance prescribed by the Greek moralists before the Christian doctrine of the flesh is totally ignored by the Wife of Bath, who stands as the antithesis of the virtuous, submissive wife. Likewise, the uprightness displayed by Jankyn turns out to be a specious imitation of the ethical ideal of self-control, of moderation in enjoying one's wife's body. The satisfaction of lust is legitimized by law, and the sacrament of marriage elevates sex, thus redeeming it. Lastly, the commitment made by both parties in the arrangement seems incompatible with reciprocal affection, mutual respect, namely the *concordia* supposed to serve as a basis for the ethical unity of the couple (Foucault, *HS III*, 216). Alisoun's biting revenge, after she has been knocked out, indicates she sets little store by the personal relationship expected to be found in a married couple. She attaches far greater importance to sex. As for her clerk of a husband, he is far from enjoying the sovereignty or "maystrye" over his wife that is warranted by his legal status. He figured he would be immune from reproach and eternal damnation while indulging in a practice, the misuse of which might be fatal for the health of his body and the salvation of his soul. The church distinguishes three categories of people whose spiritual worth can be defined depending on their attitude toward sexuality. The virgins (*virgines*) stand on top of this hierarchical representation. Then come the continents (*continents*), widows mainly and, lastly, married people (*conjugati*), who can reach only the lowest level of exemplary chastity (Le Goff, 38–39).

The Pictorial De-composition of the Body: The Display of the Flesh

The intermediary position of *The Wife of Bath's Prologue* in *I Racconti di Canterbury* between *The Miller's Tale* and *The Reeve's Tale* is not fortuitous. Holding his crotch, Nicholas embraces the carpenter's sensuous wife, exploring the most intimate part of her anatomy with the other hand. The scene takes place in the kitchen, where a dead pig is hanging from the ceiling as a symbol of flesh ready to be consumed. The love declaration then cannot be taken seriously either by Alisoun or the spectator:

> Alison, Alison, se non posso fare quello che voglio, la passione che ho di te mi farà morire! ... amami fin da questo momento, se no io morirò![10] [*Sceneggiature*, 257]

His alleged passion actually boils down to his sex drive whetted by the sight of the amply low-cut dress of the young beauty, whom he is burning to make short work of. His insatiable carnal appetite, entirely concentrated in his swollen crotch, foreshadows the Wife's. Twice she is shown licking her lips lasciviously before and after her husbands have paid their marital debt to her. The same lust drives the students in *The Reeve's Tale*. They, too, wear bright red clothes, emblematic of the nature of their desire. Exhilarated by their temporary freedom from the college, they are "worse than monks, arses tight and pricks hard!"[11] The coarse comparison employed by John directly expresses with no rhetorics what they are really up to. On one side of the windmill two naked female backsides can be seen jutting out. They belong to the miller's wife and daughter. Either real or the fruit of the youths' fantasy, this shot summarizes again in *Racconti* the simplistic idea that men have of women, whose faces in this scene are disclosed only in the following shot. Dismembered, the female body is equated with a piece of meatloaf displayed in a stall. The buttocks are exposed to view, especially to the concupiscent look of the two companions in a dehumanizing pictorial de-composition. As if twins, John and Aleyn ride the same horse like "two who shit through the same hole,"[12] one of the 118 aphorisms illustrated by Bruegel the Elder in *The Netherlandish Proverbs*.[13] The clerks are taking part in the same quest for an opportunity to have it off: "You'd like a good screw, John?"[14] This is the proper reason for their bunk. They mean to outwit the dishonest miller, first by ensuring they are not robbed of their flour, then later by seizing the opportunity to satisfy an urge as untameable as that of a rutting stallion after some mares. The animal metaphorically stands for unbridled sexual vigor.

"This is obvious" (Hagen, 37) is the second meaning of the Bruegel-inspired vision of the two bottoms sticking out of what looks like a makeshift wooden toilet overhanging a ditch —"comme chiottes sur un fossé" (37), as the Netherlandish proverb has it. The scene evokes defecation indeed, an additional clue of the debasement of the female body, the vaginal and anal orifices of which are mistaken for each other. The situation has strong scatological connotations given the posture of the women, although there is no excremental emission whatsoever. The tableau vivant nonetheless is intended as an aesthetic effect, as confirmed by the bleak, sunless English countryside wrapped in the morning haze. The diegesis is momentarily suspended by the parasitic visual parenthesis. Even without understanding the allusion to Bruegel, the viewer cannot possibly be shocked by the unexpected deviation of the narrative, a possible reminder of the filmmaker's presence in the saucy yet not obscene retrospective hint at *The Miller's Tale*, which lays bare two provocative backsides. There is nothing offensive nor rude about Symkyn's daughter's rear. On the contrary, it foretells a touch of eroticism in the night sequence later on in *The Reeve's Tale*, when the ardent Aleyn takes pleasure with Malyne under her sleeping father's nose.

Pasolini's Malyne is much prettier than Chaucer's,[15] and she is treated more humanely by Pasolini, who changes her into an infatuated fine-looking girl. The lovebirds say their farewells at dawn, exchanging pledges of love, words uttered in earnest for once.[16] She kisses him and says: "Go away, my love, go away!"[17] (288). This is the only act of sexual intercourse in the film that is accompanied by true mutual feelings. We see nothing but their faces as they look at each other, whereas their lovemaking throughout the night is discreetly occulted on the screen. As proof of her ardor, Malyne clinches a deal with Aleyn by showing him where he can find the bread made by her father with the stolen flour.[18] Then she gives him one last passionate kiss. After the fight between the young man and his furious quarrelsome host, she rushes to open the shutters. The daylight filters in to reveal the whole truth about the mistake as well as her attractive naked body, the innocent grace of which is highlighted by the childlike look of surprise on her face. She waves at her one-night lover wistfully: "Ciao amore! Ciao amore!" This gesture of tenderness betrays sincere emotion, yet it does not totally obliterate the feeling that the student is given double compensation for all the trouble he has been through. On the one hand, he has a taste of the miller's attractive daughter, and on the other hand he runs away with the cake, a material alimentary reparation which reduces the female body to a mere delicacy meant to satisfy the frustrated male hunger.

The Scandal of Denatured Sex

The treatment of the body reaches its lowest level when nakedness is associated with scatology. The undressed body may also be insulting and offensive by making an indecent gesture. Alisoun in *The Miller's Tale* displays most impudent behavior. She challenges Absolon with an insolent fart as an answer to his advances. She resents his manners and affected language saturated with clichés borrowed from the courtly romance: "What are you doing, honeycomb sweet? Alisoun, my fair bird, my sweet cinnamon, wake up, speak to me,"[19] he whispers at the lady's window. In reply he gets nothing but a discordant sound devoid of sense — as well as the essence of the *mal d'amour,* which he claims consumes his heart. The wooer's rhetorical pretension is crushed down by the outrageous detonation, smashed into an insignificant nonentity, comparable with the explosion resulting from the alchemical mixtures described in the interminably in *The Canon's Yeoman's Tale*. The accumulation of technical terms drawn from the vocabulary of this mysterious science saturates the narrative. Likewise, the artificial sham language employed by Absolon to impress the carpenter's wife is unjustified and of absolutely no effect on her heart. Pasolini pushes the indecency even further when he transposes on the screen the affront endured by the bashful suitor. In Chaucer's text, the cheeky Alisoun merely puts her rear on the squeamish admirer's mouth. In the movie, she goes as far as to inflict a disgraceful "blow" on the importunate visitor. The mortification is not only tactile but also olfactory, which worsens Absolon's humiliation and disgust. The harder the fall, the more efficient the remedy for his blind determination to conquer the belle. What his lips and extremely sensitive nose[20] rest upon calls for an answer as coarse and burning as the affront. The hot coulter which the offended young fellow thrusts into Nicholas's backside penetrates him with the aggressiveness of a sodomite penis. The punishment was meant for Alisoun, whose fart he cannot tell from his rival's. Both lovers show themselves to be irreverent and salacious. The clerk and the adulterous wife behave equally grossly. As a reaction to the lyrical style of the *fin' amor*, Chaucer's story with its strong scatological whiff stands at the opposite of the courtly erotics that offers:

> a picture of love and sex embodied by the fairies, ladies living in castles and who seduce the knight errant in quest of adventure, or the damsels that lords and squires present their visitor with.[21]

Pasolini stresses the sauciness of such counter-literature as *The Miller's Tale*. The fabliau can be described as a response to the ecclesiastical moral rigor. Jacques Rossiaud quotes the *imagines mundi*, some medieval cosmographies that depict forbidden practices judged immoral and therefore monstrous, like polygamy, sodomy, and bestiality. Such representations locate the aforesaid behavior in imaginary remote, symbolically marginal countries. The gender difference no longer applies in a context where heterosexual intercourse is negated and subverted into an act of sodomy. Still, Nicholas's rushing out of the bedroom, shouting "Water! water!" with his hands on his burnt backside awakes the gullible carpenter. Without thinking, the latter instantly cuts the rope on which the kneading trough is hanging from the ceiling, and it plummets with a deafening sound. The quick denouement, the posture of the clerk holding his sore rear, and the dumbfounded, cuckolded old husband make the story seem a slapstick comedy. The burlesque touch at the end of *The Miller's Tale* saves us from the scatological register into which the film threatened to sink.

The film version of *The Pardoner's Tale* subverts sexuality in another way. The emission of semen, presented in various situations in the brothel opening sequence, takes on a degenerate form. The fake preacher—one of the five blackguards who indulge in lust—suddenly produces his penis to urinate on the customers downstairs in the tavern. The sexual function of the male member is travestied into an unproductive act, the ineffective liberation of a soiled infecund liquid. The idea of sterility is already implied by men's impotence or premature ejaculation, as well as by the joyless prostitutes' inexpressiveness in the dreary house of ill fame. In the epilogue, the three scoundrels collapse in a state of utter physical and moral decadence, with one vomiting and another defecating. The tragic fall of these bodies is the result of the depravation of their sinful souls. The youth who suggests to his companion that they should kill the third "sworn brother" once he is back from town, where he has gone to buy some wine, is precisely the one who remains hopelessly unmoved while the prostitute in the first brothel room is doing her job. His impassive, cruel face lights up when he eyes the treasure, the only sight that causes him to have an erection. The second rogue, who was riding his "sweet dove" in the initial scene, seizes the third one from behind and pretends he wants to play. He addresses him with the same love words he spoke to the bawd in his mock-courtly style: "My love!" He even feigns to be titillated by such "a lovely arse,"[22] and starts wrestling for fun in a kind of physical game which serves as a prelude to homosexual intercourse.

In brief, when it is not impotent or full of (homosexual) desire, the male organ in *The Pardoner's Tale* fulfils a low urinary function. Uttered by the first victim of the Thief called Death, the castigation of the Seven Deadly Sins flows down along with the jet of urine on the madam, the gamblers and heavy drinkers, all spending their lives in this den of vice. In Chaucer's tale, the Pardoner, who is the narrator, condemns the following sins: "the fyr of lecherye" (*The Pardoner's Tale*, 481), "That luxurie is in wyn and dronkenesse" (484), "Corrupt was al this world for glotonye" (504), "A lecherous thyng is wyn, and Dronkenesse / Is ful of stryvyng and of wrecchednesse" (549–50), "Now wol I Yow defenden hasardrye. / Hasard is verray mooder of lesynges, / And of deceite, and cursed forswerynges"[23] (590–92). The caricature of a sermon with eschatological rings to it illustrates the body's subversive scatological potential, a theme that appears again in the infernal vision as *Racconti* draws to a close. The red fiends milling around against a very dark background (the scene was actually shot on Mount Etna, the famous volcano in Sicily) exhibit their sex in obscene postures. They gamble, show their tongues, and fart. They laugh their heads off at the sight of the torments inflicted on the undressed bodies of the damned, who are either mutilated, hanged, forced to work themselves to death or sodomized. Corrupt and sullied, the body is ruthlessly chastised. This is anticipated in *The Friar's Tale* scene of the sodomite burning at the stake for not having been able to redeem an act considered shamefully unnatural and therefore objectionable, such as the avarice, covetousness, gluttony, or vanity staged in the final tableau vivant.

A Dark Vision of Mankind in the Farcical Mode

Obscenity and the Scum

The base, servile body reveals man's bestiality. His animality comes out in the erotic convulsion, which sometimes lapses into obscenity. The policy and poetics of adaptation chosen by Pasolini in the case of the *Canterbury Tales* brings to the fore what may first appear obscene. Let us quote, for instance, the opening of *The Pardoner's Tale* in the brothel. The sexual behaviors exposed seem shocking. The rakes make use of the girls as mere tools meant to provide them immediate pleasure and attain this unrestrained freedom that releases them from respect and human feelings, and denies the existence of the other and the self. The cold cruelty with which they indulge in anomalous, deviant irregular erotic practices plunges them into an upside-down world, where the vital energy is wasted in vain in the "disorders of a destructive sensuality,"[24] strangely similar to what Sade imagined. The insubordination flaunted by the five scoundrels betrays a dissolute life, both in the literal and figurative sense. They are so intent on satisfying all their most basic drives that they wander away towards death-reeking depravity. The momentary faintness of the body in the orgasmic climax becomes a permanent flavorless state.

> Thus the limpness of an immense derision freely creeps into the heart. To reach this state, it is sufficient to steal, even kill if necessary, lazily remain alive by conserving one's strength, and anyhow live at the expense of other people.[25]

When writing about the underworld, Bataille describes a sinking of the humaneness of the soul. Coming back to the film, one may wonder, what makes this particular sequence of *The Pardoner's Tale* likely to shock as obscene? As Bataille reminds us, obscenity refers to a relation between an object and a subject, whose consciousness is marked by moral self-restraint. The denial of sensuality and the degrading display of nakedness (condemned by the Bible) repels the spectator precisely because it lacks restraint. The "ob-scene" excludes from the scene what cannot be shown, i.e., the genitals, the sexual functions of which are brought down to the lowest level of fecal and urinary ones. Obscenity also applies to some violent behaviors, the excessive nature of which inspire disgust, a feeling of horror due to the supreme vertigo caused by the glimpse of death. In other words, the obscene relates to what is not acceptable, that is, what one may show and see. The worst shape it takes in *Racconti* is that of the excreta or foul emissions of Alisoun in *The Miller's Tale* or the two rascals who murder their companion at the end of *The Pardoner's Tale*. Just like the hairy parts of the bodies are evocative of man's shameful animal nature, such gruesome elements fill the viewer with aversion, for they can be branded as filth and therefore corruption. *The Pardoner's Tale* indeed begins in the underworld of prostitution and vice. Because originally it was closely linked with prostitution, obscenity tinges sensuality with scandal. Bataille explains that society attributes to prostitutes and their kind obscene animal urges, considered as signs of irremediable immorality. This "upside-down" world alters voluptuousness into outrageous depravity through sexual fever and a language with no moral barriers. What defines the prostitute's turpitude is not so much her selling her charms as her coming down to the status of an animal. Since she is not familiar with or simply ignores the interdict, she lives in a world where she takes no notice of what is usually thought vile and objectionable. This is why society rejects the riffraff that populates such places. The Christian world ascribes to man a moral superiority over animals. Therefore sinners, who transgress moral principles, do not belong to God's humanity, but on the contrary partake of Satan's animality. His tail is believed to symbolize his fall. Eroticism in the Christian Middle Ages is associated with evil and social disgrace.

> Even morals elevated the people of lowly birth, the better to pour contempt upon the fallen class. The malediction of the Church weighs more heavily upon collapsing mankind.[26]

Having to face "the hard, dogmatic, theological core," the "preeminent social moral"—shaped by the Christian teaching against which it simultaneously attempts to resist—forces the church to put up with the illicit. While it imposes a stable monogamous conjugal order, the ecclesiastic authority recognizes prostitution and subjects it to a codification—prostitutes, for instance, must not be integrated in town—from the late twelfth century on, when the urban boom aggravated sexual violence on account of the increasing number of young bachelors in towns.

The Erotic Animal of a Remote Past

His animality guarantees man existence as a subject, whereas his humanity, which pertains to the organization of his world through work, conscience and reason, actually reduces him to the status of an object. The people in *Racconti di Canterbury* indulge in all kinds of excesses, precisely because they belong to a remote archaic past and have not yet repressed wild desire. Their humanity is closer to this poetic, divine body because of its animality. Behind the ebullience of sexual activity and the plethora of bodies (and the plethoric body exhibiting a "growth of organs" swollen with vitality), Pasolini seems to imply that man is the erotic animal described by Bataille. Eroticism only means something insofar as there is the interdict to be transgressed. Nakedness and the crudity of some situations or dialogues in the movie present no offensive character whatsoever. On the contrary, they are the targets of interdicts, which leave the viewer dumbfounded with fright and desire, terror and fascination. The duality of man lies in his being torn between the animality of shameless sex and the humanity of a shameful sexuality. For the pagans, prostitution used to be a sacred institution in direct contact with the interdict, Bataille reminds us. The numerous aspects of orgiastic dissolution testified to the sacrality of eroticism. The Christian doctrine denied this sacred dimension and made eroticism something entirely profane and transgressive, condemning it as the sin of flesh.

Nonetheless, Bataille compares the orgasmic cry with "an immense alleluia" (264), voicing the triumph of the human being in a paradoxical loss of the self. The intense climax of physical pleasure is viewed as unequalled and consequently elevates eroticism to the level of a religion of the human being as opposed to God, an exaltation of man. When he temporarily loses his humanity, the latter enjoys the blind animal oblivion in the detachment of his mind and consciousness. Sex entails a confusing disorder in social behaviors. It makes the individual free through a di(sso)lution of the self, which is at the same time a state of blissful plenitude, in the sense that the meeting of two bodies enables one to find again the lost continuity and completeness of one's being. Though a human activity, the erotic act is based upon man's animal nature. No wonder that the lexical field of sexuality is strongly permeated with that of bestiality. Pasolini brings out the exuberance of the explosion of the flesh (usually contained) through a fireworks of genitals which "calls for the unleashing of those mechanisms alien to the ordinary governance of conducts" (106). In the sexual act, an excess of energy pours out, being discharged and wasted away, as Foucault points out in *Histoire de la sexualité*. One's being gives itself up entirely, freely and excessively, and in so doing comes within a hair's breath of death.

Instrumentalized Sex

The orgasmic climax can be described as a free, benevolent gift, whereas the society in which the characters of *Racconti* live is governed by an economic logic of profit-making. The commodification of bodies is especially noticeable in *The Merchant's Tale*, *The Friar's Tale*, and *The Pardoner's Tale*. In Pasolini's view, a politics of acquisition and possession of material goods (including bodies) already pervades the mentalities in Chaucer's England, which foreshadows the Italian neo-capitalist society of the early

1970s despite the time and space gap between them. The generally accepted idea that the Trilogy of Life expresses a nostalgia for a bygone time of sexual freedom is erroneous. The overall dark tone of the film, the landscapes and a great deal of situations depicted, actually evince the insidious substitution of a bleak, cynical logic of the appropriation of a being by another for the generous gift of the self. In a remote past, the Eros was not yet constrained by reason and the control of human activity through work. As early as the late 14th century, sex was conceived in terms of exchanges and negotiations, as demonstrated by the frequent use of the imagery of commercial and financial transactions throughout *The Canterbury Tales*. The pursuit of profit drawn from marriage or dealings with a prostitute (in both cases, one takes possession of a body) sullies the erotic act with "the ugliness of power" ("la laidezza del domino") and "the common despicable violence of the rich" ("la volgare violenza della ricchezza").[27]

At the heart of this denaturation of love lies the obscene, the shock of the monstrous. As indicated by the prefix "ob," it antagonizes the other end of man's humanity: his erotic animal nature when he gives himself up to the immediate joy of Eros. The enigmatic ill of the nascent medieval bourgeoisie, a portent of the 20th-century reign of mass consumption, hinders the primitive spirit still undamaged by venality. The modernity (Michel Leiris speaks of "merdonity"[28]) of post-industrial society yields a disquieting, perniciously destructive power with anaesthetic effect on people's primal genuine capacity to enjoy life. The radiance of the jubilant, luminous Eros grows confusingly darker in *Racconti*, which renders the impression of a human community that "thoroughly excludes the disorder of the senses, ... denies its natural principle, ... protects its values from the violence and impurity of passions."[29] One recognizes the portrait of the asexual bourgeois humanity, as viewed by Bataille. The present world, ruled by "the time of work," has lost an instinctive approach to sexuality. Paradise and Purgatory, evoked at the end of *The Decameron* in the tableau vivant inspired by Giotto's *Last Judgment*, disappear from *Racconti*. In the second cinematographic panel of the trilogy of life, only Hell is left in an allegorical vision, far more frightening yet definitely farcical of the expulsion of an edenic Eros by a satanic flatulence. For Gianni Canova, this nightmarish representation provides an illustration of the bourgeois tragedy:

> ... the tragedy of our bourgeois identity is always the same: this is what we are, all of us. Small, very small indeed, acquisitive and oblivious. Driven away from the Eden of Eros by a gigantic flatulence.[30]

Under the threat of death in the grotesque scene just before the epilogue of *Racconti* we can read a reflection on the close relation between sex and power. Just after making his trilogy, the film auteur abjures it in the name of an instrumentalization of sex by the authorities, meant to homogenize the individual, to reify it inside a production-consumption-possession equation. Foucault underlines the necessity to free oneself of this juridical and discursive conception of power that dictates "the thematic of repression" (Foucault, *HS I*, 109). Besides, sexuality is defined in a way that creates the illusion of sexual liberation. The absolute will to know everything about sex has generated a science of sexuality, and its discourse is used as a tool to keep watch over people's sex life, upon which their social existence is articulated.

From the Theater of Cruelty to the Burlesque

Is mankind doomed to a cruel prophecy, as suggested by the (e)sc(h)atological tableau at the end of *Racconti*, where the redeeming figure of the Madone of *The Decameron* is conspicuously absent? The fantasized Hell reflects the harrowing image of death. However, this theater of cruelty is nothing compared with the degree of horror attained in *Salò*, a blood-chilling emanation of Sade's abject universe. The abode of the damned in *Racconti* is depicted by means of a pictorial pastiche of one of Hieronymus Bosch's most famous paintings. The pastiche creates a mediatory effect of distancing emphasized by the farcical treatment. The grotesque dimension in the film can be found in the looks, gaits and attitudes of the characters. The filmscript highlights their spontaneous, instinctive behavior by visualizing them through a number of brief, evocative parallels with animals. Januarie's clumsiness, which has already been mentioned, likens him to an oafish bear. In *The Cook's Tale*, Perkyn's second master, standing with his arms akimbo, and his chest thrown out, reminds us of a peacock on account of his overconfident, conceited expression. His debauched apprentice scurries away from his fury. Besides looking like the early Charles Chaplin, whose clownish pranks the actor skillfully mimics, Perkyn joins a wedding party. He partakes in the damsels' dance and starts hopping about like a sparrow, held as an embodiment of lewdness in medieval imagery. Furthermore, he performs silly antics with a mocking smile, half innocent, half mischievous. His pranks and buffoonish expressions are meant to give substance to the character's fresh ingenuity and authenticity. The young reveler is part and parcel of the motley crowd, among which Pasolini picks some particular faces (with comical, sometimes incongruous twitches or mannerisms), which either do not appear on the screen or remain in the background of the diegesis. In *Racconti* the camera eye turns away from the standard features and postures usually seen in conventional cinema. *The Miller's Tale* film sequence pictures an ugly, pot-bellied carpenter with bad teeth. The steward of the college in *The Reeve's Tale* is austere-looking and curiously red-faced. When Perkyn sings his song at the stocks, *The Cook's Tale* episode ends with a close-up of a repulsive old woman, virtually toothless, shaking what looks like a rattle. There is also a hideous man with a voluminous, hairy black hat on, playing the bagpipes. As for the young male protagonists, even the good-looking ones still have minor physical defects, which are deliberately not dissimulated, so that they are really different from the smooth, flawless physiognomies of the stars that the great majority of viewers want to see. The youngest of the three sinners in *The Pardoner's Tale* has beautiful pale blue eyes, but a close-up reveals the imperfections on his face. When smiling, neither Absolon, Nicholas, nor Damyan disclose a leading man's perfect white teeth in a grin of satisfaction. As he sings gaily under Alisoun's window, the handsome youth who plays the wooer gets carried away by his own game and laughs knowingly with his mate who accompanies him on a guitar. Their roguish charm almost evokes the country folk painted by Bruegel the Elder, for instance, with such an extraordinary potential of vitality in them that the figures seem to come to life on the canvas.

In addition, the spectator is not accustomed to see a film character break wind like Thomas in *The Summoner's Tale* or Alisoun in *The Miller's Tale,* or cock a snook like the college steward on his deathbed at the beginning of *The Reeve's Tale*, or shamelessly boast of having "the prettiest thing" in town like the Wife of Bath. The emphasis on comic exaggeration is what motivates such incongruities. It also explains why the language sometimes lapses into coarseness. The English subtitles unambiguously render or even strengthen the brutality of some comparisons or the bawdiness of some remarks. In Alisoun of Bath's ostentatious, windy self-portrait in the Southwark marketplace sequence, "quelle," a vague term, is translated by a rude word: "I can undo *all those bitches* in Ypres and Ghent."[31] Still, the indecency of the substantive quite suits the exuberance of this fierce English virago,[32] with her bellicose explosive temperament. Her garrulous, uncouth speech is strongly tinged with similes drawn from the warfare imagery. The amorous act is referred to by some indecorous verbs, and the genitals, male and female alike, by even more vulgar denominations, once by the Wife and once by Aleyn and John.

From Music to Grotesque Cacophony

Even the folk songs contribute to brighten up the dark atmosphere of the movie with a comic note, metaphorically mirrored in the grey, dreary urban and rural setting. The credits at the beginning capture the spectator's attention not so much by means of their visual sobriety (a mere succession of names in thin black letters on a white backcloth), but by the cocky accents of an English folk song, which Perkyn takes up at the stocks. Played with a wind instrument (some kind of bagpipe) that gives a funny, nasal, twangy sound, the song tells the story of a young singer from Lenhoory who lived in Ballahoory and could sing nothing but "the four muses." If not medieval, the tune sounds archaic to the 21st-century viewer's ear. *I Racconti di Canterbury* depicts a very remote, rough yet lighthearted world whose inhabitants sing naturally and spontaneously as much about flirting as about love pain. The prologue of the film opens with the Pardoner, sitting with his back against the wall, striking up a Neapolitan complaint already heard in *The Decameron,* when the two usurers and their host Ciappelletto join in a famous song from their native town.[33] Nevertheless, the red-haired Pardoner with a buffoon's face takes delight in exaggerating the tragic echoes of his tune, as he is a good performer trading on his lies. Later, the bald tattooed-faced Cook joyfully mumbles a funnily unintelligible old English ritornello-like theme in a goatish voice. All the other motifs and melody lines in the film help to create a seemingly genuine medieval atmosphere. The soundtrack is definitely instrumental in the making of the film's meaning(s), in the sense that the music merges with the motion picture in a combination that Pasolini calls "essentially poetic, that is empirical."[34] Outside any relation of subordination to the motion picture, the music in *Racconti* takes on an astonishingly poetic dimension in its essential link with the visual medium. In *The Reeve's Tale,* Malyne with a beaming smile rocks her baby while enthusiastically singing a brisk, lively Irish tune. Her gaiety echoes that of the two Cambridge students who, in the previous sequence, convinced they can easily outwit the dishonest miller, sing a jeering couplet with "son of a bitch" in it. Just as we hear these words, the camera eye focuses on Symkyn's satisfied expression, as he relishes in advance the trick he is planning to play on them. Far from fulfilling the mere conventional illustrative function, the music introduces an additional degree of comedy mixed with irony. It amazingly coalesces with the image in a twofold phenomenon of friction and fusion, which brings to mind the distance between the soundtrack and the picture, while at the same time erasing it.

Pasolini's film shots, combined with the medieval monodies and tunes, fashion an intricate network of correspondences in a subtle composition. This works simultaneously on the instantaneity of the gesture ("the horizontal application") in the shot or sequence, and the duration, i.e., the film's construction as the story unfolds ("the vertical application"). Despite a great variety of songs and instrumental pieces borrowed from the English and Italian medieval, Renaissance and post-Renaissance repertoire — an eclectism that reflects the discontinuity and plurality at the narrative level as well— the music in *Racconti* produces a kind of tonal cohesion perfectly in tune with the medieval spirit of the stories sometimes licentious and at other times grave. The kinship between this archaic tonality of the film and the farcicality of a great deal of situations is signified through the allusion to the Hollywood musical genre in the wedding party sequence in *The Cook's Tale*—this being done in a burlesque fashion. The pastiche of the burlesque movie in Chaplin's style actually drifts away towards another genre, where the narrative is momentarily interrupted so that the protagonist may dance gracefully among beautiful creatures all dressed identically. Now in this diegetic suspension, the dancing girls are stripped to the bones (except they are all wearing white bonnets wreathed with flowers), and caper around in a circle to their hearts' content to the rhythm of a 14th-century Italian melody entitled "Lamento di Tristano: Ghaeta." Still, their boisterous, somewhat disorderly movement (on account of Perkyn's intrusion) lacks the smooth, harmonious fluidity of Hollywood's graceful and sparkling choreographies. The young debauché's hops and lewd winks put the finishing touch to the comico-erotic subversion of the wedding party of the pretty blonde and her ridiculous, skinny crybaby of a husband.

The musical accompaniment eventually degenerates into dreadful cacophony during the phantasmagorical visualization of *The Summoner's Prologue*. The pilgrims in the frame-story are nearing their goal. The organs and bells of Canterbury cathedral can hardly be heard because of the damned's vociferations and the obscene noises made by their horned tormentors. The buffoonery becomes Grand Guignol. The passive viewer finds himself brutally roused from a lethargic state by the infernal clamor, so he is led to read under the surface, that is through the screen, into the text upon which a painting by Bosch is superimposed. It is by means of a breakthrough into the oneiric world that dissolves the narrative that the spectator is made aware of the aesthetic originality of the camera. The filmmaker's gaze becomes more radically innovative and different, as if to remind us that the cognitive and narative value of the film cannot possibly mask its fantasmatic role—behind which Freud describes a logic of rationality. The music becomes a travesty, a gruesome flatulence that signals the intention of an unmotivated amplification as well as nihilistic grotesque dimension, which could be construed as the opposite poles of what can be shown and seen in a film.

2

Placing *I Racconti di Canterbury* in Perspective with *The Decameron*

A Necessary Consideration of The Decameron

Reflecting on Pasolini's vision of Chaucer's work implies considering as carefully as possible the way Boccaccio's material is treated by the same film author. First of all, *I Racconti di Canterbury*, like *The Decameron*, which it follows one year later, is characterized by a visual radicality. Therefore a parallel can be drawn between both movies. Often described as radiant with "a visual music,"[1] the film of *The Centovelle* inaugurates a series of three singular picturesque motion pictures with an original anti-establishment viewpoint, a clever thematic and narrative architecture, as well as an unconventional aesthetics and uncommon style for the early 1970s cinematographical landscape. The surprise caused by this peculiar movie, consisting of a series of different narrative sketches, can easily be ascribed to the very subject and context from which Pasolini draws his inspiration. We are talking of a Middle Ages made up of pictorial touches, visual and sound impressions, virtually not historicized, as historic verisimilitude and authentificating details do not seem to be the filmmaker's primary concerns. Besides the poetic quality of the shots, the awareness of their expressive potential and the staging justify the particular attention that *Il Decameron* deserves. Its fragmentary, inconclusive structure corresponds to the experimentation of a cinema that breaks the conventions of traditional narrative and instead favors creativity. Pasolini's is a cinema of poetry in that it gives a major importance to the gaze which turns into vision. The stories are not only put into film but also dreamed. Playing Giotto's disciple, the author of the movie contemplates his dream once his pictorial fresco is almost finished. Lastly, an invigorating feeling of refreshing vitality arises from the spectacle of the ebullient, motley world of *Il Decameron* that somehow portrays an exotic time and space.

Although for Pasolini the editing phase in the making of a movie aims at operating diegetic segmentation — he chooses 10 *novelle* and arranges them in a chronology that totally departs from that of Boccaccio's text — Canova underlines the homogeneous character of *The Decameron*. He calls it a "choral"[2] instead of a serial film, for it falls into two main parts. The *cornice,* the prescriptive rigid frame that organizes and legitimizes the stories reported, is superseded by a much more flexible narrative configuration. Both parts hinge upon a representative figure: first a glib swindler with a gift for mystification, then an artist whose paintings deceive eyesight (*Il Decameron*, vol. 2, VI, 5 p. 737).[3] The reshaping of the textual material is interspersed with sequences entirely made up by the adaptor. Therefore the movie bears the stamp of Pasolini's personal creative re-reading or imaginative interpretation of his source. The two-faced figure preeminent throughout the film, the rascal and the artist, provides his own shadow and spirit in the part, over which he symbolically presides, and marks it with either his noxious or his positive influence. In Patrick Rumble's opinion, what could pass for an aleatory dissemination of the initial order of the stories actually delineates a structural allegory. "It would appear that the film's central conflict is expressed implicitly in the structural relation between Ciappelletto and Giotto's pupil: between the usurer and the artist."[4] One may wonder whether Pasolini's version of Boccaccio's work rests upon a thematic incompatibility. On the one hand, it opposes the capitalist system of exchange, an incitement to cupidity which subjects people to a rich minority. On the other hand, it conveys the notion of the generous disinterested practice of art, in which the artist offers the fruit of his work for the public to enjoy. Rumble's thesis calls for close scrutiny and needs to be qualified through the detailed study of the diegetic composition of *The Decameron.*

A Refraction of the Text

In Search of a "Transnational" Language

As pointed out earlier, the two texts that inspired *The Decameron* and *Racconti* constitute a watershed in Western literary creation on account of their innovative form of writing, their great thematic variety, stylistic experimentation, and the use of the frame-story narrative technique. Eager to reach as many readers as possible, Boccaccio and Chaucer show an acute awareness of the necessity of an immediately accessible language. The popularity of these works witnesses the essential role played by the vernacular expression in the making of a language representative of a burgeoning political and cultural identity. Now the context in which they flourish is then hardly concerned by the phenomenon described by Patrick Rumble in terms of "...historical and cultural processes involved in the later phases of formation of the nation-state" (Rumble, 9). Consequently, instead of serving nationalist purposes, the language they employ as a vehicle of expression for a literature as such becomes a *koiné* for a whole people whatever the linguistic and cultural differences from one country to another. Pasolini is particularly sensitive to the issue of the crossing of borders by a language. Cinema provides him with the means to gather a vast heterogeneous audience, for it goes beyond the concept of national identity. Because the diversity of the topics and styles speaks to anyone's consciousness and imagination regardless of their nationality, *Il Decameron* and *The Canterbury Tales* cannot bear a specific national label. This would reduce the reach of their contents and the regenerating potential of their form. For the filmmaker, the "transnationality" of these medieval works finds its reflection in the transnationality of a modern language with a high creative potentiality, rising above the social and cultural distinctions of "a possible future society" (Rumble, 9). What Pasolini has in mind is *la lingua del cinema*:

> The audiovisual reproduction of reality is an identical linguistic system or language in Italy or in France, in Ghana or in the United States.... The structures of the language of cinema therefore present themselves as transnational and transclassist rather than international and interclassist [Rumble, 11].[5]

Neapolitanization versus "Coca-colonization"

The film signifier or *im-segno* ("image-sign") has a universal import. *Il Decameron* and *Racconti* set off the universal character of the adapted stories. A complex network of echoes and correspondences circulates from one film to the other, thus implying they both result from the filmmaker's fantasy: that of a medieval reality deliberately not made real for it is aimed to be intemporal. The regional idiosyncrasies are wiped out as in a dream, where only the spirit and style of the works remain identifiable. Nevertheless, the shift from a Tuscan context to a Neapolitan one bespeaks a preoccupation with the specificity of minority identities. The Naples area is a poverty-stricken part of Italy with its own dialect and particular cult to the Madonna in place of Christ, as we are reminded of in the tableau vivant of Giotto's *Last Judgment* towards the end of *The Decameron*. When putting Boccaccio's and Chaucer's texts into film, Pasolini is faced with a dilemma.

Enthusiastically and with an insatiable curiosity, he launches out into the handling of modern technologies in a society, the alienating power of which he denounces while voicing an ideologically heretic viewpoint. He learns about film-making on the job. Cinema fascinates him; he sees it as the most mimetic medium that ever was, therefore he devotes himself entirely and passionately to it. Yet he bitterly realizes that such a language is first and foremost that of a society dominated by the global culture of mass consumption, which drowns ethnic differences and local traditions. In Italy, the official language is a legacy of the Tuscan hegemony (since Boccaccio's time) imposed on the other regions. The common, colloquial, colorful speech of the Neapolitan lumpen-proletariat is heard in reaction against the artificiality of an elitist normative culture.[6] This is the first twist to Boccaccio's text. As for *Racconti*, it is shot in English by British nonprofessional actors for the most part, then dubbed in Italian, which creates a deliberately unremedied gap, which contributes to destabilize the viewer. Pasolini's cinema is a political, conscious one, which helps to the "coca-colonization"[7] of the planet through the uniformization of film language: "…a possible sociolinguistic situation of a world made tendentially unitary by complete industrialization and by the consequent leveling which implies the disappearance of particular and national traditions."[8]

The Camera Eye, the Quill, and the Painting

This is why the Trilogy resorts to an aesthetics of the contamination of the film image by pictorial citations meant as a pastiche. Described as "stylistic oxymorons" (Rumble, 13), *The Decameron* and *I Racconti di Canterbury* are designed upon the tension between the common yet leveling language of the film medium and the modes of representation of the past, especially the maestros of the late medieval and Renaissance visual arts. Indeed, cinema owes a debt to the pictorial tradition. The amazing degree of iconicity found in many a shot in both films indirectly signals not only the evocative power of the picture created by the painter but also of the word picked by the poet. In his conclusion, the author of *Il Decameron* remarks that to the writer's clever use of speech corresponds by analogy the artist's ability to reproduce reality on the canvas. VI, 5 draws a parallel between two celebrities, both reputed to be ugly: Forese da Rabatta, a doctor of law and therefore an expert in the art of rhetoric persuasion, and a genius of figurative painting, Giotto, said to be able to achieve "such a perfect reproduction of the world for the eye that it was no longer a copy but the model itself."[9] Thanks to a fluid style and brief, effective, forceful dialogues drawn from the genuine popular idiom, Boccaccio and Chaucer manage to bring to life some ordinary situations of their time in comic stories related to the low register of the fabliau and farce. One may wonder why the filmmaker focuses mainly on this particular narrative type to the detriment of the *novelle* and tales belonging to the elevated genre (the courtly romance, the epic, or classic tragedy).[10] The answer can be found in the fact that prosaic events are more easily and spontaneously suited for a staging of the reality observed.

What matters most for the film director is telling stories by searching for the narrative's highest degree of visuality — so much so that the spectator is under the impression of reverting to the expressiveness of the picture so typical of silent movies. In *The Decameron,* Pasolini plays an artist painting a fresco, that is, a series of scenes following one another in a diegetic progression. Then, at the end of *Racconti,* the artist, a poet this time, logically finishes his work. The thematic continuity between the two films reproduces the creative process of a work of art, deliberately left unfinished in the epilogue of *The Decameron* — the third panel remains blank — only to be completed yet not concluded in the second part of the trilogy. Both movies bear the influence of the medieval and Renaissance European cultural heritage. The rich literary and pictorial background provides the appropriate ground for the blooming of creativity of a filmmaker anxious to make the spectator aware of the continuity and relevance of past artistic practices. The film shot in *The Decameron* and *Racconti* is devised as both visual and fantasmatic. The reference to some paintings assimilates the motion picture with the canvas, in that both speak from a delineated frame that functions as an operator of reflexiveness allowing the image, either filmic or pictorial, to signal itself as such and as discourse. The discourse of the simply evoked paintings (pastiched instead of scrupulously restored to look as authentic as possible) parasitizes and suspends the telling yet enriches the film with a poetic radiance. In literally picturing the very gesture of painting in *The Decameron,* Pasolini implies that he aims to move beyond the narrow boundaries of realistic figuration so as to make the visibility of the work tangible for us by allowing the emergence of this moment of pure poetry that obliterates the narrative.

An Artistic Tradition Brought to the Viewer's Mind

Concerning the relationship between painting and cinema, Jacques Aumont remarks that "up to the late Renaissance at least, the image is thought to have a magic action, a living influence."[11] The painting strikes the medieval man's mind by its forceful power of evocation and immediacy, comparable to the instantaneous impact of the words uttered aloud by the teller for his spellbound audience. Boccaccio and Chaucer share with their contemporaries a conception of the collective reception of the literary work. The transmission of a text is first and foremost oral and is experienced within a group. The street scene just after Andreuccio's adventure in Naples—which serves to introduce the following sequence—shows an old storyteller sitting in the middle of a crowd. The storyteller soon looks up from his book in Florentine (*Il Decameron*), from which he draws his material in IX, 2. He casts it aside and carries on improvising in the Neapolitan dialect, gesturing and mimicking with comic expressiveness, especially when he stresses the sinning nun's generous curves. Jill Ricketts notices that in this sequence the editing consists of alternating the old man's storytelling with Ciappelletto taking advantage of the listeners' concentration to rob someone of his money so as to buy the charms of a really good-looking young boy.[12] The hale and hearty fellow with a well-lined purse, from whom Ciappelletto steals a coin, stands facing the camera, motionless, staring at the old teller in a hypnotic state. The camera eye then slowly sweeps across the faces in the crowd, now hanging upon the old man's every word, now laughing when the young nun unmasks the abbess who is guilty of the same shameful activity. Obviously, the people listening to the anecdote are locals, extras hired for the sequence shot in Caserta, the working-class quarter of Naples. They are relishing the story, which is humorously related by a skilful narrator in a relaxed atmosphere of joyful complicity. The simplicity of these genuine people, the sincerity of their knowing smiles or the serious expression with which they drink in the man's words, give the feeling of a communion, the sharing of an experience that brings people together and makes them realize that under the surface of the narrative a hegemonic normative discourse can be deciphered. A young nun gives herself over to the delights of love on the sly until one day she is caught red-handed. She is severely chided by the Mother Superior, who embodies the precept of abstinence, which she ensures is scrupulously observed. A figure of authority in the convent, she has the power to chastise any offender who would dare contravene the rule. The trouble is that she secretly indulges in the very villainy she censures in public. She betrays her hypocrisy when she rushes out of her cell with the priest's breeches on her head in place of her headdress, so impatient is she to inflict on the young nun the punishment prescribed by the monastic rule. It is as though the experience of the narration and reception of stories reminded the audience that there exists a cultural ground common to all. Moreover, through humor, they are taught how the discourse of authority eventually prevailed. According to Rumble,

> ... the *Trilogia* presumes "una coralità, insomma, d'ascolto e di riconoscimento delle esperienze da cui è nata la deduzione della norma" ["a chorus listening to and recognizing the experiences from which the deduction of the norm was born"].[13]

Pasolini draws from Boccaccio's vast pool of *novelle* staging mischievous, double-dealing protagonists. This type of story is largely represented in the movie and, significantly enough, *Racconti* resorts to the equivalent material in Chaucer's *Tales*. A great deal of funny, often ribald episodes bring into light the deceitfulness of impostors and tricksters, either representative of an aspect of power (economic, religious, or moral) or closely related to it. Like Boccaccio and Chaucer, the film director picks some pieces of fiction that testify to a condemnable human and social reality—which an ingenious stylistic experimentation and a play on form (astutely intertextual in *The Canterbury Tales*) enable to stigmatize through irony. Furthermore, the choice of comic stories derived from the medieval low literary genre is more likely to appeal to the masses. Their cultural memory owes much to authors who managed to extend literature to a language and a register that spreads far beyond the narrow limits of the aristocratic readership steeped in courtly romance and poetry so disconnected from reality. While reading Boccaccio and Chaucer, Pasolini recognizes the "revolutionary" (Rumble, 14) potential of the cinema of poetry: reviving a tradition without which the present loses its resonance, reverting to the poetic magic of the collective reception of the narrative endowed with a visual radicality, while resisting the vacuity of "the new era of humanity."

Exhibiting the Unacceptable

The early 1970s Italian society reeks of death in Pasolini's opinion, first because it is the scene of an irrepressible wave of murders and criminal acts, whereas the consensual opinion sees it evolve on the way to modernity in an increasingly tolerant democracy. The depoliticization of the country disintegrating into a "dead body" with "purely mechanical reflexes"—"un corpo morto i cui riflessi sono che meccanici" (L'Abiura, 773)—seems to demonstrate that this preoccupying anthropological change is not temporary. The neo-capitalist power is alienating people's conscience by resorting to mass communication and mass consumption. The "irreality" of that policy, publicly denounced by the intellectual Pasolini, manipulates, violates, he says, and even denies the only remaining reality: that of bodies and a fortiori that of sex. In granting a large but fake tolerance, the power has succeeded in curbing the liberal struggle for the democratization of expression and sexual liberation. Turned into a mere instrument by the prevailing consumerist discourse, reduced to a common consumer good, the body is so manhandled that it is eventually deprived of the innocent, carefree joy of sexuality that irradiated it in a remote past still unharmed by the violence of power. The result, at least in Italy—which Pasolini views with a critical, well-informed eye, being himself the favorite target of some intellectuals and the political authorities—is that the youth finds itself dispossessed of its illusions and withers away under the effect of a blasé sexuality devoid of the spontaneous gaiety of the vital élan. The flesh becomes sad, the behaviors more and more aggressive, so that cruelty imposes itself in all its crudity. Suffice it to see *Salò or the 120 Days of Sodome*. Such degeneracy mirrors the overall phenomenon that plunges the country into a fatal acceptation of deprivation:

> In other words, Italy is going through nothing but a process of adaptation to its own degradation, from which it only pretends to attempt to break free.[14]

This is what Pasolini writes on June 5, 1975, five months before his assassination, in a letter entitled "Abiura della Trilogia della vita." Now we have just summed up the reasons why he disclaims *The Decameron, I Racconti di Canterbury*, and *Il Fiore delle mille e una notte*. Through the first two episodes, on which we have chosen to focus our attention, the film director owns he once believed he could make up for the decaying present, "a heap of insignificant, ironic ruins"—"La vita è un mucchio di insignificanti e ironiche rovine" (Abiura, 771)—by restoring on the screen the basic nature of what defines man; the physical existence of the body, whose vital force (Eros) is materialized by the genitals. Because it is distant enough from the present day, Boccaccio's and Chaucer's Middle Ages provide a utopian setting suitable for the representation of a true Eros characterized by a dark, archaic violence—"the ultimate stronghold of reality" / "l'ultimo baluardo della realtà" (Abiura, 770)—in a contemporary world going through a cultural and anthropological crisis. The choice of *Il Decameron* and *I Racconti di Canterbury* may well be ascribed to their author's intention (shared by both writers) to adopt a necessary distance from a controversial work in order to protect it against censorship. Pasolini's abjuration is strangely reminiscent of the Author's Conclusion in *Il Decameron* and Chaucer's Retraction. Although written several centuries later, the film author's disavowal of his work resorts to a rhetorics quite similar to that of the medieval *concessio*.

Halfway Between Self-criticism and Disavowal: Sincerity or (Dis)simulation?

Boccaccio's strategy consists not in a real palinody but in the self-justification of an author whose sole ambition is to entertain his "noble" young female readers. Thanking God for having helped him carry his literary enterprise through, in accordance with the modesty topos, he hopes he has been up to the promise he made in his incipit. Then he works out a defense strategy by thinking of some criticisms from some readers. In other words, he anticipates some fictive comments on the licentiousness of some *novelle*, the better to ward off any possible blow from detractors. The explanatory introduction indeed is built upon the repeated pattern (about 10 times) of the attack followed by argumentation. The author neither repents of his faults nor shows an act of contrition, but instead insists on having composed his work as a humble writer abiding by the principles of poetic creation. For instance, he ascribes the whiff of scandal about his frivolous stories to the very nature of their subject, which justifies the use of sexually suggestive language, similes and metaphors. He claims for his quill the freedom granted to the artist's paintbrush, which faithfully reproduces realistic, sometimes shocking details. Yet the author implies that the bawdy anecdotes should not be judged improper. In fact, they are told in a profane context, that of a garden of earthly delights instead of a sacred religious frame-story. As long as the ladies who read the *novelle* have not an unchaste mind, they are sure to get some moral benefit from them. Warned about the content of the stories in the very brief summaries that precede each of them, the female readers of *Il Decameron* are to expect that a literary work would draw its inspiration from both the elevated and low styles. Even the friars' homilies, the author remarks ironically, resort to jokes, puns, and coarse innuendos in delivering spiritual messages. Besides, as the faithful reporter of the historical events that led to the telling of the *novelle* by the *brigata* in their unplanned retreat in the Tuscan countryside, the author deems it is his duty to rigorously transcribe all that was said exactly as it was during those 10 days. Because it is not intended for clerks and churchmen, whose intelligence has been sharpened by scholastics (a jab at the *litterati*'s alleged erudition), the text employs more explicit, colorful language. Then the author suddenly goes beyond the limits of the accusation/defense argumentative model to hardly concealed duplicity: "Suppose that I am both the author and writer, which I am not ..." (*Il Decameron*, vol. 2, 1258).[15] This is to be read as a rhetorical precaution with which he surrounds his words so as to evade disapproval. Dissimulation and prevarication enable the shrewd narrator to sow confusion in his reader's mind as to who is actually the author of this composition. He astutely refers to the convention of confession in penitential literature. Later in his conclusion he uses the verb *confesso* twice (1260 and 1261). The avowal is always accompanied by apologies, so that the mostly defensive, even bitter tone of the defense lets some tinges of repentance show, indicating he is making amends: "I thought that this pleasant trick would suit some trivial stories written to dismiss ladies' black mood" (*Il Decameron*, vol. 2, 1260),[16] or "My language is subject to this rule (the mutability of things), as everything else, this language I hardly dare say anything about (for I distrust my own judgment and object to it concerning me)" (1261).[17]

The last lines put an end to the long confession, which consists of an exposition of personal intentions as well as self-criticism characteristic of the Christian conscience. The author of the book leaves it up to God's grace and judgment, although he does not directly name Him, using only the deictic "Colui ... che..." (1261), that is "the One ... who...." He concludes by wishing to remain in the memory of his humble female readers, whose life he may have filled with "joy," as befits the tone of humility. In this secular perspective — the last person mentioned is not the Creator but the ladies he addresses his work to—, the invoking of God's forgiveness raises the question of its "sincerity and necessity." These are Pasolini's words in his "Abiura" (*Sceneggiature*, 769). The author's conclusion in *Il Decameron* takes on a strangely ironic ring, then. A way of legitimizing the book is to draw a parallel with the Scriptures— which when read by an unchaste mind might lead to immoral interpretation — and the religious visual arts— which paint objects with strong sexual connotations to evoke sacred subjects. The author calls upon the supreme spiritual authority with a view to guarding himself against any possible reproaches from the church for its licentious tinge. "The defences that Boccaccio and Chaucer provide are themselves not devoid of irony" (Rumble, 87). According to Rumble, Pasolini adopts and adapts the self-criticism of their respective works all the more faithfully as he needs to denounce the outrageously mercenary exploitation of the treatment of the body in the Trilogy of Life by pornographic cinema. Still, his angry abjuration is somewhat toned down by irony. The "Abiura" has been wrongly and debasingly interpreted for too long.

> This genre (the journalistic essay), to which the "Abiura" appears to belong, conditions its reading to such an extent that precisely such a "meta-literary" or potentially ironic sensitivity has tended to be overlooked in preceding readings of this essay [Rumble, 86].

A Repenting Poet

Chaucer's Retraction belongs to the medieval rhetorical tradition of the critical commentary of "the makere of this book" on his work. First of all, the numerous references to his preceding texts— spreading over three of the 11 lines of the palinody (X[I] 1085 to 1087)— bespeak the author's awareness of his responsibility as a poet who educates an audience through his written work, however insignificant it may be. This is why he apologizes. Not only does he stress the importance of the didactic function of books, but he also means he does not address only the narrow world of the scholars through a hodgepodge of compositions as different as "the book of Troilus," "the Tales of Caunterbury" (1085) or "the legendes of seintes" (1087). These popular texts were written in the vernacular by a creator who was also a translator of a rich literary heritage. Chaucer's acute sense of the poet's mission accounts for the self-reflexive depth of his Retraction. Unlike Boccaccio, he admits to some stylistic shortcomings. His audience/readers should blame his incompetence. In the same line, he uses the term "unkonnynge" and repeats it almost literally in a synonymic clause: "if I hadde had konnynge" (1081). Next, despite the poverty of his talents as a writer, he seems eager to convince us of his sincere intention: "I preye hem also that they arrette it to the defaute of myn unkonnynge and not to my wyl..." (1081). His design, so he says, is inspired by the scriptural prescription according to which: "Al that is writen is writen / For oure doctrine." The wish to conform to God's word, a goal he alleges he has failed to attain, accentuates the penitential orientation of the discourse, apparently consistent with the rhetorical convention of the pious conclusion. He beseeches his audience to pray to God for forgiveness for his having produced some "translacions and endytinges of worldly vanities, the whiche I revoke..." (1084). In the second part of the "retraccioun," the tone grows even more repentant. He implores the grace of the "Kyng of kynges," "preest over alle preestes" (1091) so that despite the invitations to sin found in his worldly works he may eventually find himself among the blessed "at the day of doom" (1091). A large number of words relate to pious penitence and the imploration of godly grace, echoing *The Parson's Tale* which displays the rich homiletic rhetorics:

> Crist for his grete mercy foryeve me the synne [1086]; ... oure Lord Jhesu Crist and his blisful Mooder and alle the seintes of hevene [1088]; bisekynge ... to biwayle my giltes ... [1089]; the salvaccioun of my soule, and graunte me grace of verray penitence, confessioun and satisfaccioun ... [1089].

A Mock-abjuration?

Irony underlies the text of the "Abiura." Under the guise of compliance with the rhetorical rule of the writer's humility in face of God's perfection, its author feigns to leave it to the ultimate judgment of the authority of the Book to take some distance from it. Thus the reproaches likely to be leveled by religious men can be evaded. The maker of *The Canterbury Tales*, "thilke that sownen into synne" (1085), is after all nothing but the modest author of a little vernacular "tretys," which would excuse his shortcomings to the Christian ethics. Nevertheless, the latter's character of absolute reference finds itself questioned by the advent of another literature.

> And just as both Boccacio and Chaucer address their "apologies" to those in power, and rather rhetorically distance themselves from their often transgressive material in order to protect it, so does Pasolini's recantation have a similarly rhetorical ring to it.... Pasolini communicates two antithetical messages at once [Rumble, 87].

The "Abiura" explores still further than the Retraction the contradictory, litigating expressive potential of irony. "Everything is fine," Pasolini exclaims in the last part of his public confession. Then he reminds us that Italy bursts with delinquent, neurotic young people on the verge of estrangement. A few lines below, he adopts a falsely satisfied, reassuring tone: "Everybody has adapted by refusing to realize anything or practising the most inert form of dedramatization."[18] The stylistic monstrosity built upon the oxymoron figure reaches its climax at that point. The last paragraph starts as follows: "But I must admit that my having realized it (he means the collapse of the present day) or dedramatized it does not preserve me from adaptation or acceptance. Therefore I adapt to degradation and accept the unacceptable."[19] The irony grows more bitter, and so does the resentment that leads to the abjuration. The author of the Trilogy of Life asserts he will no longer be able to make this kind of film, for now he hates bodies and sexual organs on account of the numerous pornographic continuations to *The Decameron* and *I Racconti di Canterbury*, which have perverted Eros. Lastly, after evolving from anger mixed with disillusionment to hopeless bitter realization, the Abiura closes on sorrowful renouncement:

> I manoeuvre to reorganize my life. I forget what things were like before. The dear faces of yesterday start fading. Ahead of me — little by little without an alternative lies the present. I readapt to my commitment to a greater legibility — *Salò*?[20]

"Autolesionistic," as Patrick Rumble puts it, Pasolini's re-writing of Chaucer's Retraction deviates towards the heretic pole of self-mutilation though "the line of demarcation separating complicity and transgression is never entirely clear" (Rumble, 98). In an intertextual interaction (also a play) with *Il Decameron* and *The Canterbury Tales*, the meaning of the "Abiura" feeds on the underlying irony of its hypotexts, and as a consequence reaches still deeper in the performance of a two-voiced discourse. The promise of a greater legibility is reminiscent of the amends Boccaccio starts making and that Chaucer too ostentatiously makes to the supreme Judge. In the context of the 1970s Italy, God is no longer the reference. He is superseded by the dominant ideology of a power that strives to repress the creativity of dissident voices in a standardizing model.

From Text to Film: Narrative Metamorphoses

After attempting to demonstrate the legitimacy of considering Chaucer's text in the light of Boccaccio's, we will now set about closely examining the film version of *Il Decameron*. The idea is to draw attention to the many alterations entailed by the making of a literary work into a film.

Such changes, whether at the structural, diegetic or thematic level, produce new specific meanings sometimes likely to drift away from those of the source. The screening of the *Centovelle* largely shortens the narrative, but also introduces noticeable modifications and, to a lesser extent, dilatations and additions.

The Systolic Visual Reading of I, 1

Except for the anecdote of the abbess lecturing the nun about a sin she herself is guilty of, none of the other nine *novelle* selected by Pasolini retains the slightest trace of the narrator's speech. The preambles and comments in the conclusions disappear. The most obvious illustration of this is found in the very first *novella*. The invocation to the maker of the universe at the beginning of I, 1, which initiates every single human work, is suppressed. So is the indication in the following sentence of a godly miracle in the story to come. The context of the story-telling game played by 10 young members of the *brigata* is totally absent. This explains why the filmmaker passes in silence over the page-long overture (about 30 lines in the Italian text). For identical reasons, the movie dismisses Ciappelletto's last deathbed words at the end of his mock confession, when he expresses the wish to be buried in the church so the faithful may pray for the salvation of his soul, and begs for Extreme Unction. The narrative also omits the detail of the decision made by the friars in the monastery and the watch over the body. With no transition whatsoever, after the comic "Yes! No!" exchange between the naive priest and the deceitful, allegedly contrite penitent, the former delivers a sermon to the congregation, showering praise upon the dead swindler. Inside the crypt, the homage paid to the "saint" by the crowd of worshippers is played up. This passage is proportionally treated as insistently as it is in the text, in which a whole page evokes the fervor of the devotion to the fraud's body. Lastly, there is no "Thus lived and died Cepparello da Prato"—"Cosi adunque visse e mori ser Cepparello da Prato" (*Il Decameron*, vol. 1, 69)—the stereotypical conclusive formula taken over by Panfile in a comic hint at the literary genre of the saint's life. Pasolini rids the ending of the superfluous final comment on the necessity to revere the Lord, who in his infinite goodness takes into account mainly the earnestness of the faith, even though the Christian worships the wrong object.

I, 1 provides another illustration of the elliptic film rendering of the text. The iniquity of the influential Musciatto Franzesi, who hires Ciappelletto's services, occupies one-third of a page. On the screen it is cleverly suggested by the connivance he shares with his associate during an interview. This conversation marks the actual beginning of the sequence. The adaptation amputates the *novella* by almost one-third. In a few sketches only, Pasolini manages to depict the protagonist, upon whom the first part of the movie hinges. As a substitute for the recurrent references to his dishonesty, duplicity and vileness over a whole page, the film director has Musciatto remind Ciappelletto of his countless exactions, which make him most unwanted in his native town. He has made so many enemies that he urgently needs to go abroad, where his bad name is not known yet. Among all the vices he is reputed for, four are selected in a metonymic evocation. He pours out abuse upon the two usurers, to whom he has been sent by Musciatto on a shady mission (in Germany instead of the text's Burgundy), he spits contemptuously on the table, then bursts out laughing in a joke. Yet he is prone to swearing and disloyalty, which is borne out by the rude gesture he makes during the confession, without the priest's noticing it. "I kept but half to live on, giving the other half to the poor," he pretends while giving the finger on the sly! The other three sins he has indulged in are evoked in some tableaux vivants that precede and prepare for the Ciappelletto sequence. Before the spectator is introduced into the diegesis of I, 1, the film opens on the villain's suddenly emerging from the dark to commit a sordid murder, as dumb as a stone as later when he listens to his commissioner's recommendations. Significantly, while Musciatto is speaking, the corrupt businessman and his equally crooked accomplice progress from darkness into broad daylight. This corroborates the evil nature of a character whom we see killing fiercely and then stealing money to have sex with a young boy who he has spotted in the audience of the old Neapolitan storyteller. In the first part of *The Decameron*, the filmmaker proceeds by successive touches, as if he were painting. In the second part, he turns into a maestro making a fresco with the help of his assistants, just as a film director makes a movie with his crew. The selection of the four sins is sufficient to portray actor Franco Citti as the embodiment of Hell. His silence and disdainful look reinforce the perception of his villainy. No wonder he plays a hellhound in *The Friar's Tale* sequence of *I Racconti di Canterbury*.

One last glance at the screening of I, 1 brings extra evidence of the systolic reading of the *novella*. The numerous speculations made by the usurers worrying about the consequences of their wicked host's sudden death in their house spreads over a whole page. The film ignores it, but in the following passage the treatment of the feigned confession corresponds to the truncation of some six pages. In Boccaccio, its length is due to the high number of the faults committed (nine in all). Nothing is shown of Ciappelletto's inclination to anger, perjury, and deception, whereas avarice inaugurates the sinner's confession in the film. It is followed by lust, gluttony and blasphemy — including flaring up at his own mother. Lechery and greed come only after the confession of his dealings with the despicable usurers, whose cupidity he severely castigates.

Clear Cuts and Significant Modifications in VI, 5

The other largely curtailed *novella* is VI, 5, about how Maestro Giotto smartly replies to the famous man of law, Forese da Rabatta's remark on the shabby figure the artist cuts. Never would the latter's puny body and seedy dress indicate that he is the best painter in the world — "il migliore dipintore del mondo" (*Il Decameron*, vol. 2, 739). Pasolini reduces the body of the text by half. The preamble and the portraits of Boccaccio's two well-known contemporaries are not rendered either. The reason for their presence in the anecdote is the ugly faces and ludicrous appearances they share. Caught in the pouring rain, the two personalities borrow a poor plowman's rags to continue on their way to Florence (Naples in the film). The film director also cuts Giotto's scathing answer as he pays Forese back in his own coin at the end. The concluding sentence that follows the repartee is dropped. The reader is supposed to draw the morality from the anecdote. The portrait of Forese is strikingly short (two sentences) and comically stresses his repulsive features. On the contrary, at least half the page is devoted to the greatness of Giotto in a laudatory evocation of his absolute command of the art of painting, which makes him the glory of Florence. The narrator, Panfile again, adds that the humanity of the artist actually enhances the huge gap that separates him from his envious untalented disciples. Then he ends his eulogy with one statement pointing to the ugliness that characterizes both protagonists. This is why the two celebrities meet, each riding a nag.

The ellipses in the screening of VI, 5 are accompanied with a great deal of changes worth examining. First of all, the circumstances of the meeting are modified. The artist's best disciple, and not Giotto himself, is traveling with the lawyer in a cart, so it seems they already know each other when they have to stop and find shelter from heavy rain, although they are in a hurry to reach Naples. I, 1 closes on the darkness of the crypt, which contrasts with the bright immaculate wrapping round Ciappelletto's dead body, thus highlighting his supposed sanctity. The second part of *Il Decameron* opens abruptly on the dull, rainy Neapolitan countryside. We are far from the radiant white nunnery overhanging a sky blue sea in III, 1, the edenic sunny gardens in IV, 5 and V, 4 or from the luminous busy Mezzogiorno marketplace in II, 5 or IX, 10. The picture in VI, 5 on the contrary looks dark, echoing the dismal German landscape in the previous episode. It also foreshadows the more somber, even tenebrous atmosphere of *Racconti*. The sudden shift from bright sunshine to dreary rain probably serves to signal the end of I and the beginning of II, now focused on the symbolic figure of the painter. In Pasolini's sequence that follows, we return to Mediterranean heat and radiance: the sun shines in Naples. The new character played by the director takes over from Ciappelletto, assuming the main function in his turn. The unattractiveness attributed to Forese and Giotto by Boccaccio's narrator is unexpectedly displaced onto the sole character of Gennari, an old peasant patiently waiting in the shelter for the thunder shower to stop. The congenial fellow does not actually seem so repulsive as he does funny-looking with his clownish expression. Puny and skinny, he has an extremely gaunt face, a protruding chin, a scrawny neck, and only one tooth! His grotesque appearance reminds us of Bruegel's *Cripples* or *Parable of the Blind*.[21] The peasant is wearing a shapeless threadbare coat and a ridiculous hat with an upturned brim jammed tight on his head just above a pair of funny little round eyes. He is given a cue when answering the famous man of law's witty comment. To the latter, who wants to know if Gennari asked God to send a downpour, he retorts: "To me, God never says no!" This addition to Boccaccio stresses the fun of the character and directs the tone of the whole episode into comedy, good-natured joking devoid of any intention to hurt. Another change brought by Pasolini, which confirms the self-derisive spirit of the film version of VI, 5, regards the identity of the artist. The maestro, whom Forese introduces to Gennari, is Giotto's most gifted pupil from Northern Italy. From what his fellow traveler says, he is the best painter in the country, not of the world. Emphatically praised to the skies in the *novella*, the artist is demythologized and humanized through Pasolini's very features, himself an artist. His only answer to the friendly mocking remark made by Forese (in the peasant's gear) is a peal of laughter. He does not take his status as a maestro seriously. His joining in his companion's guffaw prepares for the friendly ambience in the entirely male community that forms the *bottega* — the artist and his assistants working together on the fresco later in the movie.

Differences of Meaning and Tone in IX, 2

Considerably abridged, IX, 2 undergoes an abrupt change of tone when it switches from Tuscan to Neapolitan. No mention is made of the young lady's long frustrated passion for her beloved. The refined and beautiful Isabetta — whose Christian name assimilates her with the female protagonist who dies a tragic death in IV, 5 — is turned into a nun with generous curves, who is interested only in having sex, as the truculent, even vulgar gestures of the old storyteller suggest. The ribald turn given to the narrative totally occults the pathetic, almost tragic potential of the *novella*, which threatens to burst out when the young lady is caught and condemned to chastisement by the abbess at the chapter. In the Neapolitan version, the defendant escapes the harsh reproaches leveled at her by the Mother Superior, who suddenly realizes she is wearing the priest's briefs instead of her headdress. "So you had fun, too; the priest's drawers are on your head!,"[22] she replies unabashed as she no longer fears for her lot.

The Closest to the Source: V, 4 and VII, 2

The common denominator among all the adapted stories regards the transformations of the text, the more or less important discrepancies from the original meaning, register of language or themes. Few alterations occur in the diegetic progress of V, 4 and VII, 2 put into film. The story of Caterina da Valbona and Ricciardo Manardi is undeniably close to its literary source of inspiration, in spite of a few minor deletions and a slowing down of the action that brings into light the young lady's marveling at the "nightingale" ("l'ussignolo," *Il Decameron*, vol. 2, 634, 635 twice, and 636 twice) in the terrace scene. The love plot actually takes shape as quickly as in the *novella,* and the stratagem devised by Caterina to lull her parents' suspicion is likewise successful. After a delightful night of passion — the details of which are hardly evoked by Boccaccio's narrator, Filostrato — the young lady falls asleep with her hand on her secret lover's precious "nightingale," which she so insistently pretended she was yearning to hear. The following morning, on discovering their daughter's trick, the mother and self-interested father, just as in the *novella,* punish Ricciardo, definitely a good match, by forcing him to take Caterina's hand, which the youth is of course delighted to accept. He is so happy to comply with the chastisement imposed by his future father-in-law that, as he is standing in front of the Valbona couple, he drops the blanket with which he was covering his naked body. The "bird" is disclosed again, for good this time. By means of an ingenious stroke of inspiration, Pasolini concludes the episode by repeating the pun on "nightingale" throughout the story. The wordplay functions as an epilogue, just like the final mention of the offical match which makes legal the nightingale hunt ("l'uccellò agli usignoli," *The Decameron*, vol. 2, 639).

In the jar episode (VII, 2) the action is characterized by virtually the same narrative fluidity as in Boccaccio. The posture of the secret lovers on the bed in the opening shot recalls, or more exactly announces, that of Caterina, whom we will see lying face down, tenderly holding her dear "bird" in the second part of the film. Here some ironic inversion changes the rich, respectable Ricciardo into a young rascal belonging to the Neapolitan criminal underworld. It is implied by the knife he produces and then puts back in his pocket when he has to hide inside the jar, while Peronella bewails the ill-timed return of her husband. Let us note that, as in the film version of V, 4, the epilogue of VII, 2 lays much greater emphasis on the double entendre of the instructions given by the wily, adulterous wife to her foolish, gullible husband as he is scrubbing the dirt off the inside of the jar so he can sell it. By having the action perfectly and cleverly suited to the word, the film director obliquely signals the double meaning in the woman's orders, which at the same time are hints addressed to her lover on how to satisfy her lust.

(Trans)mutation and Pastiche in II, 5

II, 5 comprises a higher number of mutations in its film adaptation. In the first place, instead of simply walking past Andreuccio, the young shrewd Sicilian woman spots him from a vantage point that allows her a bird's eye view of the cattle fair in Naples. The young greenhorn, played by Nino Davoli, therefore appears as easy prey right from the start. The camera plunges straight down on him. Richly dressed, he proudly displays his money to the horse dealer, putting on airs, lording it over him and making sure everyone notices. Little does he know he will go through a series of misadventures until he takes the initiative that will do him a good turn in the end. After getting out of the cesspool into which the wily young lady attracted him, Andreuccio is chased from the working-class quarter by the criminal mob. Pasolini stresses not so much his helplessness—it takes two pages to describe the wailing of the unfortunate youth covered in excrement—as his clownish looks. Frightened by the thugs' threats, he bolts away in speeded-up motion. This is precisely what the same actor playing Perkyn the Reveler will do in *I Racconti di Canterbury*.[23] In the last scene of VII, 2, which takes place inside the church, Andreuccio not only pulls the sexton's leg as in the *novella* but gives it a fierce bite—just as the Wife of Bath bites Jankyn's nose—and causes the dishonest churchman and his two associates to run away. The three terrified men's frantic race, also shot in speeded-up motion, is followed by the protagonist's grotesque dance, carried away as he is by the sight of the ruby now in his possession. This sequence definitely roots the narrative in slapstick comedy—which will be taken up more obviously in the narrative diastole in the adaptation of Chaucer's *The Cook's Tale*.

Diegetic Alterations in III, 1

The story of Masetto (III, 1) also goes through a series of noticeable alterations. In the film, the testing of the allegedly deaf-and-dumb gardener by the intendant of the nunnery is deleted. The nuns do not tease the handsome young man, nor do they address him with the worst indecencies (*Il Decameron*, vol. 1, 332). Nonetheless, in the kitchen scene the spectator easily guesses the kind of desire that lights up the ladies' faces at the sight of the robust new gardener, whose hearty appetite arouses their giggles and joking double entendres. When two of them experience the revelation of Masetto's mouth-watering crotch, he is standing in a tree picking fruit, instead of lying asleep in the grass as in the text. The scene is filmed at a low angle, as when Damyan in *The Merchant's Tale* is shown perched in the pear tree eager to taste May's charms. The two pretty nuns' little game soon draws the others' attention. The latter's reactions, related by Boccaccio, are brought down by Pasolini to a brief exchange of arguments shouted from one convent window to the next, probably in an allusion to the screams uttered by the angry *mamme* awoken by the unfortunate Andreuccio's fall into excreta and flight from his so-called Sicilian half-sister's home where is now more than unwelcome.

The sequence of the arrangement made between the good-looking gardener and the nuns, who eventually get something out of this bit of business, is placed in anticipation before the tired Masetto complains to the abbess—who has secretly taken him into the shed instead of her cell (in Boccaccio)—that he has to satisfy nine women at a time. Let us note that the comparison with the rooster and its harem of hens, a possible echo of Chaucer's *Nuns' Priest's Tale,* is retained in the movie. The nuns come up with a solution to the problem: regulating their dear gardener's sexual appetite so he may quell every woman's carnal vitality, while sparing his energy to carry on doing his job in the garden.[24] The Mother Superior realizes it is in her interest to accept a situation that she will take advantage of just like her sisters. She wastes no time in hailing a miracle and rings the bell as there is general rejoicing. The film sequence ends on a merrier note than in the original. The narrator in III, 1 coldly specifies that Masetto becomes the intendant of the nunnery, and begets many little monks. Once the secret has been disclosed outside the convent, years later, he takes the opportunity to return to Lamporecchio, his native village, where he enjoys happy days for the rest of his life. The movie makes no mention whatsoever of the gardener selfishly turning the situation to his advantage. Pasolini does not show him as an old man but, on the contrary, surrounded and fondled by the jubilant nuns who promise him happy days. The perfect harmony achieved in the end is somewhat reminiscent of the friendly unity of the artist with his assistants as they put the finishing touch to the second panel of the triptych inside the church. The two effeminate *fraticelli* who have eyes only for Giotto's disciple ring the bell of Santa Chiara in Naples to celebrate the event. In the epilogue of *I Racconti di Canterbury,* the sound of the distant chime of Thomas a Becket's shrine can be heard too, marking the end of the pilgrimage and the pleasurable journey through fiction.

Interference Caused by Non-narrative Sequences in IX, 10 and VII, 10

The film transcription of IX, 10 lays bare several profound diegetic changes. The half-page-long introduction by Dioneo, who acts as the buffoon amongst the "white doves" in the *brigata*, is dropped. As a preamble to the anecdote presented as a warning against mistakes in magical practices, the film plunges us back into the cattle market, as in the opening of II, 5. Giotto's pupil watches the onlookers, hoping to find some faces for his fresco. His eye is suddenly caught by a quite old peasant kissing his mare passionately until he leaves Naples in the company of a priest who has a wily, lewd expression. Retrospectively, with the story in mind, we can suppose that Pietro da Tresanti has just sold his wife — turned into a mare by Don Gianni, which would account for the amorous strokes and kisses lavished on the animal under the amused gaze of the cleric, who has deceived the gullible rustics. Such an interpetation could be deduced from the logical outcome of the plot, had Pietro not ruined the so-called enchantment by his objecting to "the tail." The reader of Boccaccio consequently notices a reshaping in the structure of the adapted story, as the preliminaries in the film signal the mystification theme. Likewise, the evocation of the context of the plot in the expositional part of the *novella* is placed in the mouth of the loquacious, smooth-tongued Don Gianni, as he rides by Pietro's side on their way back from the fair. The viewer understands that the two men have already taken this route together, and the priest has already put up the churl. When Don Gianni feigns to remark innocently that they are nearing the peasant's house, the latter falls into the trap. He earnestly offers him his bed, from which he will send away his pretty young wife Gemmata, who can sleep at her neighbor's. The camera then discloses the libidinous priest's bitter disappointment shown in his big, protruding round eyes. The other modification of the text concerns the neighbor. Her name is changed to Zita, and she is getting married on that particular day, which makes it impossible for her to find a bed outside her home. Then, momentarily, the diegetic progression is interrupted by the vision of Zita's wedding feast, strongly evocative of Bruegel's paintings. The ones that come to mind in particular are *The Peasant Wedding Dance*[25] and Bruegel the Younger's version of the same theme. As the camera eye scans across the party, the spectator recognizes the comic face of Gennari, who gave his rags to Forese and Master Giotto's disciple. Another wizened, grotesque-featured old fellow lets out an ironic comment, which will actually turn out to be true at the end of the episode: "Tutti cornuti!" ("All cuckolds!"), he blurts in a drunken belch. Furthermore, the pot-bellied priest who asks the bride for a dance echoes Don Gianni's lechery, noticeable as soon as the latter lays eyes on the buxom brunette's figure. Pietro's bonny wife shows herself to be much milder and more submissive than in the *novella*. The only reproach she levels at her husband for ruining the "magic" charm performed by the cunning priest is conveyed by a sorrowful look expressing her regret at having lost the only opportunity of getting rich: by changing into a mare so as to help her husband carry their goods to the market. Emphasis is laid upon the exploitation of credulous ordinary people, easy prey for the representatives of ecclesiastical authority.

In the construction of the movie, VII, 10 succeeds to IX, 10. Both share the same thematic ground through a common oblique indictment of the pressure exerted on people's conscience by the Christian doctrine and its precepts scrupulously defended by churchmen who misuse their power of persuasion when dealing with simple souls. The treatment of VII, 10 resorts to even more subtle variations, which bend the meanings of the *novella*. Tingoccio and his inseparable companion are not in love with the same woman in the film. The director leaves out the whole passage about the circumstances in which Tingoccio becomes enamored of a friend's wife and wins her favors, while being unaware that Meuccio, who also falls for the lady, suffers in secret. Opposite the church of Santa Chiara, in the marketplace carefully observed by the maestro,[26] the two fellows are busy weaving baskets while addressing lascivious winks at two flirtatious, slinky women selling vegetables. The men are symbolically surrounded by mouth-watering round fruit (melons of all kinds) evocative of female curves. A bit later, after having sex with one of the two women, the sensuous Tingoccio gets up from his bed, hungry for a piece of bread. As he is standing and eating, just behind his head can be seen two round pears that look like a pair of breasts. Meanwhile, Meuccio wonders about the other world, especially about the price to pay for a sinful life (of lechery). This is why he will be seen later saying the rosary to guard himself against the temptation of fornication, anxious as he is to save his soul. His friend, on the contrary, remains untroubled because he believes that the sinner who repents at the last minute will be forgiven. Consequently he indulges in lust without the slightest remorse. Only Meuccio is really fretful, whereas the narrator plays up the two fellows' fright on hearing the priest's sermons on the Purgatory torments. In the movie, to reassure Meuccio, Tingoccio offers him a deal. They swear that the first one to die will visit the other on earth to satisfy his curiosity about what happens to the soul in the next world. In other words, the beginning of Boccaccio's plot is simplified.

Still, when Tingoccio casually gives himself over to sex — he says another intercourse will not make the difference anyway — the diegesis goes through two dilatations that cause the action to slow down and disconcert the spectator. First Tingoccio's sudden decease, disposed of in only three sentences, is treated in an unexpected development which echoes the last sequence of the first part of the movie. Just as the latter closes on I, 1, the second part ends with VII, 10 in a comic parallel. Like Ciappelletto, Tingoccio has a vision while breathing his last. The shot of the dying sinner on his bed — separated from his virtuous fellow in prayer by a cross on the wall — is followed by a shot of the artist, lying on his bed, too, all of a sudden awoken by the same vision of the Madonna. Next, the funeral scene interrupts the action again. We follow the slow procession of mourners walking behind the corpse, which is wrapped in white bandages (just like the fake saint's at the end of I, 1) through the dark alleys of Naples (through which Ciappelletto carried his victim in a sack in the overture of *The Decameron*). Nevertheless, the solemn, dignified tone that befits the pathos of the situation soon lapses into derision. The incongruous detail given by Meuccio on the daily frequency of the sexual intercourse between the late Tingoccio and his girlfriend (nine times a day!) puts the register of language poles apart from the style of the saint's life. When he comes back to bring evidence of his experience in Purgatory to his friend as promised, Tingoccio remarks that some sinners find themselves in fire, others in water or ice, and others in excreta.[27] This addition by Pasolini can be read as an ironical allusion to Andreuccio's unfortunate fall, whereas he had come to Naples to inhale its fragrance! If, in each of the 10 *novelle*, the filmmaker eliminates, summarizes, or contracts some elements of the narrative, he also introduces some details or inserts some features of his own invention, thus reorienting the tonality of the story or deviating its thematic direction through the proximity of other stories. VII, 10 sounds more worldly, even colloquial. To his fellow's question about the penance for forniaction with one's girlfriend in Purgatory, Tingoccio bluntly replies: "Don't be scared, you prick! They don't take girlfriends into account up there!"[28] It seems that the vision of the Madonna, supposed to elevate the narrative to the sublime level, cannot be taken too seriously at face value. It cannot be attributed any teleological ring. The Virgin Mary indeed has a slight mocking (?) smile on her face. The terror of the Last Judgment, that so far has stopped the righteous Meuccio from enjoying the delights of the flesh, stems from his imagination, fired by the priest's horrendous evocations. Paradoxically, some suprahuman manifestation (his friend returning from the dead for a short visit) brings Meuccio back into the everyday world (as opposed to the netherworld that obsesses his distraught mind), where rushing to one's naked girlfriend waiting for him in bed, as he eventually does in the final shot, is not a sin: "Non è peccato!" (218), he exclaims.

A Miscellany of Narrative Transformations: IV, 5

The last story under scrutiny combines all the possibilities of textual metamorphosis in the screening of a literary work. In IV, 5 the adaptation leaves out both the prologue and the epilogue. It also eliminates Lisabetta's tears that make the basil grow. Besides, the film chooses to show neither the theft of the vase by the three brothers (where they finally find their victim's head) nor their flight to Messina, nor the disconsolate girl's illness leading to her death. A great deal of narrative elements are either eclipsed or replaced. The half-page-long paragraph that exposes the situation right after Filomena has announced a tale as heart-breaking as the previous one is superseded by a few silent shots of nothing but the pot of flowers on the windowsill (as a prefiguration of the basil, upon which the episode will close), then a bed where the secret lovers lie, young Lizabetta and Lorenzo, in charge of the rich family's gardens. Shortly after, when finding out about their sister's passion for the steward, the three brothers who ambiguously share the same bed give free vent to such deep fury, as testified by the violence of their insults, that we expect a murder to be committed. In Boccaccio's text, the dishonored young masters' reaction is more sedate and calculated, for the one who saw the lovers part at dawn informs his brothers only on the next morning (*Il Decameron*, vol. 1, 528). As for the murder, it takes place off camera. The spectator is suddenly denied access to the barbarous scene, after he has attended the long chase in the huge orchard where the sunlight filters through the vines. The brothers have convinced Lorenzo to take a so-called break from work. This sequence lasts for several minutes, during which the camera tracks down every single knowing smile and look exchanged between the criminals, as well as the expressions of cheer mixed with fear on the lover's face, while they run and indulge in different physical games and teases. For instance, they are shown jumping over a ditch and coaxing the wary Lorenzo to join them, feigning to treat him as their equal. They also invite him to urinate with them, contending that such an activity is shared by all men, whatever their social background. A bit later, the better to allay the young man's distrust, one smears his brother's face with grapes for fun. The stratagem employed to attract Lorenzo into a hidden place to kill him unawares provides an illustration of narrative dilatation. In this sequence, the longest in the basil episode, Pasolini stresses the escalation of that seething wild male brutality on the verge of exploding into an act of cruelty. One of the brothers (all sensuous, good-looking youths), produces a knife while pretending to chase Lorenzo, whom he menacingly urges to partake in the "game." The murder is deliberately omitted, for the savage anger, with which the young lords of the estate previously swore to get rid of their sister's lover, has already prepared us for an easily imaginable pitiless bloodshed.

The tragic event is in fact implicitly symbolized in the following shot, when the focus returns to the pot of flowers, a kind of morbid, obsessive motif that portends the beheading of the dead victim. At the window looking out on the courtyard, the worried Lisabetta desperately longs to catch sight of her beloved, whom she has not heard from for several days. A high-angle shot reveals the black figure of a wizened old person sitting with his or her head buried in his (her) lap — an incarnation of death? The character seems prostrated, as the girl will be in the final shot when, after burying Lorenzo's head in the earth underneath the basil, she will remain seated, motionless with her arms around the pot in a hieratic pose. The pathos of the sad end of Lisabetta is somewhat toned down in the movie, where no mention whatsoever is made of the popular song about the basil thief which concludes Filomena's story. The sordid details of the exhumation of the dead boy's head are discarded. Let us point out that, as in all the *novelle* selected, IV, 5 is related to the others by means of correspondences and echoes. The preternatural sequence of the late Lorenzo's apparition, in which he informs Lisabetta about the identity of his murderers, brings to mind Tingoccio's momentary return from Purgatory. Lastly, the actor who plays Lorenzo is also Pluto in *I Racconti di Canterbury*, whereas in *The Merchant's Tale* he is amused by the outwitting of poor blind Januarie by his wife and her secret lover. The scene also takes place in a natural, bucolic setting, an English garden, yet is quite different from the luxuriant sunlit orchard where he finds death in *The Decameron*. Pluto strolls about the green alleys with the same happy smile as Lorenzo. The young handsome divinity's light-heartedness is indirectly conveyed through his innocent nakedness in the idyllic context. The medieval garden metaphorically refers to the earthly delights enjoyed in a *locus ameonus* as in *Le Roman de la Rose*, translated by Chaucer. Pluto saunters by Proserpina's side, she wears nothing but a crown of flowers in her hair. Her pretty face is also that of the fresh, sparkling Caterina, beaming with happiness after a whole night spent with her dear "nightingale" in V, 4. The presence of both actors in *Racconti* probably corresponds to Pasolini's wish to evoke the graceful lightness of V, 4 embodied by Caterina's smiling face and, at the same time, Lorenzo's grave expression in IV, 5. The vigor of amorous desire runs through May's veins, but her lover and herself would certainly know a tragic end if the pretty goddess did not intervene at the right moment to give her the cue that definitely dispels her jealous husband's suspicion.

Forms and Meanings in Pasolini's Decameron
Introduction

After analyzing the transformations undergone by the *novelle* in their visual transcription, we should examine the macroscopic structural modifications in the movie as a whole. Unlike in *I Racconti di Canterbury* where there remain scarce traces of the frame-story, the narrative pattern of *The Decameron* cannot but puzzle anyone familiar with Boccaccio's work. The *cornice* is altogether overshadowed. The filmmaker not only ignores the circumstances of the storytelling — the retreat of the merry brigade away from plague-ridden Florence — but also suppresses the presence of the narrative voices. As a result, the effect of seriality is enhanced, and one has the feeling of a juxtaposition apparently devoid of transitions and a guideline of miscellaneous elements which one may think have been picked at random by the adaptor. However, we would like to demonstrate that the narrative technique of the frame-story — the putting into film of the (re)counting of the 100 stories in 10 days — is replaced by a different strategy that embraces the various components of Pasolini's film fresco. The latter is made up of 10 episodes. Ten is the symbolic number, the square root of 100. It constitutes a perfect mathematical reduction of Boccaccio's vast literary edifice. But let us first attempt to elucidate the glaring absence of the *cornice* in the movie. We will see that it corresponds to a choice made by the director from a specific artistic and ideological perspective.

Literary Formalism and Textual Structuring

As previously pointed out, Boccaccio's *Decameron* offers an innovative kind of writing in the vernacular, highlighted by the amazing virtuosity of the form. However ingenious the structural configuration of the 10 days of 10 *novelle* each, thematically arranged, the whole work is characterized by some degree of literary formalism, described by a number of critics as rigid. The wide range of narrative possibilities finds itself quite circumscribed by the fact that the authority of the king or queen of each day supervises the telling activity and defines the limits of what can be actually told or not:

> Boccacio offers an image of a self-regulating society, which articulates its own rules of comportment, and in which power is identified with, or is derived from, the delimitation of the sayable, the act of imposing a frame upon the field of narrative possibilities: an act of exclusion.[29]

Dioneo and Emilia temporarily disrupt the order in the organization of each day. Such subversive intrusion in fact functions as a means to legitimize the rules of the game to be observed. Likewise, the bawdiness of quite a large number of stories is meant to contain the erotic potential of the particular context of seven maidens and three youths cut off from the rest of the world in a pastoral setting that encourages the gratification of the senses. Lastly, for Patrick Rumble, the rigorously mathematic application of this structural, narrative and thematic delineation goes hand in hand with the author's intention, as stated in his *Proemio* (Preface) and reiterated in the conclusion. He humbly wishes, he claims, to comfort his lovesick female readers. This allegation most probably conceals an attempt to exert a form of supervision on the marginalized women, likely because of their melancholy and frustrations, to wander outside the social mold that confines them to the roles of daughters, sisters and wives entirely dependent upon their family or husband. The *Proemio* emphasizes the virtue, or more exactly the therapeutic use of stories that the author offers these idle ladies as a treat. The desires and fantasies that the promised entertaining narratives are sure to arouse in their vivid imagination will actually worsen their subjection to a restrictive social role. Rumble remarks that the verbs *ristringere* and *racchiùdere* are employed in the exposition of the reasons why the author of *Il Decameron* dedicates his work to this specific audience: "By the way, are they not *defeated* by the will, whims and orders of their fathers, mothers, brothers or husbands? More often than not *cloistered* in their bedrooms..." (*Il Decameron*, vol. 1, 7–8).[30] The great variety of enjoyable stories are most likely to cure or at least alleviate this affliction. The excuse put forward by the author betrays "an image of literature in the vernacular born of a regulatory impulse, as a technology of gender or a ritual of subjectivation" (Rumble, 116). An interpretation of *Il Decameron* in the sense of a marginalizing social structuration, which mirrors the textual arrangement of the work, may seem excessive, though. Although the private reading of such fiction with a moral message in the late Middle Ages functions as "*...control of the imaginary* to stabilize subjectivity in a society undergoing radical sociocultural transformations at the end of the age of feudalism,"[31] one should refrain from seeing in Boccaccio's work only a systematic enterprise of channeling the transgressive energies of marginal elements. Concerning *Il Decameron*, one should rather speak of an unprecedented regenerative use of a language accessible to simpler readers:

> Ladies, who can enjoy all the moments you do not devote to the delights of love. Be sure that none of your sisters lives a life of study in Athens, Bologna or Paris. Therefore you need to be addressed in a more explicit way than those whose mind has been sharpened by scholastics.[32]

The Proletarianization of Boccaccio's Florentine Society

The thriving merchant middle class in 14th-century Italy gave shape to an ideology that increasingly prevailed throughout the centuries until it became ossified in the late 20th century, when Pasolini made his *Decameron*. In Boccaccio's time, the new social category that acceded to economic power and appropriated the aristocratic culture by adapting it to its own tastes and mentality set itself free from the feudal values typical of the early Middle Ages, dominated by clerical authority. The nascent petite bourgeoisie still carried the hope for "the new human era" that Pasolini dreamed of. It embodied the antithesis of the post-industrial, neo-capitalist society of the 1970s, upon which the Italian artist and intellectual cast a critical eye. When he shot *The Decameron*, he had in mind the triumph of a contemptible decadent bourgeoisie. Consequently, he denounced its preeminent model of conformism as well as its policy of mass consumption and the leveling of thought. As a reaction to the bitter realization of a benumbing, decaying culture, Pasolini shed a favorable light on the working class, the only one he saw as still endowed with the vitality necessary for a salutary renewal of society. This is why the film does not include II, 7, IV, 4, and X, 3 (originally planned in the filmscript in three parts). These are *novelle* with an elevated subject and a lofty style, peopled with sultans, princesses, or rich, highborn, noble-hearted munificent lords and gentlemen. He retains only stories about merchants, gardeners, peasants with deceitful or naive spouses, a swindler and impostor, an artist, a man of law, rich landlords, and clerics. All fill the screen with their physical presence, comic gesticulation, expressive faces or "mugs" in some cases, loud voices and flippant, cheeky speech. Pasolini deliberately selects one aspect of the ebullient motley crowd depicted by Boccaccio throughout his collection of stories: "...the director's exclusions are potentially as significant as his inclusions" (Rumble, 117). He enhances the commonness of this medieval fauna by "Neapolitanizing" the largely Tuscan original context. The film sets most stories in Naples or the city is referred to. Because the revolutionary potential of the Italian bourgeoisie became outmoded in the 20th century, the action takes place among the ordinary people of Naples and "proletarianizes" Boccaccio's mainly Florentine world:

> That is why you did not find the characters of Boccacio, because I reduced each to a schemata and then filled them out with the reality of Naples, of a sub-proletarian world, and not a bourgeois one.[33]

In this perspective, Rumble deduces, Pasolini's *Decameron* cannot be called an adaptation of a literary source but instead a "critical reading of Boccacio's text, a devotedly antagonistic, as it were, cinematic *imitatio* of the original."[34] Making this film in 1971 the artist vulgarized his cinema which then became accessible to all, not only the educated audience familiar with ancient myths (*Edipo Re* in 1966, *Medea* in 1969) or with the Bible (*Il Vangelo secondo Matteo* in 1964). He restores cinema to the masses, for originally it was intended as a form of popular entertainment before it evolved into an art. Pasolini dreamed of getting the working class to discover a major Italian cultural work by depicting ordinary people in a farcical mode. Besides, he offers escapism through the temporal rather than the geographical exoticism of a Middle Ages that is more poeticized than historically true. Boccaccio adopted a similar approach, except he did it not through film but by way of the vernacular so as to enlarge the stylistic and thematic horizons of medieval literature and its audience.

Narrative Sabotage and the Blurring of Diegetic Delimitations

The author of *Il Decameron* was eager to have an overall view of his material through an elaborate construction built on the number 10, which provides the key and points to a perfect self-sufficiency of the literary artifact. The compliance with the thematic and social constraints established in the *cornice* rules the narration as well as the arrangement of the *novelle*. Yet at the same time the *cornice* imposes a narrative pattern and a normative, therefore exclusive model of communal life. The few exceptions are there only to prove the rule. The omnipresent frame-story weighs heavily on the telling, which it subdivides and directs according to a steady regularity at the beginning of each day and in the preliminaries and moralities of each story. Not only does the adaptation disregard the embracing narrative but also eradicates all indications of the narrators' speeches (with one exception in IX, 2) and gets rid of the prologues and epilogues. It is as though Pasolini sought to suppress or at least water down the mechanisms of clear-cut demarcation or opposition between the stories, and more generally the mechanisms of exclusion of other narrative models. He devised a sophisticated architecture in two parts, resorting to the frame-story technique, but in a more flexible and plurivocal fashion. The reason for this premeditated "betrayal" of Boccaccio's plan (not in the spirit but in the form) lies in the adaptor's wish to achieve a bewildering composition more easily subject to a plurality of interpretations. The momentary diegetic suspensions, which now and then occur during the visions in the tableaux vivants or close-ups on the non-professional actors' faces as they stare at the camera self-consciously or amusingly, magnify the meanings disseminated throughout the stories within an intricate network of correspondences.

The jamming of the meaning and blurring of the boundaries between the various episodes stems from a receptivity to the poetic degree or poeticity of the film shot, which sometimes distracts from the unfolding of the plot to draw the viewer's attention to the very cinematic act in the making. In such moments, the preoccupation with the narrative comes second behind the oneiric and aesthetic potential of the motion picture then devoid of its sound and thus turned into a kind of dream as in a silent movie. The author of the film signals his mark to the spectator as the maker of an artifact produced by means of a camera more than as the director of a perfected work with a specific message. The artist turns out to be an *artifex*, or craftsman, who leaves his (pictorial and cinematic) fresco unfinished. Probably because he is part and parcel of the world he shares with the protagonists of the adapted *novelle*, the painter cannot distance himself from his work of art to grasp it in its totality. Pasolini as Giotto's disciple has the scaffolding removed in the final scene to contemplate the first two panels of the triptych. The third one remains to be done. As the scaffolding recedes from the incomplete work to reveal it, we feel we recognize a scene drawn from the life of Saint Francis of Assisi in the first panel. In fact, the picture is deliberately kept at a distance and the shot is too brief for the spectator to be able to identify with precision one particular work by Giotto. However, the blue of the sky so characteristic of the maestro's touch that it is sufficient to evoke his style. So the painting is not closely examined, but on the contrary overlooks its maker, who is shown gazing at it from afar, looking unusually small in a high-angle shot. The movie closes on the nape of Pasolini, a band around his head, turning his back on the camera, while the chime of Santa Chiara's bells can be heard. Staring at the fresco, he suddenly declares he would rather dream a work of art than create it. Unlike the author of the text, whose voice prevails again in a conclusion that decisively seals *Il Decameron*, that of the film obliterates or at least makes it less conspicuous by refraining from putting a definitive end to it or signifying the completion, of which he has an all-embracing view. This is why the movie operates by successive touches, which eventually implicitly give shape to an arrangement articulated on two axes, and which has nothing to do with the bulky *cornice* that constrains the frame which holds the stories together.

The Conscious Artificiality of the Movie

The 10 episodes in *The Decameron* are divided into two parts, each containing five stories interspersed with sequences entirely made up by Pasolini. The unmitigated scoundrel Ciappelletto projects the nefarious shadow of deceit and mendacity over the whole of the first part, which encompasses II, 5, IX, 2, III, 1, VII, 2 and finally I, 1, about the inspired impostor's trick on his deathbed. In the second half, the figure of the painter takes over in its emblematic function. Patrick Rumble draws a parallel between the confidence man and the artist, for both are exceptionally gifted at creating illusion by manipulating reality. One skillfully handles the "powers of the false" found in words, while the other successfully employs the magic of the picture as a way to produce fiction. Nevertheless, Giotto's disciple is no villain. Ciappelletto shows an amazing ability to use language as a means of persuasion, but always does so to serve a condemnable aim. He shamelessly takes advantage of people's gullibility through mystification, from which the church unscrupulously profits. The naive priest, who readily (?) lets himself be outmaneuvered, quickly recovers from the marvel of Ciappelletto's deathbed penance and delivers severe sermons to his congregation, whom he exhorts to follow the saint's example. The moralizing admonitary lecture supports the Christian doctrine that the medieval ordinary man is expected to comply with:

> Pasolini's condemnation of this character derives from the use to which language is put, to the instrumentalization of the powers of the false for the benefit of those *potenti* who dominate and exploit the people ... [Rumble, 123].

The potentates who get much benefit from the rogue's swindle by feigning to believe in his saintliness are the stately bishop, who in motionless, dignified silence presides over the adoration of the remains; and, on each side of him, the two usurers, who stand secretly rejoicing over the timely, last-minute fake confession that took place in their home. Dressed in rich finery, the bishop reminds us of the late Archbishop of Naples, Filipo Minutolo, who rests in peace in the tomb, wearing a big ruby worth 500 florins in II, 5. He also prefigures the high dignitary of the church who, with an expression of utter satisfaction and detachment, attends the burning at the stake of the sodomite in *I Racconti di Canterbury*. The hypocrisy of the ecclesiastic authority is echoed in the amused duplicity of the two creditors, who are usurpers of the ordinary people's naive faith. The church makes use of Ciappelletto's hoax to maintain the hegemony of its ideology on the masses—which have long been subjected to confession for their conscience to be controlled, as Foucault explains in *Histoire de la sexualité*. Likewise, the two moneylenders, who savor in advance the profit that the sham miracle will bring in, share responsibility in keeping the people in financial dependence. Now, ironically enough, one can notice that the clergy gives backing to the so-called marvel, which is actually the fruit of a bunch of lies from a murderer, thief, sodomite, and blasphemer at that. The parodical reversal of the hagiographic genre reaches its climax at the end of the first half of *The Decameron*.

On the contrary, the only lie or illusion in a work of art responds to no other intention on the part of the artist than that of arousing a vision. Like Ciappelletto, the maestro has the gift of creating fiction from start to finish, precisely because he can identify it. But still, his imagination, enriched with an acute sense of minute observation, does certainly not serve a dishonest plan. His skill is devoid of any trace of self-interest or venality, and stands outside the commercial transaction model that rapidly expanded in Boccaccio's time on account of the economic prosperity of the merchant class. Now the pursuit of profit fosters cupidity and dissimulation. This is why many characters in Pasolini's *Decameron* either hide or act on the sly.[35] The artist epitomizes the antinomy of this deceitful behavior prompted by the selfish gratification of some material or carnal desire. His act is equivalent to a gift, as it is as generous and disinterested as a dream may be. The figuration of the Last Judgment projected on the third blank panel of the fresco evinces an excessive degree of visuality. The hyperbolic "imageity" or iconicity of the "putting into painting" in a theatrical setting, extravagantly artificial and sham, assimilates it to some unreal scene, as only our fantasy can produce it. The work of art then becomes a fantasy indeed, a utopia, an imaginary space. When Giotto's follower and his assistants celebrate the completion of the second part of the triptych, the third one signals itself *in absentia*. In fact, the actual frescoes in Santa Chiara have been totally worn out over the centuries. One possible interpretation of this empty panel would be the suggestion by contrast of the inalterability of a dreamed work — although dreams paradoxically consist of an ephemeral series of images. Pasolini's presence behind the mask of the maker of the fresco testifies to the self-reflexive aspect of the movie, which raises the very question of the genesis of the work and its production: from the painter's vision in his inner eye to its materialization on the wall — or the page and the screen as implied in *I Racconti di Canterbury*. We have to admit that, once created, the work does not attain the visual reality of the picture originally conceived in the artist's mind. At the end of the film, the maestro is left puzzled and mesmerized by the mystery of artistic creation. The conscious artificiality of the movie, conveyed by the metaphor of the fresco in the making, is the expression of this questioning. At the same time, it reveals itself through a style that privileges form, in accordance with Pasolini's conception of a cinema of poetry. A dream strikes our attention not so much because of its buried, abstruse signification, but because of the strangeness of its enigmatic form. The staccato construction of *The Decameron*, which seems to be a series of unconnected film sketches, the unexpected interruptions of the narrative by a pictorial contamination of the motion picture, as well as the inconclusiveness of the whole work equate *The Decameron* to a dream indeed. The meanings come out distinctly only after close scrutiny of the construction. However, as when he awakes from a dream, the spectator retains some impressions, some touches here and there rather than the usual clearly defined narrative pattern of a conventional movie.

An Underlying Homosexual Discourse

As the opposite extreme of the historical fresco set in the Middle Ages, *The Decameron* is sure to perplex the spectator, invited to descry a counter-discourse. The latter is concealed inside an elaborate framework that underlies the movie. It is most likely to pass unnoticed the first time one watches the film, for it reveals itself indirectly through a homosexual aesthetics and some pictorial pastiches closely interwoven into a subtle, subversive semantic network. In other words, the screening of Boccaccio's text hides another film. The scandal caused by *I Racconti di Canterbury* as soon as it was released in 1972 is actually only the exacerbation of a staunch disapproval caused by release of *The Decameron* the year before. The gloomy representation of bodies as mere commodities dangerously flirts with obscenity in the second part of the trilogy. Yet it is prepared by the licentiousness of the first film, which conveys a more jocular eroticism expressive of the blithe spirit of Boccaccio's universe. Why, one may wonder, is sex exhibited and laid bare? Why, after being celebrated in *The Decameron*, does the unrestrained body of a past prior to the coercive discourse find itself degenerate and lapse toward anality and sexual deviances in *I Racconti di Canterbury*? Sexuality in fact is associated with physical suffering (in the stake sequence at the beginning of *The Friar's Tale*), frustration and masochism. The homosexual hypotext implicitly denounces the totalitarianism of normative heterosexuality, an arbitrary construct that prevailed during Pasolini's time. He contrasts it with a dreamed Middle Ages, in which sexuality is not yet defined in reference to an exclusive unique model. Within a "non-disciplinary" eroticism, the body responds to no requirement other than that of the immediate gratification of the senses. "A surface of multiple sources of pleasures"[36] subjected to the sexual drive, it is urged by the anarchic surge of desire, which makes it flexible and unfettered. It can also attain a liberatory, creative pleasure. Giotto's disciple, whose homosexuality is suggested through his close complicity with his young, good-looking assistants, is making a work of art in utmost jubilation. In *The Decameron*, much more than in *I Racconti di Canterbury*, the characters revel in the delights of carefree sex. Their physical presence is obvious. Their individualities are totally overshadowed by their corporeity. They embody what Foucault aspires to: desubjectivization synonymous with desexualization. In sexual intercourse, the body experiences a dissolution in both senses of the word, which transports it towards a state where the affirmation of identity loses its meaning. Changed into a surface and a volume, it goes through a metamorphosis. It is turned inside out so it eventually disintegrates: "diffuse, *exploding* and without the old hierarchical conceptualizations of internal drives and impulses."[37] In other words, the body becomes material and liberates the individuals of its subjectivation only through the most varied forms of pleasure, and a fortiori for Pasolini through male sexuality.

Maurizio Viano[38] aptly remarks that the treatment of sexuality in the

Trilogy of Life bespeaks a contradiction. The body gives itself over with grace and innocence — mainly in *The Decameron* and *Il Fiore delle mille e una notte* — to the erotic act, but there is something illicit and transgressive about heterosexual intercourse. Some wives are shown being unfaithful to their husbands; some lovers meet on the sly. The male/female relationships are always motivated by deceit, revenge, or profit. *I Racconti di Canterbury* depicts some more reprehensible encounters. As we will attempt to demonstrate, the male love affairs in *The Decameron* connote positive, noble values, like the bliss of artistic creation in harmonious teamwork,[39] in which prevails a strong genuine sense of companionship throughout the second half of the movie. The fecund talent of the maestro, surrounded by his assistants, with whom he banters in utmost serene felicity, highlights the image of homosexuality projected by Ciappelletto. In the first part, the rascal is the embodiment of sodomy linked to theft, usury, imposture, and murder. However, such a negative image at first sight should be qualified in the light of the enigmatic intrusion of a mix of several tableaux vivants by Bruegel the Elder.

Pasolini's Picturesque Shots: The Dissipation of Meaning

During their conversation, the rich and dishonest Musciatto asks his most iniquitous and ruthless agent to go to a northern country to get a tidy amount of money from a refractory debtor. The scene closes on Ciappelletto's silent approval. His partner, ironically enough, commends him to God, whereas the impostor's legendary immorality logically promises him to damnation. With a knowing wink, Musciatto expresses the wish to see him back with the money — otherwise it might well cost the scoundrel his life, the crooked businessman implies. Then, for some reason, a brief enigmatic sequence follows, during which Ciappelletto has a premonition of his impending death. In an oneiric parenthesis, a close-up shows a skull, lying on what looks like a wooden baking paddle. As he feels faint, his head all of a sudden drops onto his plate in the same position as when slightly later he has dinner with his hosts. The camera focuses again on his face, motionless and meditative-looking against a dark background. The skull signifies an untimely decease that occurs as the natural conclusion of a criminal life. He is already metaphorically dead in his forced exile in a cold, remote country. He finds himself in the hands of a pair of debased miscreants, whose ugly mugs, dark clothes and dirty nails identify them with hellhounds — which usurers are held to be in medieval imagination. Furthermore, when Musciatto assigns him his task — so he may have an opportunity to leave Naples where he is least wanted — Ciappelletto does not bat an eyelid. A grave expression on his face supersedes his typical sardonic grin.

The macabre metaphor is actually part of a set of other vignettes or playlets, equivocal representations connoting fun in a debunking of death. Among others is the shot of a bishop and some friars dressed in white, tossing a skull at one another as if it were a ball. Simultaneously, not far away in the same pastoral setting, a woman in a hieratic pose is sitting on a strange seat fixed to a wheeled wooden base. She is wearing a very high, bulky headdress probably made of woven wicker. She cuts a perplexing figure, strangely reminiscent of the epitome of abstinence and fast in Bruegel's *Battle Between Carnival and Lent*.[40] Her youthful beauty also evokes *The Allegory of Hope*,[41] in which the lady's headdress looks like a beehive, emblematic of prosperity. Meanwhile, some young men, sitting on a huge barrel, play at exchanging their hats. Nearby in the distance, others do somersaults in a cheerful, jesting manner quite similar to that in *Children's Games*, also by Bruegel.[42] It appears that at the heart of this chaotic vision of Lent and Death, life manages to resist. It is as if a futile, derisive laughter were running through the overall morbid atmosphere that darkens the baffling composition.

The presence of cripples, female penitents, dozens of skulls heaped up in a wheelcart in a pastiche of the sinister *Triumph of Death*,[43] a corpse wrapped in bandages in a wooden cart drawn by a simpleton, or a prayer chair carried up by women as if it were a holy relic in a religious procession—all help to create a disquieting, almost nightmarish climate. Lastly, though this tableau vivant is devoid of a center properly speaking, one figure in particular calls attention to itself in this film sequence under the strong influence of the visual arts. It is the female embodiment of Lent, holding a baking paddle with, on its broad flat end, a skull in place of the two herrings in Bruegel's painting. The picture of the fast takes on a deathly dimension. The viewer is faced with a disconcertingly ambiguous figuration, that rests upon the combination of two antinomic networks of metaphors. Such a baffling configuration therefore sets us wondering. We can identify Bruegel's style, but we are confused by what Jill Ricketts calls "a pastoral pastiche" (Ricketts, 143). What we have here is a jigsaw puzzle or amalgam of themes and motifs running through the Flemish master's work, yet semantically subverted by Pasolini. The miscellaneous allusions to Bruegel's iconography are set in a pastoral backcloth that serves as a stage for a great variety of scattered performances, all happening here and there at exactly the same time in a sort of disorderly *theatrum mundi* (143). The filmmaker draws our attention to the feeling of general chaos and dissymmetry that emerges from the painter's crowded pictures and opacifies their reading. Saturated, this bewildering hodgepodge of situations teems with details coming to life simultaneously before our eyes. The spectator cannot possibly encompass them all nor grasp the multitude of meanings in one single glance. The tableau vivant thus resorts to unwonted pictures to incite the intellect to decipher them. Nevertheless, it evades interpretation or at least univocal interpretation. We feel confused by this intricate exposition of antinomies (Carnival and Lent, life and death, excess as in *The Land of Cockaigne*[44] and continence). These lead to a general liquefaction of the various significations. It seems that the whole picture is devoid of any intention to make sense but instead points to the insignificance of life. We will all finish in the state of this derisory skull, as Bruegel's Lent and Hope allegories remind us. The anarchic form and absent structuring pattern in a composition where one indiscriminately passes from life to death and vice versa may refer to the ironic sublimity of the spiritual echo of the hymn heard at that particular moment.

Revision and Re-vision: A Subversive Reading

The bringing together of motifs borrowed from various Bruegel paintings partakes in a pastiche strategy that operates by means of a "collage" or sample of the artist's style. In this particular case, we are referring to a Northern Renaissance maestro, who breaks with the laws of symmetrical structuration of space. When gazing at Bruegel's bustling motley crowds in urban or rural settings, one almost feels dizzy. The reference at the center, the axis around which the whole architecture is organized, gives the impression that the latter fades into the overall chaos. We feel as if we were kept away from one single absolute meaning, as if we lost sight of God's supreme, authoritative viewpoint. In an uninterrupted hubbub we can easily imagine — though nothing but the choir of male voices can be heard — the host of contradictory signs failing to deliver one final meaning. The answer does not lie in faith in God, conspicuously absent from this vision. The other tableau vivant in *The Decameron* (the Madonna) on the contrary exhales a divine aura (in the oneiric interlude that precedes the epilogue). The pastiche of Giotto's Last Judgment suffuses the motion picture with a touch of the religious sublime. Yet it substitutes Christ for the Madonna. The slow panoramic shot of the tableau, first horizontal (from right to left and vice versa) then vertical (from bottom to top), performs a reversed sign of the cross. In other words the sense of a reference to God is subverted.

The pastiche of Bruegel's works is ascribed to the conscience of an unmitigated sinner, Ciappelletto, bound to eternal damnation for all the exactions he has committed. Now the vision that enlightens his darkened conscience elevates his corrupt mind to the perfection of the revealed mystery of life that cannot be dissociated from that of death. For all its sinfulness, his soul attains an acute yet fleeting perception of the sublime, accessible through art. To some extent the epiphany can be said to redeem the characters' viciousness. The Bruegel-inspired pastiche may signify that any work of art is likely to undergo modifications and transgressions, i.e. a revision which is also a re-vision, a different reading. Regarding the pictorial pastiche of Giotto, which carries out a superimposition of *The Last Judgment*[45] and *Ognissanti Madonna*[46] *(All Saints' Madonna)*, Ricketts writes:

> The fusion of the tableau vivant and the film of the novelle highlights the tensions and opportunities for expanding meaning through the integration of verbal, visual, and aural elements [153].

A multiplicity of interpretations become possible. The sense gets enriched by the contamination of the style (and also by the style of contamination.) Lastly, let us remark that the pictorial quotation or at least allusion in the middle of the 10th sequence (VII, 10) displays a symmetrical construction evocative of medieval painting. At the end of *I Racconti di Canterbury* in the *The Summoner's Prologue*, the chaotic, discordant sight of the Netherworld provokes the spectator's gaze in a confusing pastiche of Hieronymus Bosch. Dismal and without an easily identifiable central axis, the composition ironically contrasts with the harmonious vision characterized by a perfectly balanced figuration of celestial grace that precedes the epilogue in *The Decameron*.

The homosexual aesthetics underlying the first movie of the trilogy is more pervasive and more elaborately conceived than in *Racconti*, where the theme calls itself to our attention in a more random, sporadic way. Ciappelletto never appears in the company of women. Neither does the maker of the Santa Chiara fresco, watched admiringly by his assistants and ogled by the two womanly *fraticelli* smiling and winking at the virile artist in his tight-fitting clothes. Such details fulfill a counter-narrative function (that denies the film's very narrativity), tinged with a gay sensibilty, illustrated by the essential role given to the "homosexual cruising gaze," already mentioned when we dealt with *I Racconti di Canterbury*. The scopic drive is embodied by Pasolini as Giotto's disciple, framing the reality he watches on the marketplace or in the streets, just as a film director does with the camera. *The Decameron* distinguishes itself from conventional cinema first by the segmentation of its narrative pattern, which can be accounted for by the lability and concision of the elliptic literary form that inspires the movie: the *novella*. For Jill Ricketts, the fragmentary structure of the film is not only intentional but also overdone by means of the homosexual gaze and pictorial pastiche in the tableaux vivants. Sometimes the diegetic coherence is impaired — even exploded — and as a result the viewer's attention is distracted. Then what comes to the fore is pure, non-narrative visuality, as if the film shot rid itself of any diegetic function to retain solely what really matters: the poetry of the visual. The verbal dimension also disappears during these puzzling suspensions of the narrative and gives way to exclusively "optic" situations more often than not accompanied by a religious song or a tune. They could be described as oneiric touches, in which a mannerist aesthetic prevails over the dramatic aspect. They provide some privileged moments during which the movie takes on all its signification. They also enable the filmmaker to introduce a marginal conflicting viewpoint. This exceptional degree of visuality should not be mistaken for the mere notion of "vision" (Ricketts, 164). It refers indeed to the oblique discourse of a homosexual artist struggling against what he considers a coercive, falsely permissive power. Because of its parasitic infiltration by subversive elements, the narrative composition as a whole loses some of its cohesion. So does every single adapted story. The device of an infection or contamination of the diegesis responds to an intention on the part of the scandalous voice, to be heard both within and against the accepted, institutionalized discourse, pervaded with the dominant ideology of a homophobic society. The resorting and reverting to the quintessential spectacularity of the non-narrative motion picture can also be motivated by the wish to revive in our cultural memory an invaluable heritage of past icons. The mise en abyme of Boccaccio's literary masterpiece with paintings by Giotto, Bosch or Bruegel aims to educate the spectator's glance to the viewing and critical reception of a 20th-century work fashioned by a diffrent medium. The cultural background, fraught with the meanings of the text and the paintings, enriches and complicates the movie's hermeneutic approach. The aesthetic backcloth arouses our dulled consciousness and arms us so that we may question the present with detachment, as we find ourselves momentarily out of place in some remote, fantasized, temporal space.

3

Il Fiore delle mille e una notte: The Last Panel of the Triptych

Sexuality and a Poetic Reality

The anti-establishment voice in *Il Fiore*, a "linguistic and moral hybrid,"[1] is the expression of a counter-sexuality, the reality of which is unlike the unreality of today's civilization. What characterizes this counter-sexuality is a much more flexible use of pleasures and an extraordinary freedom to represent sex (in close-ups). René de Ceccatty writes: "after *Theorem* (1968), sex becomes the prime sign of the aesthetic mode of expression"[2] described as "the free indirect style" by Pasolini himself. The trilogy gives flesh to a kind of visual utopia, in which the references to painting and the poetry of film language prevent the image of sexuality from lapsing into pornography. The way to an unhindered visualization of sex is opened by *The Decameron*, but it is in *Il Fiore* that it is truly achieved. A metaphor of what Pasolini calls a liberating joy, sex regains its sacrality, its prehistory animality, the innocence of the time before articulated speech and rationalized behavior. Consequently, the naked body inhabits the whole movie. The carnal act is performed naturally, genuinely, and it is accompanied with the childish spontaneous laughter of carefree, happy protagonists, whose physical youthful charm is unveiled to the spectator's gaze. A subtle game on the signifier and the signified rests upon a network of metaphors to refer to sex in *Il Fiore*. Sex is given ingenious, sometimes whimsical denominations of all kinds. For instance, a sequence stages the young Munis[3] and her two female friends in a bath, dallying with the naive

Nur-ed-Din, the main male character. The three girls take delight in teaching the youth the various names of the most intimate part of the female anatomy, indirectly designated by the camera by means of an image refracted in the water precisely when they utter their witty formulations.[4]

An Anamorphic Reflection of Reality: The Mirror of Homosexual Eroticism

The figure of the wandering youth still wet behind the ears lies at the core of *Il Fiore*. He learns about sex and the magic poetry of language. His virility is increasingly aroused in his adventurous search for his beloved, Zumurrud. A recurrent motif running throughout the movie, his erected member, filmed in expressive close-ups, embodies the gay aesthetics, only diffuse in *The Decameron* and *I Racconti di Canterbury*. At the end, Nur-ed-Din is in the bedroom of the king — actually Zumurrud dressed as a man — who imperiously orders him to lie face down on the bed with his backside laid bare so he/she may enjoy the boy's body. Pasolini manages to invert (and subvert too) the typical pattern of the phallocentric conception in a heterosexual society, since it is the woman who assumes the man's active role. For fear of being beheaded, the boy submits to regal authority. He is feminized, reduced to passivity in face of a masculine Zumurrud whom he fails to recognize. The female genitals (and sexuality) are replaced by the male ones, evoked by the phallus-shaped bed feet like bombshells with silver tops, and by the stiff long golden beard worn by the girl, a young slave, as the emblem of sovereignty. The homosexual desire is conveyed through two successive citations by Zumurrud of erotic poems (*The Arabian Nights* contains some 1250 of them) praising the beauty of boys. Maurizio Viano remarks that *Il Fiore* constitutes the first movie by Pasolini

> ... where homosexuality explicitly "organizes" and "binds" the text. Instead of hiding it in subtexts or using metaphors for it, he finally succeeds in presenting homosexuality as "the conic mirror" through which anamorphic reality can make sense.[5]

The Implicit Indictment of a Unilateral Perspective

It appears that *Il Fiore* directs the Trilogy of Life towards an increasingly staunch and free affirmation of an aesthetics of Eros, antagonistic to the preeminent imagery of heterosexual pleasure. Gay eroticism is made visible in numerous shots that highlight the male physiognomy — even if never before Pasolini's cinema had projected such a status-enhancing, positive image of woman.

> The beauty of the males, the shots emphazising their organs ... are all fragments of an imaginary archive of images opposing the dominant system of visual pleasure. Not that they are shot with women's pleasure in mind. But they are there, on the screen, and they create a ricochet effect: they remind us of the extent to which we are inured to seeing the opposite: tits and ass [Viano, 291].

Far from an excessive display of the female anatomy (the object of male desire in the phallocentric discourse), Pasolini's ideal of a penis freed from the conjugal imperatives dictated by a heteronormative society is materialized by a golden phallus at the end of an arrow pointed by Aziz at Budur's vagina. The body is rid of a strictly reproductive masculinity. Nino Davoli, who plays the poseur with a well-lined purse in the first sequence (after the incipit) of *The Decameron*, is also Aziz. The arrow he is holding symbolizes the supreme phallic power. At the end of the episode that relates his sad love story with Budur, she has him emasculated for being responsible for the death of his cousin Aziza, who loved him passionately. Aziz is also chastized for being unable to decipher the hidden meaning of the language used by the two women. He is horrified by his mutilation, a dispossession of his virility. The actress who plays his cousin has thick black curly hair amazingly similar to the young man's. We may assume that the filmmaker sees Aziza as the female double of Aziz, as their names indicate. She is capable of mastering a poetic language, unlike him. In other words, man is denied this ability on account of his virility, which shuts him in one single dream, whereas the truth lies in many. As Maurizio Viano puts it, this aphorism voiced by Princess Dunya's humble gardener, if taken out of its context, may be construed as a celebration of what is basically different: "...an implicit indictment of a monotheic perspective" (Viano, 293). The message can already be found in the subtexts of *The Decameron* and *I Racconti di Canterbury*. Throughout the trilogy, Pasolini plays at confronting quite different, sometimes opposed narrative, pictorial,[6] and sexual models. This is why a jesting spirit pervades the three movies—*Racconti* to a lesser extent, though. Fun, gaiety, and laughter are part and parcel of *Il Fiore*, in which all the stories are linked by the principle of play. The unpredictable play of love and chance finds its reflection in the amazing labyrinthine structure of the third episode of the trilogy. *Il Fiore* bears out what is expressed in *The Decameron* and *I Racconti di Canterbury* through a serial construction, a stylistic contagion of the film shot, and the blurred linearity of an already destabilizing narrative. Life is actually a dream.

> I did not want to slip into surrealism or magic ... but I wanted to approach the irrational as the revelation of life which becomes significant only if examined as "dream" or "vision."[7]

II. THE ADAPTATION: A CLOSE ENCOUNTER OF THE THIRD KIND

4

The Shock of Pasolini's Trilogy

Accusations and Misinterpretations
The Severe Blow of Censorship

The complete exhibition of bodies (especially genitals and a fortiori men having erections) caused a tremendous shock concomitant with a huge commercial success. As soon as it was released, *The Decameron* fell victim to a series of prosecutions for obscenity and pornography. Within just two months, between September and November 1971, the movie got more than 30 complaints and was even distrained. The fascistic organizations reacted violently and distributed libelous handouts against Pasolini. As for the Left, some accused him of losing the sense of reality and giving up celebrating the stupendous liberal destinies of the country. The phenomenon grew worse when *I Racconti di Canterbury* came out. It was instantly suppressed on October 7, 1972. No sooner was the penalty dismissed than another confiscation order followed. Altogether, four legal actions were brought against the film director, but he was found not guilty each time. Then he was charged with slander by the church, when a friar took offense at the pastiche of Bosch. *Il Fiore delle mille e una notte* did not evade the fierce wave of complaints, but a charge laid on June 27, 1974, was dismissed by decision of the general attorney of Milan, who stated that no work of art is to be taken away from the public. The price for freedom of speech turns out to be extremely high for Pasolini, who will be deeply affected by the years of conflict with the law and the harsh criticism. The trilogy is severely censored some 20 years later when it was shown on the Italian television in March 1994. Pasolini's triptych was "slaughtered," as Gianni Canova puts it.[1] On March 13, *The Decameron* is truncated of some 20 minutes by the RAI (the third Italian television channel). Among the amputations is the close-up on Andreuccio who, once in the tomb, looking at the ugly dead bishop in disgust, exclaims: "Mortacci tua, quanto sei brutto!"—"How ugly you look now you're dead!" On the following week, *I Racconti di Canterbury* was shown to TV viewers without the final sequence in Hell, where Satan defecates a bunch of clerics in a huge, resounding flatulence. As for *Il Fiore*, it was reduced to some useless predigested "cathodic jam" meant for television—"marmellata catodica assolumente innocua, inutile e predigerita" (Canova, 39). A quarter of an hour of shots of coitus and genitals, especially male, are cut. Like Aziz, the film is emasculated.

Defining Scandal

We have just surveyed the vehement reactions aroused by the three movies on "a view of sex, whose cheerfulness makes up for — as it used to be — repression: a phenomenon that was to disappear for ever."[2] The filmmaker's words point out the contrast between an ideal remote past and a present which, being too permissive, makes sex sad and obsessive because it is compulsory and graceless. If in repressive medieval societies the scandalous, liberating representation of the naked body constitutes some innocent debunking of power, the lightness and exhilarating vitality of sex in the trilogy symbolizes first and foremost the physical enjoyment of a bygone lifestyle. What accounts for the "scandal" of the screenings of *Il Decameron*, *The Canterbury Tales*, and *The Arabian Nights*? Why are they viewed as shocking? To answer the question, we should start considering the implication of the very notion of scandal. Etymologically, the trilogy can be said to represent a "stumbling block," an "obstacle" hit by the right-thinking individuals, who, says Pasolini, "by repressing sex in [my] films, have repressed their contents, and have found them empty [for] failing to understand that there was ideology in them...."[3] "An incentive to turn away from God,"[4] according to its religious connotation, the term "scandal" can be construed in this particular case as the provocative intention to drift away from the norm, both ideological and aesthetic, which defines the conventional cinema that the spectator is so familiar with. The three movies could be described as "confusing, contradictory objects that sow dissension" in that they are the expression of a cinema that negates the audience's habits by facing them with a different conception of film. Pasolini's trilogy is thought "immoral and revolting," thus leading to indignation on the grounds that it subverts sexual ethics and bourgeois aesthetics. The work is perceived as a provocation in some respects. Pasolini's last movie (before *Salò*) refers to the corporeity of ordinary people, the epitome of the only reality that remains untouched, genuine. Consequently, it becomes a theme of prime importance for him. The absolute signification of sex in the artist's mind explains why he will devote four films to it, the last of which stands apart owing to the abominable symbolical role it confers to sex. Still, Italy in the early 1970s failed to estimate the challenge. "And as any avowal is also a challenge, a provocation also lies at the heart of my last cinema,"[5] said Pasolini. The indictment of the present, under cover of an evocation of the Italian and English Middle Ages (as well as an undated fantasmatic past in *Il Fiore*), passes completely unnoticed by an audience that, unlike what Pasolini expected, greets what they think is a contribution to the liberation of sexual comportments.

The Misunderstanding of an Original Form of Protest: Pasolini Charged with Obscenity

The success of the innovative *Decameron* gives rise to a Boccaccio-inspired line of pathetic, cheap erotic (even pornographic) movies *à l'italienne*. The critics also (intentionally) ignored the filmmaker's intentions when pulling the film to pieces in the press. The public and the intellectuals interpreted the work in a biased, erroneous way. What they prove unable to grasp, in both cases, is this "*carattere contestativo*" (Canova, 15), not so much of the Eros pictured in its most carnal manifestations as in the mode of representation. We mean the originality of the camera-eye that breaks with the hegemonic language of the 1970s, best (or, should we say, worst) illustrated in the mediocrity and futility of television. Canova speaks of "a project of spectacularity poles apart from the iconic language, which apparently prevailed in Italy in the next years and found its full emblematic expression in the futility and mediocrity of television."[6]

To the Leftist moralists who reproached him with initiating a so-called pornographic cinema inspired by Boccaccio and Chaucer, Pasolini replied that bodies are unscrupulously exploited by what he calls "cesspool television." According to him there is more reality in a lousy skin flick than in "all the television programs in a whole year" (Pasolini, Naldini, 376). The shock of the trilogy in the European film landscape raised a shower of biting, outraged comments, one seeing in *The Decameron* a tribute paid to consumer cinema, the other convinced *I Racconti di Canterbury* is in collusion with the cultural industry, describing it as "a mere archaeological work spiced with ambiguous conscious mannerism."[7] Lino Micciché presents *Il Fiore* as an exception in a "death tetralogy" (including *Salò*), where sex is tantamount to "lewd and transgressive arrogance, rude, saucy gesturing, ... low scatological instincts between feces and urine."[8] In France *The Decameron* is dismissed as an excuse for "cheeky, dreadfully licentious pranks" or an inducement to "the most animal form of ecstasy." In the newspaper *Le Figaro* of December 12, 1972, Louis Chauvet complains about "the constant abrupt changes of subject" in *I Racconti di Canterbury*, the arbitrary, desultory telling of which he deplores. Besides, under cover of "false literary and poetic alibis," the film betrays "a smutty complacency" in picturing "libidinous capers." Another journalist quotes a contemporary who writes that Chaucer has the freshness of a medieval author, whereas "we are too blasé to pick a rose and smell it as simply as a medieval man." Then he scornfully concludes that "Pasolini's roses grow on a heap of manure, which he seems to prefer to them" in *L'Express* of December 4, 1972.

In a nutshell, the detractors of *The Decameron* labeled it as "a pornographic essay."[9] *Racconti* was thought even more salacious and obscene owing to its evocation of irremediably ugly, scatological sexuality. The reprobation of *Il Fiore* concerning the indecent exhibition of sex was not so vehement. However, this film, too, was accused of sinking into obscenity. Five days after the opening night in Milan on June 20, 1974, it was submitted to the attorney's appreciation on the grounds that it boils down to "nothing more than ... vulgarity and exhibitionism of sexual organs, all very clearly photographical."[10] Maurizio Viano blames Pasolini for a smug, condescending attitude towards the Eastern world, typical of a European man who appropriates an exotic, idealized place to foster his personal fantasies.

> Only by dissociating himself from the context and by maintaining a patronizing relationship with the Orient can Pasolini exploit it artistically, enhance the mythology of Arab sexuality, and use shots worthy of a travel brochure.[11]

Jill Ricketts, who devotes a dozen pages to the scandal caused by the Trilogy of Life, ascribes the opprobium heaped on *Il Fiore* to an exoticism

> which used naked Third World bodies to figure innocence and jouissance, his bourgeois sensibility that idealized the underclass as somehow childlike and adorable in their disadvantage, and his utopian fantasy that the preindustrial past was pure and joyful.[12]

Lastly, some find exasperating the lack of natural grace in the actors' play. Carlo Laurenzi calls it "irritating and somewhat preposterous, just like the dubbing."[13]

The Trilogy of Life: A (Baroque) Cinema of Discourse

A Victimizing Mechanism Set in Motion

In the sense in which René Girard analyzes it,[14] the scandal as defined by Christ in the Gospels refers to the mimetic phenomenon of taking it out on a single victim, or scapegoat. The outraged person is actually hurt by the obstacle he or she comes up against, as if lame. Girard points out that the Greek word *skandalizein* derives from a verb that means "to limp." Now someone with a limp compulsively follows "an invisible obstacle against which they keep stumbling."[15] The obstacle has a repelling effect precisely because it looks attractive. Scandal is almost impossible to eschew. Like the lame person described by Girard, critics' fierce antagonism against the trilogy is obstinate and pointless. Scandal is also contagious. The self-deception process triggered off by aggressive opposition — symbolized by Satan in the New Testament (Girard, 199) — is due to blind mimetism. In the case of the resentment about the trilogy, the scandal stems from the inability of a majority of people to grasp Pasolini's approach that underlies each of the three movies. The complete or partial ignorance of Boccaccio's and Chaucer's works inevitably distorts the spectator's glance. Without the reference to the texts in the background, the latter mistakes the exhibition of naked bodies for pornography. The shock of *The Decameron* entailed another two crises as *I Racconti di Canterbury* and *Il Fiore* were released. When multiplied and concentrated, scandals

> plunge communities into crises that escalate up to a climactic moment when the unanimous polarization against one single victim provides the universal scandal, "the focal point for grievances" that calms the violence and puts together again the deconstructed whole.[16]

The three panels of the triptych crystallize the victimization process. The accusations of obscenity emanate from critics who repress a desire claimed by the artist: that of a different reality of the bodies, another sexuality, and a distinct, divergent (baroque) cinematic realism. It seems that the scandal, after all, can be used to show the audience there is an innovative perspective outside the established models, to which Pasolini means to offer an alternative. In an interview on French television, he declared: "I think that scandalizing is a right, being scandalized a pleasure, and that whoever refuses this pleasure is but a moralist."[17]

The Offensive Continuations of *The Decameron* and *I Racconti di Canterbury*

One may wonder whether the scandal does not lie in the way the movies under study were exploited and perverted by the porn film industry. About *The Decameron,* Kevin J. Harty signals that it inspired "an endless series of sexploitive sequels having little to do with Boccacio."[18] The first "continuation" was released the same year as its original, in 1971. By Mino Guerrini, it is entitled *Decameron n.2: Le altre novelle del Boccaccio.* It is also in 1971 that Gian Paolo Callegari in *Le Calde notti del Decamerone* makes use of "the Boccaccio stamp" to produce a poor succession of sexual misfortunes, all dull and repetitive (Harty, 66–67). The next year, Italo Alfaro with his *Decameron n.3: Le più belle donne del Boccaccio* capitalizes on the successful model. The move towards downright vulgarity becomes increasingly obvious from one film to the next, as the titles demonstrate: *Decameron proibitissimo* by Franco Martinelli, *Il Decamerone proibito* by Carlo Infascelli, and *Decameroticus* by Pier Giorgio Ferretti, all released in 1972. To a lesser extent, though, *I Racconti di Canterbury* was followed by two remakes, so to speak, that spoil the original: *Gli Altri racconti di Canterbury* by Mino Guerrini and *I Racconti di Canterbury n.2* by Lucio Dandolo in 1972.

> In this, yet another codpiece comedy with the right amount of nudity to escape being labeled hard-core, husbands are cuckolded and clerics are baited [Harty, 324].

In 1973 another two appaling porn sequels appear: *Racconti proibiti di nulla vestiti* by Brunello Rondi, and *Fratello homo, sorella bona — nel Boccaccio superproibito* by Mario Sequi. So as to benefit from the huge commercial success of *The Decameron,* all those second-rate film directors shamelessly misuse the screening of a literary work as an excuse to support an inferior, cheap soft-core cinema, unable to spread beyond Italy on account of its awfully low quality and hopeless inanity. This is the reason why it remains an extremely short-lived epiphenomenon.

> Medieval films readily offer entrée into the decadent. Medieval films that flirt with soft-core pornography.... Decadence on a higher level informs Pier Paolo Pasolini's so-called "trilogy of life" [Harty, intro., 6].

The Difference with Pornographic Cinema

This is precisely the perverted intention behind his three movies that Pasolini bitterly bemoans in his abjuration. "Nothing in what is risqué here is obscene" in this "lesson of faithfulness to the savour of a great text," writes a journalist in *Le Nouvel Observateur* (October 25, 1971) about *The Decameron.*[19] The selection of vivid, frivolous stories from Boccaccio and Chaucer does not aim at such "cheap titillation"[20] of the spectator, presented in the sequels with endless series of flatly redundant adultery situations that suggest that all men are silly cuckolded husbands and "women are either whores or saints eager to be deflowered" (Harty, 221). Unlike its numerous continuations, the trilogy transcribes naughty tales quite humorously, "not leeringly but with a healthy frankness."[21] "There's an April freshness to this portrait of the early Renaissance...."[22] The obvious lack of inhibition in the figuring of bodies is enhanced by a joyful, invigorating vitality, a snook cocked at a sexual moral constricted by the rigid principles of chastity and propriety. Neither in *The Decameron* nor in *Il Fiore* is sexuality subjected to the mechanics of the endless repetition of an act made insignificant, as in porn motion pictures. The reality on the screen is not only recorded and reproduced in its immediacy in the rough. The scene shown lies upon a discourse. The trilogy looks towards sex "to transgress cultural taboos," "approach the whole reality, without restrictions or barriers," and "refute the mystifications and lures of ideology."[23]

"Porn movies verify the definition that Pasolini gives of cinema as a reproduction of the language of action."[24] They lead to the lowest degree of identification on the part of the viewer with the objectivity of the evidence provided by live television programs.[25] Now even if it claims to be motivated by nothing but the pleasure of telling, Pasolini's cinema is "one of discourse, of the shattering..." of the cultural bourgeois enterprise.[26] Under the cover of a neutral viewpoint, the bourgeoisie conceals "reality behind *some* realites"—"la réalité derrière *des* réalités" (Amengual, 856). It confines realism to the mere detail so as to support and generalize the dominant ideology. The sublimated realism in the trilogy, on the contrary, conveys a style consisting of pastiche and the de-conditioning of the spectator, rid of his film-viewing habit. It is part of these subversive forces that the system seeks to neutralize, of these "more or less revolutionary actions that also assail it on the cultural front" (856).[27] The close-ups on the truth of sexual organs and acts claim the rights of the flesh in its crudest experiences by means of a "baroque" coarseness, in its first sense of "irregular," "shocking," "eccentric."

A Baroque Realism

The antinormative obscenity for which critics reproached Pasolini opens the door to fantasy, freedom, and the chaotic profusion of the baroque, found in taverns, fields, marketplaces, and brothels. Unlike a pornographic film director, Pasolini tackles sex not for itself but in relation with the social and religious interdicts, while always flirting playfully with a possible deviant shift of sexuality towards its most degrading variation. Pasolini's documentary style and point of view of the camera may at first sight bring to mind those of a porn movie halfway "between the perspective of a scientific film and that of a news bulletin."[28] Yet it cannot overshadow a realism transcended by the aesthetic mannerism of the film image that exorcises vulgarity. Besides, the laughter of comedy brushes aside any trace of pathos, and farce indirectly debunks stupidity and hypocrisy. "Guilty of mutilating the flesh during life on earth and promising it to the eternal fire of Hell after death," the monks are the grotesque victims of Bosch-inspired "sado-masochistic salacious antics" in a "nightmarish dreamland" at the end of *Racconti*, as a French journalist remarks (Bory). That sham lunapark, which orients the movie towards surreal farce, signals the preeminence of visuality over the subject.[29] The heterogeneity of the three motley films conveys, formally speaking, Pasolini's idea of the perception of the profilmic in a series of situations in which the individuals are confronted with everyday or extraordinary events. The spectator feels he is really experiencing existence. For one thing, the actors "play themselves" instead of "acting," particularly professionals like Citti and Davoli. The filmmaker seems to accompany them more than he actually directs them. Pasolini indeed does not attempt to reproduce reality as it truly is with a neo-realistic camera. His aim is rather to seize things themselves and make them palpable. His is not "a cinema of revelation as Rossellini or André Bazin viewed it, but a cinema bound to stumble against the sacrality of the close-up, a face, a dilated detail."[30] *The Decameron*, *I Racconti di Canterbury*, and *Il Fiore delle mille e una notte* stand as the opposite version of a proper historic reconstitution, for their author is exclusively concerned with the rendering of a humanity outside any specific era. In the first two movies, the Middle Ages appears as an excuse for and a metaphor of premodern man, whose sexuality still has not been exposed as "the institutionalization of eroticism and the transgression of Judeo-Christian morals" by porn cinema and by "the merchandizing of bodies in the industrial society."[31]

5

A Trans-semiotization: The Subversive Intention in *I Racconti di Canterbury*

After a necessary detour in the context of the reception of *The Decameron*, *I Racconti di Canterbury*, and *Il Fiore*, we will now focus on the two adaptations under study. The "trans-semiotization" or mutation of a semiotic system into a second one occurs through some manifestations of such a metamorphosis (a text put into film). One seems particularly revealing of the mechanism of adaptation.

The Treatment of Characters

The character plays a determining part in the meaning of a film inasmuch as it is a component of the narrative and fits to its logic. Not a person, properly speaking, but a signifier, it brings us back to the central question of representation that lies at the heart of film theory and practice. Still, while it boils down to a purely linguistic and typographic material in a text, it takes on a certain amount of iconic, verbal, and sound reality on the screen. From a mere semantic label or empty morpheme, progressively invested with meaning as the reader proceeds further into the reading, it fully becomes a sign "that bears multiple significations,"[1] as soon as it appears in human shape in a film. André Gardies and Francis Vanoye examine the notion of character from the angle of the distinction between four essential concepts: the "actant" (a term coined by Vladimir Propp and taken over by Claude Greimas), the actor, the part or role, and lastly the character. The latter is defined by what it is and a fortiori by what it does, for it is mainly actions the spectator watches in an ordinary movie, where "everything revolves round the hero,"[2] both the object and instrument of focalization. In other words, the character in film narrative is a cross between an actor (we are aware we are watching a perfomer) and an actant, whose actions influence the diegetic world, who is endowed with an actantial function, and triggers off fiction and sets the narrative rolling. According to Greimas, the actions of a story considered as "anthropomorphic figurative entities" "possessing differential qualifications" (Vanoye, 134) assume thematic roles determined by their actions and natures.

In the case of the screening of a book, one cannot view the film character in terms of a mere embodiment of a "paper being" with an illusory palpable existence. "In fact the literary character and the film character are two signs that differ in the signifier (in the substance and medium) and in the form of the contents."[3] The perceptible reality of the iconic signifier points to a subtle semantic construct that the words "character" and "actor" do not quite manage to translate with accuracy. This is why André Gardies suggests that the entangled relationships between the four aspects of the anthropomorphic sign (part and parcel of the textual system) be called an "actorial figure" (Gardies, 59). This denomination describes more aptly the specificity of a hybrid entity that

> partakes in the textual activity and a complex semiotization process, thanks to which it gets richer in multiple meanings. In this perspective, one realizes how wrong it would be to analyse the film character as a mere character ... [Gardies, 66].[4]

Thus formulated, the acceptation refers to the actant (identified by one or several functions of the actantial model), to the role (a kind of pattern or genre profile and operator), to the character (an essential element in the diegetic world and defining itself through the way he relates to the other components), and lastly to the actor or performer (who embodies the character). The actor however belongs to another (profilmic) dimension. If he is a film star, he may also introduce an intertextual ring to the movie on account of his or her mythic aura. In *The Decameron* and *I Racconti di Canterbury*, as far as characters are concerned, "characterization and ... psychologization ... come well behind actantialization."[5] In a text, the protagonist occupies a variable diegetic and/or narrative position thanks to a name, some adjectives and verbs especially. In a film, the materialization or reality of the character, qualified by means of a sum of features, roles, and actantial attributes, depends on the importance the film director gives it. It is first and foremost quantitatively, that is, in the number and duration of the shots and dialogues intended for him or her, that the actor/actant comes to life and actually becomes a character. In his clearly delineated sphere of action, the protagonist in Boccaccio's and Chaucer's tales in most cases strikes the reader's attention as an actant moving inside a referential universe reduced to essentials, close to the theatrical stage and yet presented as real.

Examples of Actantialization: *The Cook's Tale* and *Decameron*, II, 5

The broken construction of *The Decameron* and especially *Racconti* ingeniously help to translate the ephemeral, even immaterial nature of these shadows of paper, whose existence becomes palpable only through a small number of (more often than not stereotyped) behaviors within a limited space of intervention. As in a silent movie, Perkyn in *The Cook's Tale* is sketched through a minimal stock of comical expressions and exaggerated attitudes, pleasantly reminiscent of Chaplin's tramp figure. His impish light-heartedness is all the more cleverly enhanced as it is contrasted with the gullibility of his second boss, the irritability of the dwarf father-figure, the stupidity of the cops and the pot-bellied friar giving out soup to the destitute. All these representations of authority are caricatured. Perkyn hardly says anything in the film. His clownish behavior and funny looks are sufficient to picture him as a happy-go-lucky, cheerful trickster. We see him hop about, dance, and whistle like a goldfinch: "Gaillard he was as goldfynch in the shawe" (*The Cook's Tale*, 4367). He defines himself exclusively through an uninterrupted series of movements and short actions succeeding one another quite erratically, like Chaplin's sprightly, farcical gait. His film visualization of Perkyn perfecrtly restores the abundance of action verbs in the incomplete portrait of the young rogue, as well as the superfluous repetition of details indicative of a dissolute life: "Dauncen he koude so wel and jolily / That he was cleped Perkyn Revelour" (4370–71). "At every bridale wolde he synge and hoppe; / He loved bet the taverne than the shoppe" (4374–75). "And daunced wel ... / And gadered hym a meynee of his sort / To hoppe and synge and maken swich disport" (4380–82). Note the staccato rhythm of the last line quoted from Chaucer. It skillfully reproduces the boisterous ritornello, to the sound of which the youth seduces the bride and improvises a libertine dance in a ring with pretty undressed ladies. Perkyn/Davoli/Chaplin can be interpreted as an intertextual or, more exactly, interfilmic allusion to the Davoli in the first episode of *The Decameron* (II, 5).

Andreuccio's naïve carelessness, typical of a self-confident greenhorn, so far from imagining what the Neapolitan underworld has in store for him, exposes him from the start as the fool who is tricked and made a laughing-stock. In the *novella*, emphasis is laid upon his male pride, as he feels flattered by the interest the "gentil dona" shows in him (*Il Decameron*, vol. 1, p. 179). Nino Davoli's performance (winking and smiling at the camera) humorously renders the character's self-satisfaction. He starts walking ostentatiously, swaggering like a real Mediterranean *macho*. When a young maidservant delivers her mistress's message, he preens himself and follows her parading, then breaks into a run so as not to lose sight of her. All these flaws are implicitly stressed to encourage mockery. Yet we expect a reversal of the situation, for Andreuccio appears quite congenial after all. The plot first turns this pretentious young man into an imbecile covered with ridicule and travestied in a smelly "outfit" after coming out of the cesspool. Then he is pictured as a coward, scared stiff when all alone with the dead archbishop in his grave. While he is crying his eyes out in the text, the actor screams in fright. Davoli's expressive features distorted by terror have nothing to do with the image he is eager to project at the beginning of the episode: that of a young man, whose beaming face almost evokes a simpleton's unfailing smile.

Some Tricks That Set the Action Rolling: *The Miller's Tale* and VII, 2

In the film version of *The Miller's Tale*, the camera focuses not so much on Alisoun as on Nicholas. He is the one who takes the initiative. He triggers the plot mechanism by contriving a trick aimed at outwitting John the carpenter, his landlord. The latter's old age, jealousy and gullibility (*The Miller's Tale*, 3509, 3614) predispose him to the role of the cuckolded husband. Besides his being "a riche gnof," a fatheaded bumpkin who whistles and hums folk tunes, the actor's plump figure and ugly features help to underscore the character's silliness: "He knew nat Catoun, for his wit was rude" (3227)..." But sith he was fallen in the snare,/He moste endure, as oother folk, his care" (3231–32). When Nicholas predicts the coming of the flood, John reacts childishly almost like a simple Simon: "He wepeth, weyleth, maketh sory cheere" (3618). Right from the beginning, there is no doubt that Nicholas, a student who sings in Latin and has some basic knowledge of astrology (3514), will effortlessly assuage the wariness of an old man, whose young sexy wife he covets. In the opening of the episode, he is shown at the window spying on John as he leaves for Osney. We become aware of the young man's duplicity when he plays a character in a mise an abyme of the actor's performance: that of a clerk transfixed by the shock of the false revelation of the impending disaster. "And spaake so faire, and profred him so faste,/That she hir love hym graunted atte laste" (3289–90). His ability to convince Alisoun to be his echoes the long, persuasive speech delivered in *Il Decameron* (VII, 2) by Peronella, who manages to turn a tricky situation to her own advantage. She comes to life not so much through her acts as through her discourse, hence the stress on the overperformance of the actress, who yells, laments, gesticulates, and rolls her eyes in fury. Her virulent speech, made vivid by colorful language (*Il Decameron*, vol. 2, 800–01) sounds somewhat like the Wife of Bath's, another more famous epitome of the shrew. In the movie, Peronella appears amazingly garrulous and restlessly ebullient, which sets her in opposition to her passive half-witted husband, who obeys her with a wide stupid grin. This ludicrous hard-featured churl is guileless, unlike the lover. Craftiness is the attribute of both the adulterous wife and Giannello, a handsome blackguard. His pale blue eyes and light hair grant him a falsely gentle, almost angel-like expression like Damyan in *The Merchant's Tale*. No wonder the two good-looking actors play the secret lover who betrays the husband in his very house.

Vicious Characters: The Shadow of the Devil in *The Pardoner's Tale* and I, 1

The malevolent, immoral characters, such as the three rogues in *The Pardoner's Tale*, betray the baseness of their souls through their physical appearance, gestures and speech on the screen. In Chaucer, their harsh, laconic statements are peppered with swear words:

> "Ye, Goddes armes!" quod the riotour (*The Pardoner's Tale*, 692) ... / I make avow to Goddes digne bones! (694) ... / "And we wol sleen this false traytour Deeth" (699) ... / And many a grisly ooth thanne han they sworn, / And Cristes blessed body they torente —" [708–09].

To the extremely old man who tells them where to find the mysterious thief named Death, they retort most disrespectfully: "...What, carl, with sory grace! / Why artow al forwrapped save thy face? / Why lyvestow so longe in so greet age? (717–19) ... "thou false theef" (759). They speak aggressively and even shout menacingly. The cruelty of their tone is also reflected in their rough actions. They run, pretend to fight, and the first one stabs their younger companion after bluntly exposing in few words the cupidity that motivates that crime.

> "...And thanne shal al this gold be departed be, / My deere freend, bitwixen me and thee. / Thanne may we bothe oure lustes all fulfille, / And pleye at dees right at oure owene wille." / And thus acorded been thise shrewes tweye / To sleen the thridde, as ye han herd me seye [832–36].

Later in the tale, the word "feend" (844, 847) appears. It sounds strangely similar to "freend," already used in lines 815 and 832. The evocation of the two rascals who plot the murder of the third fellow takes on a fiendish tinge. We cannot but think of Franco Citti, whose impenetrable gaze and somber expression as Ciappelletto in *The Decameron* foreshadow the Devil's commissioner in *The Friar's Tale*. Ciappelletto does not scruple to indulge in blasphemy. He even abuses his two hosts for fun, as we pointed out earlier. At dinner, one of the usurers hints at the havoc he will wreak among his debtors, so dreadful his reputation is. He replies that they are no better than he and calls them "leeches, ghouls, ... vermin, filth, usurers," frowning at them and feigning to cast a bad spell on them. Debating on what to do with the dead Ciappelletto, the iniquitous moneylenders refer to him as a damned soul who cannot possibly be redeemed (*Il Decameron*, vol. I, 56). In *I Racconti di Canterbury* the same Franco Citti, who plays Satan's summoner, neither swears nor kills, but exults at watching the sodomite burning at the stake. He delights in the sight of the black smoke rising up. This is the only clue to his demoniac nature in the episode. Nevertheless, his feeble, satisfied smirk betrays the same cynicism as that of the crafty cheat, Accattone, in the eponymous movie (1961) and that of the despicable Carmine in *Mamma Roma* (1962). In his first two movies, Pasolini gives Citti the role of a pimp. When Mamma Roma (Anna Magnani) sees him at her door, she is scared and tries in vain to shut it in his face. He blurts out ironically: "Che, hai visto er diavolo?"[6] The actor personifies a diabolic figure that seems to run through the filmmaker's work up to *Il Fiore*, in which he embodies a red-haired demon who ruthlessly beheads a girl.

Picturing the Clergy: Irony, Pastiche, and the Grotesque

The Pilgrimage Perverted

The film treatment of the clergy, a favorite target of satire, deserves close scrutiny because it brings to light the feeling shared by Boccaccio, Chaucer, and Pasolini of a decadence of the spiritual ideals and role played by clerics in the Christian faith and religious practice.

> For when Chaucer decided upon a pilgrimage to Canterbury as the unifying framework for his story collection, he drew upon one of the most deeply ingrained images and social realities in medieval culture.[7]

The *viator*'s itinerary toward Heaven leads to some intense religious emotion aroused by the discovery of holy relics, especailly the corpse of Thomas à Becket in the Canterbury shrine. The long, exacting pilgrim's progress turns out to be a liminal experience "focused both on this world and the next" (Bisson, 110). Such an ordeal momentarily places the pilgrim at the threshold of another reality, from which he will emerge regenerated. The duality of a route both meandering — open to the temptations offered during the trip — and perfectly straight — the right way to eternal salvation — finds its materialization in the architectural layout of some churches. On the one hand, the divine tones are in total harmony, while on the other hand the penitent epitomizes human erring and groping. Furthermore, the Priest's function as a pastor responsible for showing us "the wey, in this viage" (*The Parson's Prologue*, 48) confirms the eschatological orientation of *The Canterbury Tales*, the frame story of which uses the "pre-text" of a pilgrimage to a famous English shrine emblematic of Jerusalem. As Lillian Bisson points out, in accordance with what is planned by the Host in *The General Prologue*, the procession of the merry company "is supposed to end in a tavern rather than at the shrine" (Bisson, 119). The spiritual aspiration originally meant to unite the pilgrims in their common effort toward Canterbury seems to fade away in face of some low motivations. It is as though the sublime were eclipsed by human fallibility. In Chaucer's time, though, the practice of pilgrimage — one of the most popular along with the worshipping of saints' relics — was sharply criticized. The phenomenon can be ascribed to the emphasis laid upon a deeper religious interiority known as the *devotio moderna*, or Christian will to voice one's faith in a more personal manner. Previously the privilege of churchmen, communion with God through the expiation of sins, the saying of prayers, and self-discipline initiated an inner quest among the laymen more sensible to the humanity of Christ and the Virgin Mary — omnipresent in 15th-century iconography. Laymen bought prayer books and books of hours to satisfy spiritual needs that the clerics were no longer able to meet. The reason for the growing disapproval of pilgrimages lies mainly in the corruption of the church, the ideals of which became obsolete to the benefit of secular values often inherited from feudal aristocracy. The spirit of contrition, supposed to prevail among the company of the 30 pilgrims hoping for the remission of their sins, does not strike one as clearly manifest in *The General Prologue*. We are poles apart from the serious contemplation one would expect from this kind of context. Thomas à Kemps, quoted by Johan Huizinga, believes that "those who often go on such journeys seldom become saints."[8]

The Satire of Churchmen

Suffice it to examine the last two portraits in *The General Prologue*: the summoner and his partner, the Pardoner — iniquitous associates who epitomize the abuses of ecclesiastical justice and the shameless exploitation of popular faith. The dishonest peddler boasts that he can save from Purgatory anyone who buys his pardons. In other words, he trades in hopes for redemption and cons many a credulous buyer. The theologian Pierre d'Ailly demanded that one should "ban from the Church the pardoners and pedlars of indulgences who sully its reputation with their lies and ridicule it."[9] Besides, he blamed "quantitative evil" that gnawed at the institution, within which all kinds of worship and religious orders multiplied. As a result, a puzzling diversity of practices developed and led to "exclusivism and rivalry" (Huizinga, 158). Through the portraits of the clerics in *The General Prologue*, Chaucer deals with the corruption of their estate, which grows worse and worse as we move on from the Prioress to the Monk and lastly the Friar. Donald Howard[10] devotes several pages to them and underscores the obsolescence of the lifestyle they are supposed to stand for but fail to put into practice. Far from relinquishing earthly preoccupations as their vows of poverty, humility, charity and chastity bid them to, they actually behave as the antithesis of Saint Anthony, getting away from the world in obedience to the *contemptus mundi* principle. The Prioress seems to hesitate between religion and *gentillesse*: "And sikerly ... of greet desport, / And ful pleasaunt, and amyable of port, / And peyned her to countrefete cheere / Of court ... / And to ben holden digne of reverence" (*The General Prologue*, 137–41). "Speaking of the Monk, Chaucer explicitly describes this obsolescence of 'old things' and speaks of the emergence of a new world."[11] One learns that this stout, "manly" Monk could not care less about Saint Benedict's monastic rule, which prescribes a secluded life inside the monastery, entirely devoted to ascesis, labor, and the study of the Holy Writ. Chaucer's character on the contrary shamelessly evinces his preference for values alien from the ideal of an inner struggle against vice. Like a rich landlord, he rides a superb steed, indulges in hunting and wears fine, expensive clothes. Then Chaucer proceeds to a more detailed description of Friar Huberd, a representative of the Mendicant Orders that flourished in the 12th century when monachism, which became too rigid for the profound urban and economic changes in Western medieval society. In the early 13th century under the pontificate of Innocent III, such orders transformed "the organization and functioning of the monastic and religious life."[12] The novelty they introduced was the forswearing of opulence and social life. Instead they claimed autonomy from the ordinary clerical authorities. Furthermore, the new conception of spiritual life broke with traditional religious habits. Two orders prevailed. The Dominicans, who are preachers, live in destitution and conventual mendicancy — an essential condition to attain eternal bliss. Chaucer's Friar belongs to the Franciscan Order. The narrator in *The General Prologue* "accidentally" remarks that Huberd shuns the poor and lepers (*The General Prologue*, 242–47). The religious man's taste for playing and singing ballads implies he belongs to "God's jesters" (*The General Prologue*, 235–36). The Franciscans form a brotherhood of lay penitents. Searching for food instead of money, they commit themselves to predication. They are *poverelli*, living in the joy of being indigent. The fresh innocence of their totally disinterested faith is successfully rendered in Roberto Rossellini's *Francesco giullare di Dio*.[13] In a very sober Franciscan fashion, the Italian filmmaker transcribes the graceful elation of the friars entirely engrossed in mystic contemplation, their serious yet childlike expressions highlighting their radiant humaneness. Their regenerative order indeed satisfies the spiritual expectations as well as the needs of the church. They set great store by the Last Judgment, the time when the have-nots will find compensation at last.

The Mendicant Orders: The Irony of The Summoner's Tale

The friar in *The Summoner's Tale*, grinning smugly at the end of the episode just before he is taken down to Hell, is lying in bed with plenty of victuals around him. His satisfied smirk has nothing to do with the genuine beatitude that transports Francis and his disciples in Rossellini's movie. The well-pleased look on the greedy, concupiscent clergyman's face is of a completely different kind. It could be compared with the proverbial cat that has swallowed the canary. "The Friar similarly holds after the new world. His abuses suggest the ideals of the Franciscan order — poverty, begging, good works ... 'He was the best begger in his hous' (*The General Prologue*, 252)."[14] He seems to be feasting on a gargantuan meal in advance. Nevertheless, the parallel with the saint of Assisi appears preposterous if we consider the following scene, where the hypocritical glutton ends up, like many other ecclesiastics, in Satan's bowels. Upon the image of the fleshy Mendicant, Pasolini superimposes that of the Friar on the Southwark marketplace, glimpsed in the opening sequence of *I Racconti di Canterbury*. He does not look in the slightest like the friar described by Chaucer, yet he cuts an equally ridiculous figure. First he looks daggers at the Summoner as the latter is whistling along while the Pardoner is singing his Neapolitan complaint. His expression is fraught with hateful disdain, which cleverly confirms Chaucer's detailed evocation indicative of the beggar's villainy. He is depicted as a good sort who is second to none when it comes to "muchel daliaunce and fair language" (*The General Prologue*, 211). The introductory scene of the movie shows him glaring at another dishonest individual. Ironically, the Friar of *The General Prologue* is one of the most colorful caricatures in Chaucer's portrait gallery. The hint of his malignity, in a mise en abyme through the Pardoner's baseness — and his own double, the fake preacher in *The Pardoner's Tale* episode — refers to a specificity of the late medieval mentality.

Of all the contradictions of religious life then, the most insolvable may be the avowed contempt for the clergy, somewhat mixed with the utmost respect inspired by the holiness of priesthood.[15]

At the time, the corruptibility of human nature and therefore of the social group called for a reform and a practice of charity, supposed to overstep the decline of the world. For Howard, it is the awareness of an urgent return to righteousness that gives rise to the medieval estates satire, especially that leveled at churchmen. "That is the seed of satire, perhaps the real origin of medieval satire..." (Howard, 116). Now the most appropriate instrument of satire is irony. "And the implications that things should be reformed is present in *The Canterbury Tales*—present in the minute actualities of its un-ideal characters and present in the author's irony" (116).

Resorting to the Typology of the Estates Satire

Friar John in *The Summoner's Tale* perfectly reflects the typology of friars, as he personifies all the well-known faults generally attributed to them. What Donald Howard calls "impersonated artistry" (Howard, 257) refers to the the fact the author places an indirect diatribe in the mouth of a narrator who resents the Mendicant Orders.

> Now help, Thomas, for hym that harwed helle! / For elles moste we oure bookes selle. / And if you lakke oure predicaccioun, / Thanne goth the world al to destruccioun. / For whoso wolde us fro this world bireve, / So God me save, Thomas, by youre leve, / He wolde bireve out of this world the sonne [*The Summoner's Tale*, 2107–13].

In a comically hyperbolic metaphor, Chaucer astutely conveys the insistence of the sanctimonious preacher who is solely interested in the financial profit he thinks he can derive from the sick man. The grandiloquence displayed by the confessor, whose lecture abounds in high-sounding, polysyllabic abstract terms, is echoed in "predicaccioun," "destruccioun," and "false dissymulaccioun," (2123) which efficiently summarize the real intention behind the dissembling friar's endless disquisition. The narrator's voice suddenly puts an end to the deceiver's act: "This sike man wax wel ny wood for ire; / He wolde that the frere had been on-fire / With his false dissymulaccioun" (2121–23). In the last line, the author's discourse can be perceived in the background. The duplicitous churchman becomes an obsequious, effeminate character in the movie. Whereas he takes the initiative at the beginning of the story, he soon falls victim to the churl's trick and eventually gets just what he deserves. As Chaucer intimates in line 2122, he collapses into the place par excellence where helpless victims end up: the pit of Hell, in which he is bound to be tormented forever. Chaucer's use of "the basic features of the antifraternal stereotypes" (Bisson, 94) can be observed in Huberd's quarrel with his sworn enemy, the Summoner, in the middle of *The Wife of Bath's Prologue*.[16] Relying on William of Saint Amour, who distinguishes three groups within the mendicant orders, Lillian Bisson emphasizes their hypocrisy, venality, and ability to have themselves accepted in people's homes so as to beguile them. All those flaws are embodied by Friar John, who succeeds only in probing Thomas's rear instead of his conscience. The only funds he gets for the benefit of his community come from a fundament that rewards him with an insolent fart. His dissimulation is similar to Don Gianni's (*The Decameron*, IX, 10). Manly yet sweet-tongued, the priest takes delight in fooling Pietro and Gemmata by means of his smooth speech. The abbess in the film version of *Decameron*, III, 1 also has some power of persuasion (doubled with a fierce sexual appetite), which enables her to satisfy her sisters thanks to a compromise, which she astutely presents like a miracle. Both tricks, the fake intervention of the supernatural and the use of magic, betray a tendency to tell lies, which contravenes the essential pursuit of virtuous conduct advocated not only by the mendicant orders but by all the clergy. By the way, one can notice that both Friar John in *Racconti* and the Mother Superior in *The Decameron* are overweight, ludicrous and unattractive. The former is pot-bellied and the latter uncovers fat old legs when giving herself to the young gardener.

Marcel Pacaut speaks of an ecclesiastical crisis (206) in the 14th century. The spiritual prestige of the church is on the wane. The Great Schism (1378–1418) divides Christendom into two parts and shakes the religious institution. The monks' morals begin to slacken. Are we to infer that at the end of the Middle Ages laymen became anxious to lead a spiritual life on account of the alarming depravement of clerical models? "Like many of his contemporaries, Chaucer wrestles with the problem of what constitutes Christian perfection in a beleaguered world" (Bisson, 98). The only priest who seems guileless and sincere is Ciappelletto's confessor. In the final sequence of the episode, though, he reveals a darker, ambiguous profile, as he severely lectures the crowd of worshippers, whom he blames for an excessive use of blasphemy. He almost hurls abuse at his congregation like the rascal inveighing against sin in the parody of preaching that opens *The Pardoner's Tale*.

The Incongruous Superimposition of the Preacher and Sinner Figures

As pointed out earlier, Rufo il Rosso thus named by Pasolini (and said to be "il miglior scopatore di via del Pesce"[17]) embodies the superimposition of the Pardoner and the Priest. The assimilation of the two significant figures in *The Canterbury Tales* can be accounted for first of all by their being preachers delivering "sermons," one being true while the other is fake. Furthermore, the Pardoner brings up the rear of the procession in *The General Prologue*, while the *Parson's Tale* closes the series of narratives. The young rake's performance in the brothel stages Chaucer's extradiegetic mention of an "alestake" (Introduction, *The Pardoner's Tale*, 321), in which the peddler of indulgences—sarcastically required by the Host who addresses him as "thou beel amy" (318) to tell a tale—insists on stopping for a drink and a meal while thinking of "some honest thyng while I drynke" (Introduction, *The Pardoner's Tale*, 328). We may wonder how the edifying "moral thyng" announced in the Introduction to *The Pardoner's Tale* (325) could possibly arouse any deep serious meditation in a context that invites gluttony. In this paradox lies the key to the interpretation of the character and his speech. His is an anti-sermon that boils down to some garrulous exhortation to buy pardons, supported by an anecdote about divine retribution. The wily crook who lives on that fraudulent trade personifies the medieval concept of the incongruous, which conflicts with and threatens the perfection of order, the accepted standard or norm of the good and the beautiful. These serve as the yardstick by which evil is measured and considered the equivalent of chaos and inversion.

> ... medieval art had a place for the grotesque, but it was never at the center of things—it was on the outside or the underside. Chaucer lived in a century before Bosch and Brueghel isolated this estranged world, nearly a century before the word "grotesque" came to be applied to ancient art discovered in grottos. In this time the grotesque—the disordered, incongruous, and startling element in experience, the demonic element—was antithetical to artistic ordering or structuring; its place was at the periphery, but there it was permitted to exist and did exist [Howard, 338].

According to Howard, evidence of the grotesque dimension of the Pardoner rests in the self-destructive guilty feeling of a marginal person, embittered by the awareness that what is in store for him is damnation, significantly enough just like the three rascals (a threefold projection of the narrator) in his example. In the brothel, Rufo stands above a "congregation." Yet he is far from attaining the ultimate spiritual elevation of the pastor of their souls. In place of the long "tretys" in prose delivered by the Parson about how a Christian should behave to find the right way to penance, Pasolini's rogue hurls violent abuse at the sinners, who are doomed never to reach the "Jerusalem Celestial." While doing so, the false preacher showers urine on his audience along with a stream of aphorisms and quotations from the Scriptures and the classics. The provocative performance has nothing in common with the rigorous, methodical structure of a prose treatise that falls into parts and subdivisions of fairly equal length and contains examples and vivid details intended to convey theological abstracts. The dual irreproachable preacher/irredeemable sinner figure is reminiscent of the perpetual tension between the two spiritual poles of the medieval mind quite familiar with a puzzling contradiction "that has now become almost incomprehensible."[18] We mean the coexistence of the pious and the obscene that pervades all aspects of the medieval culture, including literature and particularly Boccaccio and Chaucer.

> In the medieval consciousness two conceptions of life emerge side by side. The pious, ascetic conception attracts all moral feelings. Carnality on the contrary belongs to the Devil and takes a terrible revenge. Whatever tendency prevails, we have either the saint or the sinner. However, there is no steady balance between them but huge discrepancies instead [Huizinga, 187].[19]

Feminized Clerics and the Subversive Power of Pastiche

In *I Racconti di Canterbury* (even more so than in its source), where *The Pardoner's Tale* is obliquely mentioned only to be subverted, the clerics have a lascivious, sometimes demonic nature. The sundry portraits of priests, nuns, friars, and monks throughout the first two episodes of the Trilogy of Life stress indictment of the shameless misconduct of the clergy, such as the selling of pardons, the abusive prescription of penance, and the excessive importance given to the intercession of priests and saints. Still, if we look attentively at the movies under consideration, we realize that their respective galleries of ecclesiastics close on the comic image of funnily effeminate friars in both cases. The two *fraticelli* in *The Decameron*, gaping admiringly at the maestro working on his masterpiece, mince, smile, wink flirtatiously at the artist, and blithely sound the bells of Santa Chiara. The scene is the occasion for a comic, even burlesque act, in which the pair of exalted whippersnappers are hanging on the bell rope and soar up in the air. If one bears in mind the heresy that homosexual love (called "sodomy") represented in the Middle Ages, one can easily figure out how sacrilegious and infamous it may seem when it involves a churchman, supposed to preserve the purity of body and soul. Does this imply that the depravement of clergymen culminates in the kind of dissidence known as "the horrendous crime" or "abominable evil?"[20] The upward movement of the friars, sounding the church bell to celebrate the completion of the first two panels of the triptych, could well be construed on the contrary as a liberation of the male homosexual voice. Pasolini nonetheless adds to the comedy of the situation as well as the ludicrous behavior of the two womanly fellows. We see them side by side, the one with his head leaning against the other's, simpering coyly at the maestro—whose muscular bare chest and virile sculpted body are enhanced by his samurai-like sober dress.

Conversely, Friar John, the last clerical figure in *Racconti*, follows quite the opposite direction. Instead of rising up in the air, he is urged on down to the pit of Hell, where, horrified, he finds out that his kind are riotously expelled from Satan's anus. John's sexual ambiguity also strikes the spectator's attention. We see him purse his lips, simper, and clutch a phallic squash. The hint at the Devil's anality in the infernal vision refers to sodomy, and the fact that the shameful orifice is the Devil's strengthens the turpitude of homosexual love. The punishment imposed upon Friar John does not offer the slightest hope of remission, just as the flames inexorably consume the sodomite's body at the stake (at the beginning of *The Friar's Tale* film version) under the eye of the smug archdeacon — whose stilted air and sophisticated fine dress could indicate some degree of affectation usually ascribed to homosexuals. The image of the sissy ecclesiastic serves as a transition with the pastiche of Bosch's painting. The last pictorial allusion in *The Decameron* constitutes a vision of the sublime (the supreme godly Judgment) from a distance. The citation of Giotto is easily identifiable, as the film director puts the Madonna on the celestial throne in the place of Christ. It is not so much the eschatological import of the religious tableau that matters to him as the aesthetic message he indirectly delivers. He aims at shocking the viewer's consciousness through a heretic act of burlesque distortion of well-known, virtually revered pictures. It is as if, like the Pardoner or Ciappelletto, Pasolini reminded us about his nature and function as a crook and an actor creating a fiction — which could stand as a definition of the artist. The artificiality of the new product inspired from a renowned work of art signals itself more conspicuously at the end of *I Racconti di Canterbury*. Though grave, gloomy and apparently irrevocably devoid of hope, the grotesque tableau cannot possibly point to the ultimate vision, "the sighte of the parfit knowynge of God" (*The Pardoner's Tale*, 1079) — which can only be achieved through the correction of sin and the "verray penitence, confessioun and satisfaccioun..." (*Retraction*, 1089). To the perfect silence of the revelation of God's mystery, the artist prefers a chaotic yet colorful scene bustling with life and sounds. The sight he seems to opt for is first and foremost extraordinarily exhilarating and pleasurable. This could serve as an explanation of the selection of tales, which cleverly restores this subtle mixture of the sublime and the scatological.

6

Eloquent Pictures

The Voices of the Text
The Screening of Words

Adapting a text amounts to "creating some equivalents of writing out of the possibilities of film language."[1] The neologism "cinécriture," used by French specialists in film studies, describes a semiotic transfer, namely another form of semiotization of the literary work. A new, different textual occurrence of it is submitted to our judgment. A trans-semiotization phenomenon occurs, made possible by the visualizing of words. Chaucer happens to be mainly concerned with words or speech. *The Pardoner's Tale*, which comes last, after *The Manciple's Tale*, deals with the vision of the Heavenly Jerusalem, the goal of the pilgrimage of the soul through the meandering Daedalus of fictions, as the erring pilgrims are "wanderynge by the weye" (*The General Prologue*, 467) like the Wife of Bath. The structure of *The Canterbury Tales* resembles that of a labyrinth: "...the labyrinth had a beginning, middle, and end; was a pilgrimage to Heavenly Jerusalem."[2] One understands better why the long, elaborate demonstration of *The Pardoner's Tale* occupies the final position in Chaucer's work. Then, bringing out the sophistication of the labyrinthic design, Howard carries on

> with many turnabouts in which the path clusters now on one side, now on another, sometimes sweeping past whole areas where it has been before, and yet which through its overall form and conception encompasses all of its design and arrives at its end [Howard, 331].

An amazing intertwining of speeches precedes the Priest's treaty, a handbook of good conduct for Christians. A complex network of narratives and voices intermingling and echoing one another, the collection of tales reaches its climax in a parodic apocalypse in the denouement of *The Manciple's Tale*. For having disclosed the unbearable truth about his wife's unfaithfulness to Phoebus, his master, a white crow is "blackened." In a fit of rage, the young god — also a poet: "...flour of bachilrie, / As wel in fredom as in chivalrie" (*The Manciple's Tale*, 125–26) — murders his wife and breaks his musical instrument as well as his bow and arrows. An abrupt silence succeeds to an overwhelming flow of words: "the empty blah-blah of too much talk and the flapping of an open mouth" (Howard, 304). In accordance with the morality drawn from the anecdote, the Parson ensures his audience in his prologue that he will ward off the danger of telling fables. He seems to take into account the sententious conclusion uttered by the Manciple quoting abundantly from his own mother's recommendations: "My sone, thenk on the crowe, a Goddes name! / My sone, keep wel thy tonge, and keep thy freend (318–19).... My sone, be war, and be noon auctour newe / Of tidynges, wheither they been false or trewe" (359–60). The interminable pompous enumeration of maxims pulverizes in an ironic deflagration the supernumerary redundant words on the necessity to keep quiet, by far preferable to useless perorations. "*The Manciple's Tale* lets language itself fall beneath corrupt human nature. The rest, or at least the end, is silence" (Howard, 304). The making up of stories thanks to the magic of language thus appears unjustified. From one tale to the next, the speech act never ceases to signal itself through the excuse of the tale-telling contest. In *La lettre et la voix: de la "littérature" médiévale,* Paul Zumthor refers to medieval literature in inverted commas. As the editor puts it on the back cover, literature in the Middle Ages is the product of the voice rather than the letter. It is not a literature and even less so a "piece of writing" or "text."[3] When today's readers focus their critical attention on a 14th-century written composition, they must bear in mind the subtle and essential distinction between the audibility/visibility of a "work" and the legibility of a "text."

Chaucer's oratory poetry is composed to be performed. The recurrence of verbs relevant to the delivery of poetic speech indicates that the written words are endowed with a vocal quality. Actually, the text is conceived as the opportunity for a vocal performance. A "speaker" transmits his message to a crowd of listeners in a situation of discourse *in praesentia* (Zumthor, 42). The famous frontispiece in the manuscript of *Troilus and Criseyde* dating from the early 15th century[4] pictures Chaucer reading aloud his work to the court. The author thus becomes an actor. Despite their textual discontinuity (they are divided into fragments), *The Canterbury Tales* are conceived as a "book" rather than a mere collection or miscellany by their "makere." The presence of a voice that contrives to communicate its poetry suffices to grant unity to a massive literary product. Chaucer shares with the first Italian humanists a craze for books, rare precious things that contain not only past doctrines and authorities for our edification, but also some recorded voices that can be reproduced ad infinitum. "Bookness" and "voiceness" (Howard, 63) are the two qualities that coexist in a book. The poet's audience, metaphorically pictured in the small gathering of pilgrims in *The General Prologue*, feel that they hear the author/performer say his text, just as the tellers seem to be uttering their narratives. Furthermore, the work gives the impression of following a linear structure typical of oral delivery. Some links, breaks, prologues and epilogues nonetheless definitely contribute to build a textual arrangement reproduced on vellum pages bound into an object that the reader can use, handle, and in which he can "turne over the leef" (*The Miller's Prologue*, 3177) to revert to some particular passages or skip others. Besides being written and read, voiced and heard, the work is a material thing, a "body" that receives the stigmata or marks of the sharp point of the quill as it runs across the sheet of paper. In Chaucer's time, "literature" basically pertained to a culture of generalized theatricality. The work achieved its full realization only when the letter was made one with the melody of the voice and the performance. The teller fulfils the double function of narrator and informer. He comments upon the letter while deciphering it. Such glossing or interpreting is expressed through the performer's gestures. His theatrical play alters the meaning of the text, determining its tonality according to the effect of persuasion he intends to produce on the audience. No wonder Pasolini chooses to present two preachers in *The Canterbury Tales*: the immoral rake — a burlesque version of the Priest, doubled with the cynicism of the Pardoner — in the brothel scene, and the sly-looking friar in *The Summoner's Tale*.

Putting on a Show: *The Pardoner's Tale, Miller's Tale, Reeve's Tale,* and *Merchant's Tale*

From the 13th century on, the *artes praedicandi* flourish. In France and England, predicators enliven their sermons with verse or popular couplets as illustrations of the themes dealt with. *The Miller's Tale* makes mention of Absolon's talent for singing at the mass. The church soon realizes that homilies provide an effective instrument of ideological manipulation. As a result, ecumenical councils insist that the priest should strike the consciences of his congregation by singing moving songs or by telling jokes. An artful handler of rhetorics, the preacher turns into an actor performing a popular drama. Leo Carruthers underlines the major role played by *exempla*, a precious tool that helps the predicator captivate his flock.

> The artes preadicandi advise to use stories and parallels meant to lighten a long, tedious sermon, enliven doctrinal teaching, and pepper a much too dull, common tale.... Anecdotes make the text more interesting and sometimes even funny, highlighting human weaknesses.[5]

After 1200, Paul Zumthor remarks, the members of the mendicant orders borrow from the chanson de geste and the fabliau formulas to attract the listeners' attention. Such formulas emphasize the phatic function of language, which means they resort to vocatives and set phrases to call the audience to order or witness. Predication partakes in "drama" in the medieval sense of show. It contributes to develop a rhythmic language aiming at creating an impact. The preacher's art is closely associated with music and jugglery. The silent spectator/auditor plays a major part in the elaboration of medieval poetry. The performed work is put into the conversational form (Zumthor, 248). *The Canterbury Tales* contain a great number of dialogic interventions. The young preacher in his parody of sermon in the opening of *The Pardoner's Tale* urinates on a mock congregation of fallen individuals of all kinds, whom he shouts at just as Chaucer's Pardoner addresses his credulous victims sharply, standing "lyk a clerk in my pulpet" (*The Pardoner's Tale*, 391).

I Racconti di Canterbury stages other characters such as the wily Nicholas in *The Miller's Tale*. The latter exploits his gift for acting when he easily outwits his gullible landlord. Through a slit in the door, the carpenter watches the young clerk prostrated before his book, with his hands raised as if receiving a revelation from God. Then, when the old man asks about what keeps him so mysteriously quiet, Nicholas launches into a lengthy pseudo-theological explanation, which he pours out in a hurry, shouting so as to aggravate the carpenter's fright. In *The Reeve's Tale* Aleyn and John, the students from King's Hall College, Cambridge, attempt to lull the cunning miller's suspicions by feigning to be most interested in the different stages of the bread-making process in the mill. They exchange knowing winks and smiles, behaving like cheap counterfeiters, unaware they are being fooled by Symkyn's ingenious trick — he has just let their horse loose so that they will have to walk back. The film translation of Januarie's justifying his decision to take a fresh young spouse despite his old age also underlines the performing aspect of discourse. Finely dressed, the old lord enters the reception hall of his abode and sits down to deliver an apology of marriage in a self-confident tone, smiling knowingly, frowning and rolling his eyes. His audience (that is, his court whom he has summoned for the occasion) seems completely indifferent to the specious argumentation delivered in a sentential tone. A shot of the counsellors, Placebo and Justinius in Chaucer's text, reveals that one is looking up, bored stiff, while the other throws a chicken bone over his shoulder.

In *The Decameron*, Ciappelletto with a contrite imploring expression persuades the priest of his holiness, and the successful show put on by the shrewd performer takes in the crowds even after his death. Exhibited to be gazed at and worshipped, the body is literally displayed as on a stage. Words are no longer necessary for the smooth-tongued swindler to give evidence of his purity of soul — which is the dream and paradox of the actor. The tricksters turn out to be excellent performers, such as Andreuccio's alleged stepsister, who accompanies her lies with tears. Peronella never leaves her silly husband the slightest opportunity to answer her attacks, since she fills the space of her house with abuses poured out in a shrill voice. She even goes as far as to call the heavens to witness in a possible parody of a diva. Endowed with the same talent of persuasion though not as wildly garrulous, Don Gianni performs his conjuring trick, never ceasing to talk while gesturing in a puzzling, allegedly esoteric manner. Yet his preposterous gesticulation comically betrays his lust for the buxom Gemmata, whom he pretends he can change into a mare.

The Significant Example of the Wife of Bath

The addition of the old Neapolitan storyteller in *The Decameron* foreshadows Pasolini's intention to retain some traces, however scarce, of the frame-story in the incipit of *Racconti*. The spectator discovers or recognizes some of the 30 pilgrims, among whom the Wife of Bath exposes herself as a narrator. She depicts herself performing a dance number before a young, disheveled, affected cleric, who is listening to her attentively, somewhat intrigued, almost fascinated. Alisoun is wearing a burdensome bright red dress that swirls around her as she ostentatiously steps backward, forward, and sideways. She occupies the whole space of the frame and faces the camera in a frontal shot. Her radiant corporeal presence serves as a reminder that a voice emerges from a body, some postures of which the church strongly disapproved of. Jugglers, male and female alike, are just as disreputable as prostitutes because they trade on their physical abilities. The Wife exudes and exalts her femininity through lascivious gestures and winks. "Gestures along with the voice help to fix or at least fashion the meaning" (Zumthor, 273). The gesture is highlighted by the bright colors of the performer's habit. The flashing red worn by Alisoun of Bath stands out noticeably against the dark gray hues of the English marketplace. Alisoun catches our eye and the camera focuses on her longer than on any other pilgrim. Her appearance on the screen is even preceded by the sound of her voice, which little by little fills in the whole film shot. The incessant gesturing of the insatiable speaker testifies to her need to be in the limelight, where her speech is enhanced by an underlying network of looks, smiles, and silent pauses. The non-verbal manifestations of a character addressing us directly are highly significant in that they take us back to our prior remark on silence being a surplus of words emptied of their meaning. Saturated with meaning until the message explodes into naught, Januarie's never-ending monologue full of contradictions eventually invalidates his pseudo-*disputatio* in favor of marriage.[6]

Speech and Silence in I Racconti di Canterbury *and* The Decameron

From Words to Crude, Expressive Motion Pictures: *The Miller's Tale*

Throughout the 23 tales prior to the Priest's sermon, words are used in quite different ways. The films of *Il Decameron* and *The Canterbury Tales*, however, tend to truncate the dialogues, cut down the stream of words uttered, or replace it completely to with eloquent silences. Pasolini gives a visual translation of speeches, which only subsist as gestures, expressions, or postures sufficient to sketch a character within a minimal narrative unit strangely evocative of silent movies. The protagonists of the filmed tales are mainly defined by their actions, like mere puppets that disappear from the stage as abruptly as they pop up. They follow and serve a specific actantial pattern (consisting of a quick succession of actions) in which the discourse neither outshines nor suspends the diegesis—except in the adaptations of *The Merchant's Tale* and *The Pardoner's Tale*. Closely linked to the low or intermediary style, the stories hold the filmmaker's attention precisely because of their brief introductions and conclusions as well as the great number of action verbs. These help to increase the fluidity and vividness of the actors' play typical of comedy. *The Miller's Tale, The Reeve's Tale, The Cook's Tale, The Friar's Tale, The Pardoner's Tale*, and *The Summoner's Tale*, save a few digressions of the narrator or the characters, differ from the other *Canterbury Tales* on account of the simplicity and effective vigor of the conversational form and spoken language. The spontaneous short dialogues relate to the prosaic register in which that type of light-hearted, unpretentious, sometimes saucy stories are told. A search for the raw expressiveness of the motion picture attempts to offer an equivalent of the language employed by Chaucer. Drawn from common, hackneyed imageries (animal, agrarian or commercial in most cases), the metaphors and similes in the text are highly suggestive and often bear sexual connotations.

The portrait of the sensuous Alisoun in *The Miller's Tale* associates her with a prancing kid, which can be read as echoes of sexual capers: "Therto she koude skippe and make game, / As any kyde or calf folwynge his dame" (*The Miller's Tale*, 3259–60). Her florid, overelaborate dress brings out the harmonious curves of her anatomy: "Fair…, / As any wezele hir body gent and small" (3233–35). She wears a little apron and a blouse trimmed with black embroidery that sets off the whiteness of her complexion. In the movie her dress is not as overwrought. Still, Alisoun looks just as appealing with her excessively low-necked gown. Besides, she has the same "likerous" eye and announces Alisoun of Bath, who nostalgically evokes her happy youth when, tipsy and gay as a popinjay, she had nothing but Venus in mind: "A likerous mouth moste han a likerous tayl" (*The Wife of Bath's Prologue*, 466). The young wife's beautifully arched eyebrows make her look like a graceful doe. The animal's agile, elegant movements seem to be reproduced in the way she nimbly hops about to escape from Nicholas's repeated amorous assaults. The cunning clerk soon gets the better of the wench's weak resistance: "As clerkes ben ful subtile and ful queynte; / And prively he caughte hire by the queynte" (*The Miller's Tale*, 3275–76). Note the double entendre on "queynte," which means "shrewd" as an adjective and "female genitals" as a noun. The burlesque cat-and-mouse chase — a metaphor applied to Absolon's concupiscence[7] — resembles a comic dance number quickly concluded by the "melody" that the hot admirer plays for her: "He kiste hire sweete and taketh his sawtrie, / And pleyeth faste, and maketh melodie" (3305–06). The musical image in the text is unambiguously rendered on the screen. The student indeed falls upon the girl and eagerly hitches up her skirt. "Let go of me, Nicholas, or I'll scream!," she replies but hardly resists.

The Text as a (Female) Body: *The Miller's Tale* and *The Wife of Bath's Prologue*

The female character in *The Miller's Tale* has an undeniable erotic aura. This is suggested in the way she is portrayed or "read" by the narrator (and the author). It is as though Alisoun were the embodiment of a *text*, the *textus* of the readable body dressed in *textile*: "…the female body becomes consubstantial with the body of writing."[8] The physical description of the carpenter's attractive wife that comprises more than 37 lines (*The Miller's Tale*, 3233–70) turns her into an alluring, cocky creature, whose anatomy is described in fragmented parts, each of which is fetishized. Seth Lerer indeed speaks of "a fetishizing of the body parts into objects of erotic attraction."[9] This is a rhetorical phenomenon typical of medieval and Renaissance literatures:

What is ostensibly symbolized here is a phenomenology of desire that entails a dismemberment of the female body, one that conjures up detached body parts or fetishized objects, whose wholeness is entirely phantasmatic.[10]

Nicholas the student owns a few books, "(h)is Almageste, and bookes grete and smale" (3208). In *Racconti* we see him through his landlord's eyes, when he is shown engrossed in the study of a book he feigns to have been reading for days on end, shut in his room. His ability to decipher texts and interpret heavenly signs predisposes him to examine carefully Alisoun's body, which he dreams of reading — he is supposed to know how to read the stars (3514). He sings religiously with the help of his prayer book as if communing with God. By the way, no close-up reveals whether this is a prayer book or a treatise of astronomy. However, the sole presence of the book, the symbol of the authority of what is written, suffices to beguile the naïve churl. The strong erotic connotation of the book as a fetish also manifests itself in the anecdote of the stormy beginnings of the Wife's conjugal life with her fifth husband. The episode obliquely points out the sensuality of the contact with the book. On the wedding night, Jankyn is expected to consummate his spouse's body/textus. Instead he is lying on the bed in his nightshirt. Alisoun of Bath comes into the bedroom in her nightdress too, carrying with a dignified air her sweet husband's slop pail. As she passes by, one can notice her red clothes scattered about the floor as a sign of her keenness to put her beloved's amorous talents to the test. The stiff man with a standoffish expression ironically brings to mind May's impassible, resigned face on her own wedding night, when the libidinous Januarie walks towards the bed where she has just been brought. The old man's lewd eye looks the same as Alisoun's — except that in the Wife of Bath sequence the roles are reversed. It is the man who proves to be indifferent and passive. The Wife's discourse equates the sexual relationship in a married couple with a contract. As she sits down by Jankyn, she stipulates that she hopes she will never have to regret having imparted all her property to her new spouse, bound by the covenant that obliges him to pay her his marital debts whenever she asks for it. As pointed out earlier, sex is ascribed a merely mercantile value in *The Wife of Bath's Prologue*.[11]

The Language of Action: An Instrument of Characterization in *The Reeve's Tale*

The genuine colloquial English spoken by the two students from Strother (in the north of England) in *The Reeve's Tale* is cleverly transposed in concise dialogues that nonetheless betray each protagonist's interests. They act more than they talk, in fact. The language found in Chaucer's tale is precisely adjusted to the coarseness of the subject. Chaucer, who reports what is said and done during the journey to Canterbury, warns his audience: "Blameth nat me if ye chese amys. / The Millere is a cherl; ye knowe wel this. / So was the Reve eek and othere mor, / And harlotrie they tolden bothe two" (*The Miller's Prologue*, 3181–84). The large amount of oaths and curses,[12] sayings,[13] and unflattering comparisons borrowed from animal and agrarian imagery[14] are an index of a predilection for the clearly common language of the ordinary people. Furthermore, Chaucer's transcription of the students' northern dialect sounds authentic. What Aleyn confesses to his companion John, as Symkyn, his wife and daughter are snoring in unison, summarizes the passage (4168–210), in which the young victims of the fraudulent miller's trick speak of getting even with him. They draw from the vocabulary of material compensation closely linked to that of commercial and financial transactions (also underlying *The Merchant's Tale*, *The Wife of Bath's Prologue*, and *The Shipman's Tale*). In lines 4178–86, Chaucer puts some crude speech in the frustrated Aleyn's mouth. He is totally devoid of the courtly noble ideals that urge on Emilye's suitors Palamon and Arcite in *The Knight's Tale*. The young man's cue in the movie is curtailed in comparison with both the text and the filmscript. It is reduced to: "Who wants to sleep tonight? I'll be damned if I don't hump that wench. I'm entitled to some compensation for the grain that's been stolen from us."[15] The verbs "swynken"[16] and "swyven"[17] (4178, 4266, 4317) — an echo to the conclusion of *The Miller's Tale* (3850) — occur several times and add to the crudity of the reparation that the youths find in the arms of the miller's daughter and wife. Purely sexual, the indemnity they treat themselves to under cover of the dark motivates the action in the second part of their visit to the mill. The venal interest that tinges the narrative with sexual innuendos, contaminated by the lexical field of payment, is conveyed in Aleyn's remark on his erection. He even takes his fellow's hand under the blanket so that he may feel his turgescent penis. In his turn John invites him to do the same, as he, too, feels an irrepressible desire rise inside him. The situation of the two youths sharing the same bed may appear dubious. It is indeed reminiscent of *The Miller's Tale* film version, when Absolon is lying sensually on his bed while his companion is playing music. An extradiegetic sequence inserted by Pasolini between *The Friar's Tale* and *The Cook's Tale* shows a youth lying naked, stroking a cat by Pasolini/Chaucer's side. Once again, the physical reality of the swollen male member both suggests a homosexual relationship and epitomizes the network of sexual metaphors upon which rests the diegesis.

Aiming at a Genuine Spoken Language in *Racconti*

In an interview in *Jeune Cinéma*, talking about *I Racconti di Canterbury*, Pasolini declares:

> I tried to do what I did with the *Decameron*. I set the whole of the *Decameron* in and around Naples and I made all the characters speak in the Neapolitan dialect of today. I could not use Chaucer's English, so I have used the most simple vernacular possible, with some dialect elements. I've used Chaucer's words but translated them into modern idiom. For instance, in *The Pardoner's Tale*, which is the one about the three boys on the margins of society, living on their wits, etc., I found three boys like that on the road. Completely by chance all three happened to be Scottish, so they will be talking with Scottish accents. I shall be shooting *The Cook's Tale*, the story of Perkyn, in the London docks, so that one will be in Cockney. I'm making it into a homage to Chaplin. And then when I was down near Bath and Wells, I really liked the way people spoke down there, so some bits will be in a Somerset accent. I am using live language, with a lot of different dialects put together.[18]

Pasolini's preoccupation concerns the orality of a performed language. Its multiple manifestations throughout *The Canterbury Tales* can be found in the display of a wide range of ways of speaking, dialects, or common, even coarse parlances. Chaucer's language sounds genuine thanks to this "palatable colloquialism that contributes to the impression of a conversation or confidence."[19] For a deeper insight into the "textual existence" of the tales, the reader must be aware of their "discursive existence" (Zumthor, 237) and submit it to his judgment as a subject of analysis. Many a passage testifies to a reference to some types of narrative discourse inherited from a long oral tradition. The rogue's pseudo-homily in the opening of *The Pardoner's Tale* in the movie is structurally and linguistically built on the rhetorical model of the sermon, drawing numerous examples from the Ancients and the Bible, as Chaucer's Pardoner does: "Thanne telle I hem ensamples many oon / Of olde stories longe tyme agoon. / For lewed peple loven tales olde; / Swiche thynges kan they wel reporte and holde" (*The Parson's Prologue*, 435–38). Shortly after the tale comes a long-drawn-out, sententious parenthesis. The sham preacher castigates the sins he observes among the customers of the tavern. A stream of vocatives and laments lard his exhortations to moderation, which spread over nearly 200 lines (483–660):

> O glotonye, ful of cursednesse! / O cause first of oure confusioun! / O original of oure dampnacioun (498–500) / ... / Allas a foul thyng is it, by my feith, / To seye this word, and fouler is the dede (524–25). / ... / O wombe! O bely! O stynkyng cod (534) / ... / Looketh the Bible, and there ye may it leere [*The Pardoner's Tale*, 578].

The language is that of a sermon, which borrows from invective, shocking similes and strings of common exclamations and phrases. Another significant indication of the oral dimension of *The Canterbury Tales* is provided by the countless proverbs. The "formulism" of aphorisms, as Zumthor puts it, makes more palpable to the audience the subject of what is being said through topoi. Characterized by "a high number of signifiers for a small amount of signified" (Zumthor, 217), a saying "brings to light the roots that any formulistic speech plunges into the traditions of an oral world."[20] Zumthor speaks of "a strongly functionalized and formally stylized redundance" (221), which often peppers the dialogues and moralities in the tales. Sometimes proverbs even threaten to undermine the discourse and leave aside the context in which it is delivered. The narratee is thus kept at a distance from the message of the text. *The Merchant's Tale*— in its hints at Teofrastus (1305–06), misogynous literature (1418–22), as well as Justinus's sanctimonious words (1541–43, 1553, and 1567–68)—*The Manciple's Tale* (318–62), *The Summoner's Tale* (1944, 1967, 1989, 2086–87, 2206)— and also *The Wife of Bath's Prologue* (389, 413–15, 655–56, 775–79) all contain a great deal of occurrences of commonplaces, maxims and generalities, which can be reiterated to infinity, and aim to be universally understood by means of metaphors referring to concrete things.

Aphorisms in *The Cook's Prologue,* *The Cook's Tale* and Bruegel

The Cook's Tale is of particular interest on account of its astounding concentration of sayings. Their abundance proportionally to the brevity of the unfinished narrative gives the feeling that the discursive nature of the text breaks with the diegetic context of the anecdote. As early as *The Cook's Prologue*, in his comment upon the lesson drawn from the Miller's bawdy story, the Cook cites a maxim (attributed to Solomon) on the danger of putting up strangers (*The Cook's Prologue*, 4329–34). His reply to the master of the tale-telling game, who tauntingly accuses him of being a fraud, contrasts with the Reeve's mean, embittered requital to the Miller. Hogge of Ware (*The Cook's Prologue*, 4336) sounds like a match for the Host, whose authority fills him with excessive self-importance. The two colorful characters engage in verbal sparring in a good-humored, high-spirited tone that relieves the tension caused by the Reeve's rancor: "Now telle on, gentil Roger by thy name. / But yet I pray thee, be nat wroth for game; / A man may seye ful sooth in game and pley" (*The Cook's Prologue*, 4353–55).[21] Roger astutely falls in with the Host's game and ripostes with a Flemish proverb to pay him back in his own coin. The situation reverses to his advantage; he starts teasing Harry by mockingly begging him not to bear a grudge against him for telling a story about an innkeeper. "But 'sooth pley, quaad pley,' as the Flemyng seith. / And therfore, Herry Bailly, by thy feith, / Be thou nat wrooth, er we departen heer, / Though that my tale be of an Hostileer" (4357–60). The Flemish origin of the truism voiced by the Cook brings to mind Bruegel the Elder's *Flemish Proverbs*[22] previously mentioned.

Because it is brimming with tiny details that saturate the restricted picture frame, this painting implies that there is a risk that the discourse may be absorbed and contaminated by the linguistic "primal anthropological" manifestation of formulism (Zumthor, 221). From *The Cook's Tale* (4391) onward, the teller adopts a ponderous didactic tone and launches into a series of truisms with a view to warning against the danger for a master to have an unscrupulous apprentice: "For sikerly a prentys revelour / That haunteth dys, riot, or paramour, / His maister shal it in his shoppe abyde, / Al have he no part of the mynstralcye" [*The Cook's Tale*, 4391–94). Then ensues a moralizing enumeration of substantives describing blameworthy behaviors: "For thefte and riot, they been convertible, / ... / Revel and trouthe, as in a lowe degree, / They been ful wrothe al day, as men may see" (4395–98). One day as the master works out his benefits, he thinks of a truism in the form of a vegetal metaphor: "Wel bet is roten appul out of hoord / Than that it rotie al the remenaunt. / So fareth it by a riotous servaunt" (*The Cook's Tale*, 4406–08). He gives Perkyn the sack only after ruminating over this conclusion. The adverb "therefore" which opens line 4411 conveys the idea of causality, signifying that it is the authority of common sense that incites him to get rid of the rot that has already set in the fruit. One may find it surprising that a proverb instead of the ne'er-do-well's pranks should entail the master's decision; this actually strikes us as most improbable, actantially speaking. Yet the intention behind the discourse, which is to warn and lecture first and foremost, is obvious even before the plot gets under way (only in line 4413!).

> We share with all the users and hearers of proverbs in *The Canterbury Tales*—from the Parson to Chauntecleer—the desire for lore, sentence, and doctrine, and share with them the grounds for judging and disputing *auctoritees* [Howard, 188].

The Paradox of the Silent Motion Picture

All of a sudden, *The Cook's Tale* puts an end to the first fragment or series of Chaucer's tales. The plot is hardly triggered when it is abruptly left incomplete as early as the 57th line without a single explanation. Still, if we consider it in the light of *The Knight's Tale, The Miller's Tale*, and *The Reeve's Tale*, we become aware of some thematic and stylistic continuity with the three preceding narratives. The situation (a young lady coveted by two rivals) is exploited for the fourth time but according to "a degenerative movement" (Howard, 245). The continuous recycling of the Knight's courtly plot and values by the churls (the Miller, the Reeve, and the Cook) suggests a declination and degradation of the same pattern to infinity, which would account for the incompleteness of *The Cook's Tale*.

As we move from ideals toward realities, Chaucer's voice disappears from the tales.... He has left us on our own in a world from which civility has disappeared. After two concatenated pairs plus a fragment, the theme is abandoned; and the effect would likely have been the same if *The Cook's Tale* were complete [Howard, 246–47].

Pasolini changes the order of the three parodic deviances of *The Knight's Tale*. They do not follow one another. The tales contain no hint of the knightly plot inspired by courtly romance and classic epic. However, the diegesis vanishes as in the text, though differently. The ineffective redundant display of didactic formulas and set phrases put in the mouth of Perkyn's master is replaced with a static shot of the smug merchant, standing stock-still in a disapproving attitude. His offended look is focused upon for a moment — while a derisive tune can be heard in the background — but fails to convince us of the moral superiority of his judgment. Indeed, we have just seen him follow an alluring prostitute after leaving his apprentice to keep an eye on his stall. Once back, he literally gives Perkyn the boot, kicking him while holding him by the collar. The vain, sturdy fellow struts about like a peacock and bombastically utters an adage. The comical, affected tone in which he delivers his empty, pompous message makes it impossible to take seriously. The long introductory evocation of the Revelour's vices in Chaucer is visually turned into a purely slapstick comedy sequence, which takes the spectator back to the early years of film. The silent motion picture constitutes the paradox of the "talking screen." The sketch of the undisciplined happy-go-lucky gay dog, so similar to the impish, cheeky Mediterranean good-looker[23] causes a dislocation of the narrative. In the movie it amounts to a concatenation of vignettes and very short juxtaposed scenes, as in a burlesque silent film, where stress is laid on the actors' grotesque postures and funny physiognomies.

The "Imageity" of the Film Shot, the "Pictoriality" of the Painting

Film Rendering of the Medieval: The "Archaicizing" Effect

In "Una chiave di lettura per il *Decameron*," Vittore Branca underlines the fact that Boccaccio's work is rooted in contemporaneity and speaks of the literary making of "una geografica linguistica dell'Italia trecentesca."[24] He provides many examples of the expressiveness of a language with colourful sonorities, idioms, and regionalisms typical of the social background portrayed. The linguistic authenticity is made plain even at the phonetic, lexical, and grammatical levels, where the dialectal and cultural particularisms (Neapolitan in VII, 2 and Sienese in VII, 10, for instance) become the most obvious. Boccaccio's "programmatic plurilingualism" (Branca, xxiv) encompasses and spreads beyond

> ... the dialectal or regional varieties, ... the influences of the different cultures, ancient or modern alike. He had an acute awareness of a social diversity linguistically speaking quite as deep and vast at the geographical, chronological and cultural levels.[25]

The "commedia umana" (viii) of *Il Decameron* is written in the nascent language of the bourgeois epic, which benefits from the contributions of other idioms. Furthermore, the "literary ironicization" (Branca, xxxix) (the imitation of styles and registers) not only revitalizes the narration but also helps to render a medieval tonality. *Il Decameron* brings evidence of the transition between an aristocratic literature and a language with its own themes and new narrative modes. "The heroes become more human for more humble readers, and therefore can speak a more direct, immediate language, richer in resonance for the common run of people" (Branca, xv). As for Chaucer's text, even though Pasolini has indirect access to it through its Italian translation, Pasolini manages to grasp its linguistic heterogeneity, its stylistic inventiveness, as well as its surprising theatricality. Yet there remains an extra dimension to which the film author seems most receptive: the archaism of Middle English, the apparent roughness, the puzzling oddness of the forms and phrases of a remote time. *I Racconti di Canterbury* makes frequent use of frontal shots that produce an "archaicizing" effect.[26] The characters appear on the screen in situ, transfixed within the picture frame, especially in the inaugural sequence. The pilgrims' faces seen in the marketplace in some way retain the figurativity of the medieval tradition of the literary portrait.

> The portraits of Chaucer's pilgrims nevertheless owe a great deal to medieval traditions of literary portraiture.... The hypocritical friar, the hunting monk, the thieving miller and others are familiar types in medieval *estates satire*....[27]

Like Boccaccio, who personally illustrated his *Decameron* in 150 drawings and watercolor sketches over some 20 years,[28] Pasolini successfully translates in a few shots each protagonist's specificities "with a satiric emphasis on their vices peculiar to their stations in life."[29] Regarding the first sketches by the author of *The Centovelle*, one may notice the archaic aspect of the pictures and especially the dresses and architecture of his time. The words are literally visualized. Only the key moments in the plot are retained because they "best serve the ultimate meaning of the narrative."[30] The illustrator employs "a continuous narrative method suited for short cycles of three or four episodes ... heralding the new trend that will develop in the fresco cycles and the altar retables of the late Gothic period."[31] "The late Giotto style of urban and rustic landscapes"[32] in Boccaccio's drawings betrays a deep sensibility to the iconography of the time.

Pasolini's Figurative Pictures: *The General Prologue*

The same allusive force permeates the visualization of Chaucer's words in *I Racconti di Canterbury*. The film picture is peculiarly expressive thanks to a selection of eloquent details of comic realism. The caricatural Miller in *The General Prologue* has a red beard "as any sowe or fox was reed, / And therto brood, as though it were a spade" (*The General Prologue*, 552–53). In the movie, where he only puts in a brief appearance, he is depicted as a matchless beefy wrangler. Once the fight is over, a close-up shows him facing the camera triumphantly brandishing his trophy (a goat!): "The Millere was a stout carl for the nones; / Ful byg he was of brawn, and eek of bones" (*The General Prologue*, 545–46). The almost initial position of the adjective "byg" in the line emphasizes the fellow's powerful build. The somewhat colloquial "stout carl" confirms that the portrait is closely related to the estates satire. The structure of the following lines brings to the fore the Miller's quarrelsome temperament. His churlish manliness is heightened by the hard-sounding "cam"/"ram" rhyming couplet: "That proved wel, for over al ther he cam, / At wrastlynge he wolde have alwey the ram" (*The General Prologue*, 547–48). Pasolini need not picture him bashing into a door with his rocklike head. Suffice it to consider the wild animal way in which he swoops down on his opponent. It must be pointed out that he is even imparted a nightmarish resonance in the text when assimilated with Hell: "His mouth as greet was as a greet forneys" (559). The forceful comparison can be explained by the medieval liking for morbid and infernal frightening images:

> ... around 1400 indeed sculpture and painting acquired the means of realistic expression necessary for the treatment of this topic (the horror of rotting bodies and death).... The graves are decorated with hideous pictures of naked, decaying corpses with stiff wrists and feet and a wide open mouth.[33]

This is strongly reminiscent of the furnace painted by Bruegel in *Dulle Griet*.[34] The archaic pictorial motif is in keeping with that of Chaucer's evocation. The portrait of the Reeve, whose profile the camera eye discloses in a static shot, transposes in as much detail the leanness of the aging "sclendre," "colerik" man (*The General Prologue*, 587). Lines 591–92 strike the reader by their redundant adverb "ful" and synonyms like "longe" and "lene." In addition, the harsh, unpleasant "staf"/"calf" alliteration (*The General Prologue*, 591–92) adds to the dryness of his soul. A disorderly succession of worldly, even crude metaphors—the horse deprived of its fodder, the spoiled fruit, the cold ashes, the lifeless member, and the thin streak of life wasting away (*Reeve's Prologue*, 3867–97)—are aimed at stressing his effete stiffness. In the movie, Oswald is played by an actor who is slightly younger yet with a bony, unlikable face and a haughty expression. The appearance-consciousness that somewhat feminizes him may well suggest sexual impotency. He combs his scarce hair very slowly as if his movements were decomposed (as in a sequence of photographs) and finally addresses us with a slight, contemptuous grin.

Eloquent Frontal Shots in *The Merchant's Tale* and *The Friar's Tale*

As soon as it starts, *Racconti* reveals an "aestheticizing" or rather expressionistic intention meant to offer a visual reading of *The Canterbury Tales* in a quasi-dialogue between words and pictures. It is as though they could in turn "capture what the other is not always able to represent, thanks to their respective integration."[35] Therefore the pictorial aspect of the image is shown up, especially in frontal shots. In *The Merchant's Tale*, after Januarie's speech on the blissful state of marriage, which is peppered with quite a few coarse innuendos, comes a close-up that literally lays bare pretty May's lovely backside. It seems to emerge from the lewd old man's fantasy fired by the mere thought of a young wife. The dream that repeatedly haunts him—"Ther passeth thrugh his herte nyght by nyght" (*The Merchant's Tale*, 1581)—gives way to a brief funny shot in the movie, which implicitly puts down to chance the reason for Januarie's elaborately justified choice and consequently ridicules it. The camera adopts the protagonist's point of view. The mirror he metaphorically takes with him about the marketplace in search of a girl[36] becomes the prism of his own consciousness—in the spirit of Pasolini's free, indirect style applied in his earlier movies. Here the shot goes through a pictorial treatment, for the camera slowly sweeps across a crowded street, where the physiognomies are strangely evocative of Bruegel's peasants. Nevertheless it is not May's pretty face that kindles Januarie's heart—"For if that oon have beaute in her face" (1589). The hypocrisy in the metonymy is ironically rendered by the filmmaker, who discloses the other side of the "ideal" spouse.

The beginning of *The Friar's Tale*, disproportionately extended in *I Racconti di Canterbury*, meticulously reproduces a pictorial composition in a long static shot portraying church dignitaries, facing the camera, attending the public burning of the sodomite. In the foreground stands the stilted archdeacon, whose elegant, dazzling purple habit sets off the paleness of his severe features. His wide-brimmed hat signifies how influential he is. He plays a major part in the administration of ecclesiastical authority: "An erchedeken, a man of heigh degree, / That boldely dide execucioun / In punysshynge of fornicacioun" (*The Friar's Tale*, 1302–04). He faces the spectator, so dignified, as solemn and motionless as the statue of a saint. The shot, only a few seconds long, seems suspended in time. It summarizes the stunningly lengthy accumulation (over some 20 lines) of pompous polysyllabic terms used to conjure up the importance of the archdeacon's power. Behind him we catch a glimpse of his henchman, the most iniquitous summoner who ever was: "A slyer boye nas noon in Engelond" (1322). He, too, stares at the camera, impassive. His position in the background, like a mere shadow among the influential representatives of the spiritual authority, bespeaks his duplicity, implied by a subtle lexical network in the tale centered on the theme of dissimulation (1321 and 1345): "As any hauk to lure," (1340), "They tolde him al the secree that they knewe," (1341) "prively," (1343) "His maister knew nat alwey what he wan" (1345). Later in *The Friar's Tale* a shot discloses the devil's mysterious handsome features, when he asks the summoner to pledge loyalty to him. "Give me your hand" materializes the symbolical oath he takes (in accordance with the knightly romance code): "Everych in ootheres hand his trouthe leith, / For to be sworne bretheren til they deye" (*The Friar's Tale*, 1404–05). His marmoreal face with a somber look stands out against a dark landscape, whereas his fellow traveler is always outlined against a lighter background. The naivety of the summoner's abrupt questions on the mysteries of the netherworld[37] is contrasted with the metaphorical answers given by Satan's agent: "Brother, quod he, fer in the north contree, / Whereas I hope som tyme I shal thee see" (1413–14). Only the gist of the dialogue (*The Friar's Tale*, 1384–1580) remains in the film: "And therfore by extorciouns I lyve. / For sothe, I take al that men wol me yive" (1429–30).[38] Then slowly he looks up and eventually satisfies the rogue's curiosity. The shadow over the enigmatic man is at last removed: "Io sono un diavolo, e la mia dimora è l'inferno" (372)—"I am a feend, my dwellyng is in helle" (1448). The truth is told without prevarication. The long evocation of the clichés concerning Hell[39] (1461–1512) vanishes. A preternatural aura emanates from the secretive, uncanny character. Citti's melancholy expression and almost sepulchral voice virtually elevate him to sacredness. The chiaroscuro shot is strangely bereft of details. In addition, from the background raises the same choir of crystal-clear voices as the one heard at the end of the stake sequence earlier in *The Friar's Tale*. Demons are of a divine kind indeed, as noted in the text.[40]

Conjuring Up the Middle Ages: Songs and Paintings

Pasolini's movie responds to a search for a certain Middle Ages. The soundtrack offers a wide range of songs and instrumental pieces from English, Irish, and Scottish folklore, which grants them an archaic popular ring in the spirit of the eight adapted tales. In an interview the filmmaker recalled:

> I always chose folk music in England when I was there, shooting. I bought a lot of records and listened to a lot of music, English and Scottish folk songs.... Morricone simply adapted that music for some musical instruments. All he did consisted in a technical transcription for particular instruments. In some specific cases only did he compose from folk themes. I did exactly the same while making *The Decameron*, in which all the musical pieces were borrowed from Neapolitan folklore.[41]

Absolon and his companion light-heartedly sing under Alisoun's window:

> We know by the moon that we are not too soon, / And we know by the sky that we are not too high. / We know by the stars that we are not too far, / and we know by the ground that we are within sound.[42]

The allusion to the moonlight echoes the text: "The moone, whan it was nyght, ful brighte shoon, / And Absolon his gyterne hath ytake; / For paramours he thoghte for to wake" (*The Miller's Tale*, 3352–54). Still the couplet is rid of the courtly style imitated by the pretentious suitor: "He syngeth in his voys gentil and smal, / Now, deere lady, if thy wille be, / I praye yow that ye wole rewe on me" (3360–62). The two youths holding each other by the shoulder sing in a natural merry fashion, quite unlike Chaucer's stilted Absolon, whose piping voice pesters the belle and her husband. The lumbering Januarie in *The Merchant's Tale* makes a fool of himself in dancing about the bedroom, carried away by his (pathetic!) sexual performance. The old self-satisfied oaf starts humming a song. The actor is undoubtedly dubbed by an aged, quavering voice that sings laboriously. This increases the clumsiness of his ludicrous hopping about. "As I went up to my garret, / No mirror could I find...."[43] The structure of the sentence, which reverses the verb and complement order, is to some extent comparable to Chaucer's verse in Middle English. Another indication of the medieval spirit suffusing *The Canterbury Tales* regards the allusions to the late medieval and Renaissance painting. Pasolini "remakes famous paintings, explores, deconstructs and constructs them again, pushes them to their limits, experiments some variations, combines and simplifies them. To put it in a nutshell he puts them to work and to question."[44] This is "cinématisation" (as opposed to "cinétisation") that is painting turned into cinema and not just some vague movement in the making.[45] The three examples we can draw from the movie illustrate the visual dimension of the motion picture, which signals its own iconicity (since it is inspired from early Renaissance painting). Words and ideas take on a visual evidence. The final shot in *The Pardoner's Tale* focuses on the three lifeless rascals in the grass around the treasure in the position of the three sleeping peasants in *The Land of Cockaigne*[46] pastiched in Ciappelletto's vision (*The Decameron*, I, 1). It also echoes the shot of Masetto (*The Decameron*, III, 1) and the former nunnery gardener fast asleep at the foot of a tree. The episode of the three hoodlums in *I Racconti di Canterbury* closes on the picture of the third youth, stiffened by a violent death with cold, fixed eyes. The languid male bodies are totally devoid of sensuality. The ending of the sequence looks as harsh and brutally short as in Chaucer: "Right so they han hym slayn, and that anon. / ... For which anon they storven bothe two" (*The Pardoner's Tale*, 881–88). The film picture abruptly puts an end to the stream of words in a frozen silence. The vision of Hell — "How that a frere ravysshed was to helle / In spirit ones by a visioun" (*The Summoner's Prologue*, 1676–77) — aptly renders the apocalyptic dantesque evocation in *The Summoner's Prologue* by means of one of the major post-medieval representations of the horrors and turpitudes of the Inferno: the part devoted to Hell in *The Seven Deadly Sins* by Bosch.[47] The brisk animated dialogue (*The Summoner's Prologue*, 1683–99) between the angel and Satan in a familiar tone becomes a well-known tableau that comes to life. Crude terms such as "tayl" (1687, 1689, and 1699), "ers" (1690, 1694, 1698, 1705), "Hold up thy tayl, thou Sathanas!" (1689) resound in a seemingly endless sonorous fart accompanied by inhuman shrieks.

Picturing the Poet Writing

The third example in *I Racconti di Canterbury* concerns the self-representation of the author of the film (and of its literary source) in two short extradiegetic sequences. One occurs between *The Cook's Tale* and *The Miller's Tale*, the other between *The Reeve's Tale* and *The Pardoner's Tale*. The former shows Pasolini/Chaucer in his wooden seat reading Boccaccio's *Centovelle*, then resuming his work after dozing off at his desk in the latter. "The metalinguistic consciousness is stronger in these two films than in the previous ones," declares the director.[48] He translates the self-reflexiveness of Chaucer's writing on the screen in a hieratic scene highly evocative of the visual arts. The setting, patterns on the carpet (large black and white triangles in Vasareli's style), the silence and isolation of the artist absorbed in his difficult task all bring to mind several figurations of the late Middle Ages/early Renaissance. For instance, in *Saint Luke Painting the Vir-*

gin, by Rogier Van der Weyden,[49] the artist is wearing a brown (instead of a white) bonnet. The floor is decorated with similar square or diamond-shaped patterns. In *Portrait of Erasmus Writing*, by Hans Holbein,[50] the philosopher is seen in profile tracing letters with a quill. The same action is represented in *Erasmus of Rotterdam*, by Quentin Massys.[51] Erasmus's less bulky, more bony face slightly resembles Pasolini's. He is writing with his right hand. Seven big books lying on a shelf at the level of his head highlight his erudition and the essential role played by books in his life.

By adding the writing dimension to the motion picture (itself influenced by painting), the filmmaker signals the literary awareness of *The Canterbury Tales*. In a medieval interior,[52] Chaucer asleep with his feet on the desk is unexpectedly admonished by his wife. He yawns, stretches himself and takes his quill again. Pasolini acts and at the same time offers a personal reading of Chaucer's text. The act of poetic composition is pictured four times in *Racconti*, thus reminding us that the movie is a fictional artifact that emerged from an imagination nurtured on the authoritative texts of the past. The silent, static shots of the author in profile or facing the camera either in quest of inspiration or putting into words the mental images that come to his mind could be construed as an amused and detached consideration of the notions of authorship and reception of a work. The Gothic era represents a turning point in the evolution of the visual arts toward a progressive acknowledgment of the artist's creative role as a mediator between the real world and the figurative level. Pasolini grants the written word an extra specificity. The author in *The Canterbury Tales* indeed takes shape on the surface or "canvas" of the screen, itself a mise en abyme of some Renaissance visual masterpieces. The tour de force in the visual arts in the 20th century consisted of introducing a third virtual dimension; perspective found itself questioned. Contemporary artists, especially cubists, began to wonder about the plane bidimensional space specific to painting. Despite the perspective that adds to the depth of the study, in which Pasolini/Chaucer is composing his work, the illusion is achieved thanks to the diamond-shaped patterned floor that gives the impression it is sloping. The picture then looks vertical and flat. Furthermore, the narrative seems momentarily "frozen," because of the stillness of the tableau.

Cinema and Painting: The Question of Representation

Extradiegetic in-between sequences, the tableaux vivants throughout the fragmented narrative progressions of *The Decameron* and *I Racconti di Canterbury*, indicate an authorial signature, confirmed by the author's physical presence in both movies. Featuring Giotto's best disciple and Chaucer,

Pasolini signs his name, "the trace of ... the artist's having been there when the creative act of enunciation was being performed, and the trace of his disappearance vanishing behind the work that now re-presents him."[53] The filmmaker leaves his signature as early as the credits, which represent a "hors-d'œuvre"—what precedes the work and belongs to the extradiegetic (de Mourgues, 144). What lies outside the picture frame actually invites one to reflect upon the screen that is so closely related to the painter's canvas. As François Jost points out, the "transposition of paintings" does not function as "the narrative germ of the story."[54] It is rather planned to attract our attention to the distinction between the motion picture "leaving its print on the screen" and the artistic representation that cannot be seen because it arises in the viewer's perception. There is more to cinema than a mere reproduction of reality, as suggested in the bewildering structure of *The Decameron* and *I Racconti di Canterbury* as well as in the intrusion of painting. Hence the general impression of watching some unusual, incongruous work by an artist who borrows from another semiotic system, wondering about the pictorial relevance of the page and the screen. The reference to one or several Old Masters—and painting per se in *The Decameron*— rests upon a critical perspective on the the cinematic device consubstantial with a meditation on the *Quattrocento* pictorial device especially. The viewpoint and its multiplication, the camera and its mobility, the editing and its extraordinarily rich power of signification revive the awareness that the image results from and induces a reflection. For Walter Benjamin, cinema fragments "the image of the organic wholeness."[55] Instead of a space synthesis of several moments as painting does, cinema operates a temporal synthesis so that "the rules of composition are disturbed by the editing through a succession of shots."[56] The pictoriality and imageity[57] constitute the common ground shared by painting and film.

> ... each art must seek with its own means the expression of its plastic essence, and it is only when the "purity" has been attained that an "imbrication will become possible which will reveal the unity of the different arts by bringing to the fore their common points."[58]

The purity of the picture is to be found in its intense expressiveness, to which Pasolini aspires. In these singular moments when the telling "freezes," the film shot, superimposed with the canvas, manifests itself as a pure "effet d'image clos" (Kessler, 86). Still it threatens to transform the work of art into "a sort of kitsch cabinet de curiosités" or reduce "the action of the film ... into an illustrative anecdote" (Kessler, 86). Giotto's *Last Judgment* at the end of *The Decameron* or the descent into the Bosch-inspired Hell in *I Racconti di Canterbury* ascribe the ornamental, static function of painting to the pictorial citation. The wigs worn by some of the extras—

the youth carrying a miniature model of the Scrovegni Chapel, the exaggeratedly bright colors that tend to divert the spectator's attention from the subject — or the gold-colored cardboard halos around the heads of the singing angels standing on either side of the Madonna create the impression of a gaudy imitation of the original, somewhat remote from the marial sublime. In other words, the film shot is devoid of the pathetic vocation defined by Eisenstein. The spectator's emotions are neutralized by his awareness of watching a pastiche, a form of imitation, itself linked with the problematic tradition of representation. Throughout these sets of pictorial motifs drawn from the Old Masters cited in the tableaux vivants, Pasolini is anxious to reassert in the manner of Eisenstein the escape of cinema "toward the unrepresentable that can never be attained and is perpetually signalled and postponed."[59] Film materializes a cinematic concretization of the essential question of figuration. It makes possible "a way of looking cinematically at the figurative tradition by discovering a new exemplarity" (Montani, 68). Beyond the Boccaccian and Chaucerian material adapted with an unusual freedom of tone, the spectator realizes that the singular pictorial constructions fulfill a specific function: showing "representation coming out of itself ('ex-stasis') to seize a non representable sense" (Montani, 72). In other words, the unwonted motion pictures aim at attracting our attention to the fact that film "produces a more unknown, less structured reality of the cinematic event."[60] It is "the discontinuous, unforgettable weight of hardly translatable pictures that persists beyond the stories."[61]

This theory of the film shot and the author corresponds to Pasolini's film practice. His shots do not systematically play a narrative role. They just are. They rise above the "obscenity of the double affirmation of excess and total emptiness"[62] characteristic of the "flat" pictures in the rushes.

The Pursuit of "Another Middle Ages"
Making the Concept Visible

Is the visualization of Boccaccio and Chaucer's Middle Ages betrayed or, on the contrary, revitalized, distorted or regenerated? The remote era is described as the matrix of present society by French historian Jules Michelet in the 19th century. Jacques le Goff[63] sums up four successive perceptions of the medieval period, delineated in the 19th century by Michelet. He deems it necessary that "the medievalist should know how to remove the scaffolding of figures and find out a Middle Ages as such, namely approximative, huge, fearing God for counting too much...."[64] That past, both familiar and alien, also fascinates a film author who, like a historian, removes the scaffolding of scholarship (especially the medievalist's reading), once the work is completed. The artist's assistants precisely remove the scaffolding at the end of *The Decameron*. Contemplating his fresco, the maestro claims the right to the power of dream. Pasolini's choice of an immersion into "a time which, thanks to imagination, was able to erect upon its lacks and weaknesses such a great civilization of the dream.... What initiates the crusades is the call of an imaginary Jerusalem...."[65] The Middle Ages that interests the filmmaker is of another kind, so different from that traditionally conjured up in the movies. The first example that comes to mind is *The Knights of the Round Table* by Richard Thorpe (1953). It was the first cinemascope MGM production, starring Ava Gardner as Guenever and Robert Taylor as Launcelot. The photogenic stars wear impeccable costumes with dazzingly bright colors set off against an immutable, spotless blue sky. The settings look sumptuous but artificial, compared with the dark, sometimes shabby world of the ordinary people in *The Decameron* and *I Racconti di Canterbury* in particular. Lastly, such conventional movies on the Middle Ages stage stilted characters in hieratic poses. The performers act in a stiff, theatrical fashion, using affected diction. Many American movies with a medieval subject[66] mirror the function generally attributed by our 21st-century optical distortion to the abstract the period represents. As Giuseppe Sergi remarks, it is from the perspective of the present day that we look at that time, for we perceive first what is close to us before creating an image falsely identical to what is remote.[67] The result is a double vision of a phase simply preparatory to the Enlightenment, dark, remote, characterized by indigence, epidemics, and endless wars on the one hand. On the other hand, it is held as a world of heroes and fairies, tournaments, courtly life, and the marvelous. Sergi imputes to the last two centuries of the thousand-year era the negative image — inherited from Renaissance humanism — that we still have today. The medieval man notwithstanding strives to overreach himself (Sergi, 100), because he believes that the intermediary penal time of Purgatory (promulgated by theologians in the early 13th century) will allow him to wash himself of his venial sins. After his first death, he thinks, he stands a chance to live eternally in Heaven. The "in-between space of man's eschatological destiny,"[68] Purgatory probably best epitomizes the duality of the medieval mind torn between an earthly surge toward the profane and a spiritual elevation summarized in the pilgrimage metaphor: "...the medieval tendency to blur the line between the holy and the profane."[69]

The Eccentric and the Grotesque

In the Middle Ages, the history of mankind can be apprehended in terms of a symbolical itinerary towards salvation. Man's fallen nature determines the progression of his soul in three main stages: the Last Judgment, Purgatory and, lastly, redemption. Despite the advent of a sense of personal and subjective duration, the different times—which before being laicized, that is, appropriated by the peasant and then the bourgeois, belonged to God only—"eventually slip, soar up, and crash down toward the eschatological time of ... the Last Judgment leading to the end of time itself, to eternity."[70] What inspires Pasolini is the paradox of an era when the preeminent discourse of the Christian doctrine and the official culture in Latin does not prevent the lay voices from being heard. People's growing awareness of their ludicrous image and grotesque potential favors the flourishing of a parodical, even satirical vision, a culture of the laughter that bursts out in the margins of the church, namely in the street and on the marketplace, as Mikhail Bakhtin demonstrates.

> Michelet discovered an eccentric Middle Ages of the margins, of the periphery...."It is a feature of the Middle Ages that it always confronts the very high with the very low," he exclaimed...." God and Satan, the witch and the saint, the diagonal rib and leprosy."[71]

The film director of *I Racconti di Canterbury* may be blamed for ignoring the "noble storie(s)" (*The General Prologue*, 311) such as *The Knight's Tale*, an elaborate composition related to the highest poetic genre and drawn from Boccaccio's *Teseida* and Boethius's *De Consolatione Philosophiae*, among others. Pasolini also chooses to disregard the pious tale, halfway between romance and the saint's life as in *The Man of Law's Tale*, as in the very moral *Clerk's Tale*, replete with pathos. The marvelous, as in the complicated unfinished oriental tale told by the Squire, is cast aside too. So are the Breton lai with an affected courtly tone in *The Franklin's Tale*, the example in the Physician's "pitous tale," or the hagiographic *Second Nun's Tale*, and The Prioress's miracle of the Virgin (preceded by a liturgical exordium). Chaucer's mock performance in *Sir Thopas*, initially planned in the filmscript, is discarded in the final version. The filmmaker does not retain the moral collection of *sententiae* in *The Tale of Melibee* nor the Parson's prose treatise on penance either. Turning away from the serious grandiloquence of the noble genres, Pasolini is anxious to break with a literary norm, in comparison with which the other poetic forms are deemed inferior. The selection of stories in the uncommon motley material brings evidence of a preference for farce, what some call "bawdy Chaucer." Albeit it is a *tempus medium* symbolically situated halfway between the Incarnation and the Last Judgment (which will mark the end of mankind), the Middle Ages is characterized by a comic, festive dimension, due to a long oral tradition and pagan folk beliefs gradually assimilated by the church. Laughter implies celebration. Festivals, which serve as the foundation for communal life and originate from highly pagan practices, are instrumentalized by the clergy, which doubles with a commemoration the most significant times in Christian life — especially Christmas and Easter. The Christian appropriation of the comic spirit inherited from ancient sacrificial rituals equates the notion of the profane with that of the sacred, what Lillian Bisson refers to as "holiday" and "holy day."

The Canterbury Tales: A Festive, Licentious Form of Writing

The Canterbury Tales partake in the carnivalesque spirit in their stunning juxtaposition of genres. Pasolini's adaptation is focalised on the fabliau-derived narrative type. Close to the exemplum because of its brevity and its diegetic rooting in the contemporaneous world, the fabliau contains "an aspect of the promotion of the successive ... time, of a story, a segment of narrative, historical, linear and divisible time."[72] The narrative pattern of these anecdotes presented as veracious definitely influences the structure of Pasolini's movies, made up of consecutive segments. The link between the saucy tale and the exemplum, an instrument of Christian edification, is made obvious in the filmmaker's decision to screen *The Pardoner's Tale*, in which "reality" merges with "the eschatological adventure."[73] *The Summoner's Tale* responds to a similar theological intention, but declines the genre in its most subversive aspect: the extravagance of the Grand Guignol. However, *The Decameron* and *I Racconti di Canterbury* emphasize laughter, "a phenomenon that expresses itself in and through the body," and coarsely breaks the silence of monastic humility. The laughter that rings out in both movies has nothing in common with the beatitude of Saint Francis of Assisi. On the contrary it stems from an erotic, scatological deviance. Pasolini bears in mind the Aristotelian tradition, which acknowledges man's natural urge to laugh. To this the Middle Ages opposes another attitude, for it condemns the giving vent to hilarity on the grounds that Jesus Christ is supposed never to have laughed. Besides depriving man of his reason, laughter is thought to dishonor speech and hinder asceticism and salvation. Therefore, it must be held in the prison of the body. The Christian moral of behavior hinges upon three main notions: a vertical movement, introspection, and a moderation of gestures. What arouses mirth is exactly the opposite: all forms of excesses, in the body and its gesticulation, associated with the depravity of the devil. The undressed or ridiculed bodies in grotesque postures in *The Decameron* and *I Racconti di Canterbury* parody the spiritual ascension — like the carpenter in his kneading trough in *The Miller's Tale* episode — or conversely collapse — like Andreuccio into the cesspool — or hide inside a big receptacle in a burlesque echo to the descent into Hell literally conjured up in *The Summoner's Tale*. At the end of *Racconti* prevails the depiction of chaos, a general ear-splitting confusion so remote from the inner elevation advocated by the medieval Christian ideology. The hedonistic materialism of the fabliau reverses the poetic norm of the epic and the romance set up by the Knight's performance in Chaucer. The subversion of the genre in the following tale gives an idea of the parodic role played by Carnival in a system of thought resting upon the exegetic reflex, which attributes to concrete things and everyday events the function of signifiers of an invisible abstract reality. The stress on anality in *The Summoner's Tale* put into film betokens Pasolini's awareness of his riotous, undermining role as a "Lord of Misrule," which allows him to clear himself of any charges of indecency. Literary and film writing become entertainment and allows a euphoric license that rules out any form of punishment. "For in *The Canterbury Tales* (Chaucer) does not simply incorporate many elements of the carnival world *into* his fictive world but makes the carnivalesque the principle *of* the world he creates" (Bisson, 258). At the core of *The Decameron*, the narration is unexpectedly interrupted by a pictorial interlude, a pastiche among others of *The Battle of Carnival and Lent*. The 21st-century spectator cannot fully grasp the meaning of this medieval vision if he or she fails to take into account the contemporary reprobation of laughter. The veer to bawdiness and licentiousness in *I Racconti di Canterbury* confirms its author's bakhtinian sensibility to the Carnival-like dimension of a work shaped in such a way as to imitate the very structure of the medieval feast: "fitting the patterns of action in the frame and links to a model of oral group performance thoroughly familiar to his contemporaries ... Chaucer reshapes literature into festival...."[74]

Carnival: Celebrating the People

As a reaction against the repressive authority of Lent, which starts on Ash Wednesday — when the dead are commemorated and the living prepare for the Last Judgment during an ascetic period of fasting, penance, and prayer — man feels the need to liberate himself from the weight of orthodoxy. The norms and interdicts are transgressed by means of a valorization of the depraved body, emblematic of the derision of the spiritual. The stress put on the shameful parts of human anatomy such as the mouth, the nose, or the belly, the genitals and the anus, functions as the belittling of perfection and the definite. In connection with eating, urinating, defecation and copulation, such organs materialize the notion of transmutation from one state of being to another — the idea of "process" as opposed to the final "product." This distinction is applied by Lillian Bisson in her reading of *The*

Canterbury Tales. Their deliberate inconclusiveness can be justified by their author's keen interest in the creation of a work in the making rather than in the final result. The fluidity of the text evocative of a "rhizomatic labyrynth," the apparent absence of a clearly identifiable plan in the whole loose structure made up of surprising clusters of stories, and the thematic recurrences throughout the composition could well be imputed to Chaucer's preference for a writing in progress, just as his pilgrims are on their way to Canterbury. The novelty of *The Canterbury Tales*, as pointed out earlier, derives from the fact that their maker senses that the univocal perspective of his time is being questioned. Thus the central position supposed to be occupied by one of the religious and scolastic authorities is insiduously pervaded by the perverse potential of the Carnival forces. After the long festive interlude of all the preceding tales, *The Pardoner's Tale* might be read as the ultimate reaffirmation by Chaucer of the established hierarchies "in returning his pilgrims, and his pilgrimage, to the orthodoxies and apocalyptic framework..." (Bisson, 259).

One of the most significant contributions of the 14th century regards the appearance of what Le Goff calls the "Jacques" figure, namely the humble peasant (epitomized by Piers Plowman), who gradually emerges from the mass. Furthermore, Christianity promises and proclaims the elevation of ordinary people to the first ranks of mankind in Heaven. From this angle, one understands why Pasolini declares his *Decameron* highly popular. The people are the main protagonists in the movie indeed. Their free, happy sexuality grows sad and gloomy in *I Racconti di Canterbury*, where the characters live in a virtually bourgeois context. "Maybe in Boccaccio there is not the problem of sex, whereas it is there in Chaucer, who to my mind announces the 'petite bourgeoisie.'"[75] The film director makes an essential distinction between unhindered joyful sex as embodied by the Neapolitan population in *The Decameron*, and what he designates as "eroticism" about *I Racconti di Canterbury*—in an acception quite different from Georges Bataille's. This definition is to be construed as the transformation of sexuality in the late 14th-century English "petite bourgeoisie" (Pasolini, 85), whose spirit already pervades the sociological backdrop of *The Canterbury Tales.*

The Medieval Context: The Pretext for an Artistic Ideological Project

Despite their differences between *The Decameron* and *I Racconti di Canterbury*, the ordinary people in both films have a common liking for or proneness to transgression. The screen brims with individuals outside the norm: miscreants, prostitutes, adulterous wives, sinful clerics, demons, and

Sodomites who end up at the stake. Talking about the margin, Carolyn Dinshaw builds a clever argument on the poetic genre of the romance. She demonstrates its instrumentalization by a policy that promotes heterosexuality in an innovative reading of *Sir Gawain and the Green Knight*.[76] She draws a parallel between the unattributed poem and Quentin Tarantino's *Pulp Fiction* (1994), on the diegetic and thematic levels. The Middle Ages marks the beginning of the construction of heterosexual masculinity, in the name of which homosexuality is ruthlessly checked after the 12th century. Against the mechanisms of repression, laughter provides a means of resistance. This is precisely the postulate used by Pasolini and Michel Foucault in the justification of a heretic discourse in favor of liberation. Dealing with the Middle Ages or, more exactly speaking, from the medieval perspective allows the anti-establishment voice of the minority to refer to a time prior to the major interdicts—dating to the 17th century, Foucault reminds us. The filmmaker employs the medieval context actually with a view to supporting "a discourse that combines the fervor of knowledge, the determination to change the laws, and the longing for the garden of earthly delights."[77] Because it insists on individual confession, the medieval era paradoxically begets a discourse better suited to formulate the sexual act. At that time the individual is still devoid of a sexual identity that subjectivizes him or her. This pre-modernity, where only acts matter instead of identities, Pasolini is anxious to revert to so as to express a free will that consciously transgresses the laws by claiming the use of sensual pleasures whatever they may be. His conception of history is similar to Foucault's in other words. There is not one single history but a story or, in the case of *The Decameron* and *I Racconti di Canterbury*, a series of fictions inspired by a remote reality. An authentic past (the late 14th century) is fictionalized through the film medium. This age of transition or *media aetas* serves as a springboard, "an empty space" (Foucault), from which Pasolini fashions his personal artistic and ideological project. His quest consists in bringing back to life an alternative Middle Ages, likely to liberate the individual from constraints not only through laughter but also through dream, "closely watched and even punished"[78] for belonging in an in-between marginal space.

The Dialectics of Inversion: The Land of Cockaigne

Because "chaos prevails over a rational design"[79] in the oneiric field, the dream makes it possible the parallel existence of a compensatory universe projected by the folk utopia that conquers an increasingly large territory, where the allegedly "superior" rationality is out of place.[80] Oneirism lets out the overflowing folk imagination, one of the most representative manifestations of which is the Land of Cockaigne. The upside-down world of a profusion of food, of unchecked leisure and total sexual freedom is a medieval theme likely to be interpreted as the expression of an objection to the social and cultural system. This fascinating "nowhere" counterbalances the daily regular routine. No wonder Pasolini contaminates the narrative in his *Decameron* with a hint at Bruegel's *Land of Cockaigne*. The painting probably embodies the heretic potential of a motif from popular imagination in the pursuit of an upside-down world. "It is the idea of heaven on earth, the golden age that precedes our time, and ... like a return to the origins, instead of a future horizon."[81]

7

A Defense of Adaptation

Text and Film: Intersections and Transmutations

Taking Liberties with the Source

> Alberto Grimaldi
> presenta
> Un film di PIER PAOLO PASOLINI
> IL *DECAMERON*
> Da "IL *Decameron*" di G. Boccaccio
>
> Alberto Grimaldi
> presenta
> un film di PIER PAOLO PASOLINI
> I RACCONTI DI CANTERBURY
> Dai "Canterbury Tales" di G. Chaucer
> PRIMO PREMIO ORSO D'ORO
> FESTIVAL DI BERLINO 1972

This is how the virtually identical credits of *The Decameron* and *I Racconti di Canterbury* begin. They appear in thin black letters on a white background that looks like a blank page. In both cases, the filmmaker's name precedes that of the author of the literary source of inspiration. Does this mean that the value attached to the texts is minimized? The mention of the writer's name in the credits reveals something about the intention behind the film transposition of his work. The title is certainly no guarantee that the movie will be close to the textual reference. It comes only after "un film di Pier Paolo Pasolini" indeed. In other words, it seems that pre-eminence is given to the film version made a posteriori. Pasolini's name takes precedence. Only then does he refer to the writer: "Da *Il Decameron* di G. Boccacio"/"Dai *Canterbury Tales* di G. Chaucer." In the opening sequence of *I Racconti di Canterbury* on the Southwark marketplace, Chaucer is invoked or "summoned" again, this time physically in the person of Pasolini himself, whose guiding presence and self-citational function are brought to light. So the figure of the "makere" of the Tales is called upon twice. Yet then it is swept aside. The redundant enunciatory marks ("un film di...," "dai..." and the embodiment of the poet) create a distance from the source, as if the literary work were being kept away. Now analysing the credits from this angle leads us to wonder about the type of adaptation Pasolini has in mind. The Italian "dai" meaning "following," "in the fashion of," "according to," signals a screening supposedly true to the text and the author's motivations. The indication that the movies are "adapted from" Boccaccio and Chaucer does not vouch for a faithful transcription of the original. "Faithfulness" is a term that revives the debate on the legitimacy of this criterion used to assess the screen version of a book. The faithfulness/betrayal dialectic regarding the literary source remains closely related to the study of film adaptation. André Gardies[1] claims this is not a proper issue in itself. The essential notion upon which our reflection is to be articulated is rather that of the textual gaps, divergences or deviances and sometimes the doing away with the author. In a press conference at the Berlin Festival in 1972, Pasolini unambiguously exposed the reason why he took such daring liberties with the Chaucerian material. His rendering of the fictitious universe of the English medieval poet never aimed at achieving a historically accurate reconstruction.

> The pleasure of telling stories implies a play with what one is narrating, and that implies a certain liberty vis à vis the subject matter. This liberty regarding the material requires that the Chaucerian reconstruction be visionary, and that it should not be used as a pretext for a reconstruction of the historical period. History in this film is strictly visionary. Therefore, I forget Chaucer in order to make the film as my own visionary game, my personal game as the author.[2]

A Problem of Definition

Thinking in terms of faithfulness to the original provides too narrow a perspective from which we wish to consider the passing from text to film. The adaptation should not be apprehended solely as a reading that undermines, amputates or spoils the source. What strikes us as more fruitful an approach is reflecting on the specificity of film language, what it adds in particular to the literary work, instead of simply thinking in terms of what the work loses, of what it is dispossessed in its cinematic version. We could thus avoid the commonplaces and sterile stumbling blocks of a viewpoint that too systematically opposes the two means of expression specialized in the art of telling. Our analyses of *I Racconti di Canterbury* and *The Decameron* especially raise the question of the very definition of adaptation. Is it a recreation, a metatextual comment from the hypertext, a total rewriting, the projection of a dream on the mirror-screen of film, a mere illustration of the original or a complete eviction of it? Millicent Marcus calls Pasolini's *Decameron*[3] a cinematic imitation, notwithstanding a scandalous subversion of the structural and formal rigour, the thematic progression of the original, and the narrative pattern of the Boccaccian *novella*— an anecdote with a preliminary part and a morality that comes after the denouement. In a respect/irreverence dialectic, the movie succeeds in capturing the meta-literary depth of *The Centovelle* as well as its spirit. Pasolini conceives of the key figures of the artist in *The Decameron* and the poet in *I Racconti di Canterbury* as arbitrary characters who bear "the meta-linguistic meaning of the film" (Pasolini, 73).

> It is in this meta-literary sense that Pasolini's imitation most authentically captures the spirit of the original. [...] The political revisions may be harder for Boccacio to swallow, but he could read these as just one more index of the vast cultural and historical gap which gives this imitation such a rich and mutually revealing relationship to its source [Marcus, 180].

The visualization of the text offers a different work of art as such, less an adaptation than an imitation rather emerging from the databank, that is the literary source. The film version is basically unlike the text, because it results from a series of complex transformations from one state of facts to another. Paradoxically enough, the discrepancy between the two mediums is precisely what brings them together: "their only common denominator is the soul."[4] In spite of the obvious "ontological discordance" (Bazin, 119) between them, literature and film can be reconciled in the adaptation process, in which they closely interact through the "dynamics of exchange," described by Keith Cohen.[5] He postulates that the film exists side by side with its literary source of inspiration. Thus, adaptation rises above the restrictive debate that sets closeness to the original in opposition to the liberty of creation. It can be viewed in a new light in terms of a dialectic of cinema and literature. Another work is erected "on the book through the film medium" (Bazin, 124–26). The adaptation then forms "un être esthétique nouveau," "a kind of text multiplied by cinema" (Bazin, 126). In Bazin's conception, the rendering of both the letter and the spirit establishes the essential double parameter through which to assess an adaptation. Because it consists of a subtle phenomenon of influences, equivalences and correspondences between two aesthetic structures, a cinematic transposition may wander far from the text, while surprisingly remaining close to the spirit. This is what Jean Renoir achieves in *Une partie de campagne*, also examined by Bazin. Still his "sovereign independence"[6] notwithstanding, the French filmmaker admits "a priori the transcendence" (Bazin, 82) of Guy de Maupassant's short story. The literary work that the film takes possession of is reconstructed and therefore recreated. Not only does the adaptation make it easier to understand the various narrative models and transformations from one medium to the other, but it also allows the exploration of the mechanisms of creation. A creative reconstruction is then achieved.

The Birth of an "Alien"

In his analysis of Robert Bresson's film of Georges Bernanos's novel by Robert Bresson, *Journal d'un curé de campagne,* Bazin speaks of "a ceaselessly creative respect" (97)—"un respect sans cesse createur." The antinomy denotes the paradox of the adaptor's work, which takes possession of a material and re-structures it so as to fashion a separate final product. Such a task appears all the more delicate as it pursues a twofold objective: "offering an accurate translation while creating freely."[7] Consequently the relations between the two semiotic systems cannot be described as analogical, as both narratives merge, intermingling into one single work beyond analogy at the "screenization"/"écranisation" level, the aim of adaptation.

> The topic is rethought, revisited by the filmmaker. There is no translation, no equivalence or metamorphosis. There is an allusion to the content, a transcoding of the narrative devices and a reincarnation of the same work [...] a sort of [...] second birth of the initial story.[8]

We would be tempted to add that the textual source is transcended. The limits of adaptation have inspired various theoretical positions. George Bluestone[9] and Jean Mitry[10] are convinced that the intricate mechanism of transformations from book to film cannot possibly be attained. Other theoreticians such as Nelson Goodman[11] apply themselves to distinguishing in both modes of expression some elements with similar functions. Keith Cohen and Christian Metz adopt a virtually scientific approach in examining the possible connections between both arts. To them the codes in novel and narrative fiction film are strangely congruous, in that they work at the level of implication or connotation. Anyway the notion of adaptation is to be qualified. Some precisions appear necessary so we may tell between the different degrees of closeness to or remoteness from the original, in the mutations entailed by the passing from one medium to the other.

One satisfactory solution would be to make a distinction between "adaptation," "free adaptation," and "transposition." Neither too close in the first case nor too remote in the second, the transposition "does not betray the film nor the novel because it is situated at the boundary between two forms of artistic expressions" (Garcia, 203). In fact, adaptation is a question of style. The style refers to the artists's vision. He is actually his own style. This Proustian conception is in keeping with that of Pasolini, for whom the subject of the movie matters less than the expressiveness and personal stamp of its maker.

Dudley Andrew considers three aspects of relations between novel and film. First of all, respecting the spirit as well as the letter of the original constitutes a criterion that involves the specificity of each of the two signifying systems. One should bear in mind the equation established by Christian Metz between the text, which goes from signification to perception, and the film, which goes the other way around. The original becomes the signified in a fairly accurate transcription, whereas it is nothing more than a referent in an "inspired by..." type of adaptation. Then the second and most common form of adaptation concerns mere borrowing. Lastly comes the "intersecting" concept, which strikes one as noteworthy on account of the emphasis laid on the specificity of the source. Yet this does not preclude the specificity of the cinematic medium, in which it is transferred in a mise en abyme. "An original is allowed its own life, in the cinema" (Andrew, 423).

The Literary Work Seen in the Light of Cinema: Trans-semiotization and Visualization.

Such a perspective pertains to a modern aesthetic because it rejects the limited view of adaptation that requires the movie to follow the book scrupulously. On the contrary, it points out the otherness of the original, compatible with that of the screen version. Andrew gives the example of *Il Vangelo secondo Matteo*, *Medea*, but also *The Decameron* and *I Racconti di Canterbury*, which he calls "adaptational events in the intersecting mode" (423). These are not adaptations strictly speaking, precisely because they seek to bring out "the otherness and distinctiveness of the original text, initiating a dialectical interplay between the aesthetic forms of one period with the cinematic forms of our own period" (423). Cinema records its confrontation with an uncompromising text, the particularity of which is not only preserved but also displayed. The difficulty for the adaptor is to imbue his movie with the substance of the book — every single page, paragraph, or chapter of which is bound to be inaccurately rendered nonetheless. The discrepancy between the written text and its visual version in an idiom with its own mode of expression deserves particular attention. Narration represents the most delicate aspect of the enterprise of adaptation. Therefore close scrutiny of the transfers in the arrangement of the narrative from text to film appears necessary. Passing from words to motion pictures entails the indispensable mediation of the script which operates selections and orientations in the text that all lead to interpretation rather than just translation. Still, condensing the narrative on the screen does not mean impoverishing it. The filmmaker creates an autonomous form as such, borrowed yet distinct and new. If the term "film adaptation" becomes "riduzione cinematografica" in Italian, the art of putting to film does not boil down to mere curtailing or truncating. On the contrary, it lies in the ability to find a satisfactory compromise between the letter and the spirit. Talking about his project on Saint Paul, Pasolini stresses the necessity "to capture the spirit via the letter, and restore the letter by developing and making personal use of the spirit."[12]

In other words, the screening should go beyond the cinematization of a text, as André Bazin conceives it. It should refract the original instead, as Bresson manages to do so in his *Journal d'un curé de campagne*, where "the film is the novel seen by the cinema."[13] To borrow the metaphor of the crystal chandelier and the crude flashlight, we could claim that from the intersecting of Pasolini's camera (the flashlight) with the "chandelier" of Boccaccio's and Chaucer's works results an "experience of the original modulated by the particular beam of the cinema" (Andrew, 423). A large part of the literary work remains in the dark, and what is lit is *Il Decameron* and *The Canterbury Tales* seen by film. As we have attempted to show, it is upon the visualization process that the passage from text to film rests. The trans-semiotization is motivated by a quest of pictures, shared by poetry, painting and cinema, intimately linked in Pasolini's mind. As early as his first movie, *Accattone*, his cinema is imbued with past pictorial models. The film director's "rapport *indirect en acte*"[14] with the visual arts can be explained by a "figurative coup de foudre"[15] that he experienced when he was Roberto Longhi's student. He was then working on a M.A. dissertation on contemporary Italian painting. Fascinated by the natural (even carnal) reality of the world and its (trans)figuration through art, Pasolini developed a predilection for close shots that compress and flatten the depth of field of the film shot — obvious in his scenic recompositions of famous works by Old Masters. This search for pictorial figurativeness can be already traced in *La Ricotta* (1963), in which Orson Welles plays a filmmaker obsessed by the excessively scrupulous reconstruction of Pontormo's *Deposition*.

The Aesthetic Rapture: The Linguistic Illusion Given Shape in the Picture

A few years later, *The Decameron* reiterated Pasolini's "fulguration figurative"[16] in his self-representation as Giotto's best disciple engrossed in the painting of his fresco. It is as a "flamboyant popular fresco"[17] that the visionary artist views his trilogy. His liking for frontal shots mirrors his conception of filmmaking as something like "slipping from the abstraction of words to the figurativeness of pictures" (Gérard, 84). While shooting *Mamma Roma* in 1962, Pasolini confessed:

> And I just cannot conceive pictures, landscapes, and faces outside my first pictorial, medieval passion, entirely focused on man. As a result, when my pictures are in motion, they are so as if the film camera drew closer to them on a painting. I always see the backdrop of a painting as a setting, and this is why I always attack it frontally [...]. This is why my camera sweeps across backgrounds and figures mainly felt as motionless and sharply highlighted by a chiaroscuro treatment.[18]

Among the stylistic particularity of his movies are the works of Italian and Flemish Old Masters of the late Middle Ages and early Renaissance, which provide Pasolini with a visual model serving an expressive technique. The objective (in the literal and figurative senses of "camera eye" and "aim") opts for the antithesis of the real-time continuity of the naturalistic sequence shot, that is the endless succession of brief shots, an editing made up of small units. *The Decameron* and *I Racconti di Canterbury* reach an unusual degree of self-signaling editing, which gives the films a paratactic construction, like a series of paintings that succeed one another without transitions. For Millicent Marcus, the mechanism of the division of a film into sequences is metaphorically signified in the three panels of the Santa Chiara fresco, itself an echo of the film in its photographic sense.[19] The filmmaker's wish to visualize the words can be likened to the poet's dream of creating the illusion of pictures. In other words, the film transpositions of *Il Decameron* and *The Canterbury Tales* "picture" or even "figurate" the texts. Adaptation then becomes figuration. The picture bestows an illusory shape on the linguistic illusion."[20] Albeit distinct from that of literature or painting, the mediation of reality by means of cinema rises from the same creative will. "The quest of images results in face of reality from an inner state that inclines you to be open to whatever is likely to arouse the intuition of an image."[21]

Textual Images and Motion Pictures: A Fruitful Interaction

The sight of the empiric world contains the promise of an aesthetic pleasure for the writer and the filmmaker. They achieve it differently though.

The contemplative temptation provoked by the poetic image that springs up is due to a dynamic of the gaze, shared by the two modes of artistic expression.

"In the end, the inner space or field of writing meets with the infinite space of the motion picture, but technically speaking their processes and effects are not compatible."[22] It would be appropriate indeed to wonder about the divergences between both forms of writing in order to ultimately highlight their enriching encounter on common ground. The postulate that the frontier between them is irreversibly closed thus finds itself invalidated. The textual image takes shape in the reader's mind only once he has gone through the whole description. The epiphany is neither concomitant nor consubstantial with the text that fashions it. Defective because it only partly translates "the lines and volumes of the real world" (Drevet, 60) the linguistic tool nonetheless makes palpable the presence of the world under scrutiny.

It is quite the reverse in a movie, in which the evidence of reality appears immediately. Its instant reconstruction has the effect of a shock: that of a revelation of the "compactness" and "fullness" of things. For Pasolini, what basically constitutes the difference between text and film is the latter's ability to seize some snatches of reality explored by his camera. This is what he calls "cinema in nature." The components of reality, what he calls the "cinems," stand for the smallest units of film language. The motion picture directly seizes these fragments of the real world. The artist's search of the immediate poetic nature of the picture, along with an instinctive film practice make it easy to attain a "plastic density" (Drevet, 87), a corporeity that words are unable to materialize. Paradoxically, the choice of a reference to the literariness of the text enables the author of *The Decameron* and *I Racconti di Canterbury* to attain the unmediated genuineness of the motion picture, found only in the moments of grace of these "situations optiques et sonores pures" (described by Gilles Deleuze) in the movies. In other words, both signifying systems could be associated in a relationship of contiguity and interaction. Cinema brings us back to literature, which itself raises new questions about cinema. It seems legitimate, then, to formulate differently the literature/cinema relationship in terms of a "transmutation" or "change in nature."[23] The semiotic systems under consideration can "enter in translation with each other."[24] In spite of a change of medium (from the page to the screen) and of formal and narrative structure, some semantic isotopies circulate from the literary source to the film version. The choices made by the film director aim to respond to a minimum degree of continuity and coherence with the original.

A Vampirization of the Literary Source or an Inventive Imitation?

An *Auteur* Policy: The "Homo Pasolinius"

> Dracula is (thus) a figure whose destiny is inseparable from the destiny of cinema, which begins in the flickering of black shadows against a white screen.[25]

This metaphor of the quintessence of cinema (a contrast of shadows and lights) might well be applied to a reflection on adaptation. We pose the question in these terms. Does the film object vampirize the work it is inspired from? Or does it content itself with sucking the gist out of it with a view to serving a separate project of artistic creation? It seems that *The Decameron* and *Racconti* stand not so much as "excrescences" of the texts they emerge from as works of reinvention or inventive imitation by means of the visual medium. Siegfried Kracauer[26] reminds us that the essential function of art consists in helping man to grasp the real world. Cinema especially succeeds in bringing him closer to this concrete reality that the spectator can feel by proxy through the mediation of the camera eye. More than any other mode of expression, film depends on the raw material of reality, which it arranges into a formal composition. It has its own picture-and-sound vocabulary, its own syntax and aesthetic structures. As an art of representation, cinema plays on the "fiction of reality and the reality of fiction."[27] The expressive power of film lies at two levels, as it is the art of reality in its denotative function of photographic and phonographic designation on the one hand, and an art as such in its aesthetic connotative use on the other hand. In addition to showing reality directly, film also comments upon it by indirection. The "represented world" conceals an "expressed world": the artist's style, a recognizable stamp, "a universe of connotation," as Metz puts it in *Essais sur la signification au cinéma* (vol. 1). The natural expressiveness of the empiric world is put in the service of the aesthetic expressiveness of the author's style.

Defined in 1954 by François Truffaut among other young French filmmakers, the *politique des auteurs* rests upon the theory of the artist being the master or author of his own work characterized by "these marks of directorial authorship (that) will manifest themselves in all of a true auteur's films, even as he works with different writers, cinematographers, and stars."[28] The *auteur*'s films may indeed be seen as artifacts fashioned by a person — so long as the artistic creation may be considered as the work of one single individual, for a movie is the fruit of the collective effort of the shooting crew, as remarked earlier.[29] Peter Wollen[30] enriches Truffaut's reflection on the individuality of film creation with a structuralist and semiological explanation of the meaning of the movie. An *auteur*'s movie calls for deciphering, which entails a distinction between a film made by an auteur and one made by a director. In the former, the style (which conveys the meaning) is part and parcel of the movie. An *auteur*'s work possesses a dimension not only formal but also semantic, so much so that the meaning of his movies "is constructed *a posteriori*." The work of a film director limits itself to a transcription through the purely cinematographic technique of a preexisting text. This is why Wollen speaks of a meaning *a priori* typical of that type of film. The *auteur* theory, he believes, allows one to spotlight the structure that underlies the movie and gives flesh to it, making it a coherent whole.

> [...] The purpose of criticism thus becomes to uncover behind the superficial contrasts of subject and treatment a hard core of basis and often recondite motifs. The pattern formed by these motifs [...] is what gives an author's work its particular structure, both defining it internally and distinguishing one body of work from another.[31]

The relevance of the *politique des auteurs* finds its justification in its structuralist approach, in which the critic writes about the movie as part of a whole work: "[...] it is only the analysis of the whole *corpus* which permits the moment of synthesis when the critic returns to the individual film" (Wollen, 600). A "homo pasolinius" emerges out of a whole range of thematic isotopies and motifs that constitute his aesthetic universe, identifiable in each one of his movies. The distinctive features of an *auteur*'s style — he spends his life producing variations on the same movie — define a recognizable type. Roland Barthes's formula of "homo racinius," from which we have borrowed, indeed suggests both the singularity and the universal scope of the artist's work.

An *Auteur*'s Adaptation: The Example of *The Decameron*

"The auteur theory," Wollen continues, "[...] insists that the spectator has to work at reading the text" (603). The film text is meant for the viewer, who not only receives it but also reads and interprets it. The trouble is that there is not one single authoritative meaning. As a result, the study of a movie cannot pretend to fix its senses in a permanent, definite way. Behind the first obvious message in Boccaccio's or Chaucer's stories adapted to the screen lurks a second movie, in which Pasolini adds in a superimposition effect his own aesthetic and ideological preoccupations. In *The Decameron* and *I Racconti di Canterbury* a conscious style strikes our attention, especially in the pictorial pastiches, the stylized non-historical costumes, or the presence of non-professional actors. The two movies are characterized by a style that seeks to signal itself. After having watched the *Trilogy of Life*, the spectator recalls the film *auteur* more than the original author. The analysis of the cinematic transposition of a text is necessarily articulated upon the question of the type of adaptation. One has to wonder if the film director retains mainly the plot, the setting and the characters, or conversely if he goes deeper into the intersection with the text, its spirit, structure and style, which he is keen to restore. As regards *The Centovelle*, the *cornice* or frame-story that contains and constrains the 100 stories is deliberately eradicated, as if Pasolini asserted his determination not to adhere to a principle of structural order to the work as advocated by medieval scholastic thought. The filmmaker ignores the original arrangement of the *novelle* as well as their thematic progression. Millicent Marcus speaks of a desacralization in Pasolini's handling of the literary masterpiece produced in a cultural and aesthetic context so remote from the modern conceptions of the world and the work of art, especially in the early 1970s.

> By rejecting the *Decameron*'s meticulous structure, Pasolini is perhaps scolding Boccacio for clinging to a vestige of a scholastic order [...]. But the criticism goes both ways, for Boccaccio's ordered cosmos points to the very impossibity of such ordering in the modern world. Pasolini thus endorses Frederic Jameson's argument that literary genres are predicated on the ideological possibilities offered by a culture at a certain point in its development. Boccacio's culture offered (if somewhat nostalgically) the raw material for complete, coherent narrative forms, while Pasolini's obviously does not.[32]

Lastly, the *brigata*, composed of some representatives of the 14th-century Florentine aristocracy and thriving merchant class embodying the ideal of courtly behavior, is superseded by a dual figure which takes over the extradiegetic function of framing the stories. Neither the impostor Ciappelletto nor Giotto's humble disciple — who hardly speaks throughout the second part of the movie — belong to the Tuscan privileged social category epitomized by the 10 young people in the *cornice*, who reconstruct the hierarchical civilized order in their idyllic bucolic retreat. Pasolini's (iconoclastic?) rendering of *Il Decameron* thus operates not only some profound alterations in the narrative construction but also bends the meaning while successfully seizing the very spirit of the original, its light-heartedness and vital élan. He does so by infiltrating the narrative with a veiled intrinsic ideological message — the neapolitanization or popularization of a collection of stories originally aimed at a bourgeois readership/audience — and by playing with form and resorting to other means of artistic expression such as painting.

The Sagacious and Playful Film Re-writing of *The Canterbury Tales*

The author of the movie does not pretend to emulate nor transpose the text as accurately as possible at the diegetic, discursive, and poetic levels. However, although he appropriates the source in a somewhat cavalier fashion likely to shock the informed reader of Boccaccio, Pasolini's *Decameron* with its aesthetic and thematic preferences stands as a self-contained work, an independent form that claims its existence beside the text. Gérard Genette in *Palimpsestes*[33] remarks that any hypertext can be read for itself without any reference to the hypotext or source of inspiration. It is precisely the autonomy of the final product from the model that distinguishes the notion of hypertextuality from that of intertextuality. We could contend that the film hypertext, *I Racconti di Canterbury*, like the first episode of the Trilogy of Life, originates from the filmmaker's propensity to "tinker about, make something new out of something old and worn out"—"faire du neuf avec du vieux."[34] What Genette has in mind is the art of getting "objects that are more complex and delightful characterized by a new function that adds to and intermingles with an older structure, and the dissonance between the two coexisting elements makes the whole composition so particularly interesting."[35] *Racconti* is subtly linked to Chaucer's vast literary work. The special relationship is ingeniously summarized by Genette in the "lucidité/ludicité" anagrammatic doublet (452), which means clear-sightedness or sagacity and recreation or play. A meaningful whole clearly separate from *The Canterbury Tales*, the movie denotes a lucid reading of the spirit and initial program of its hypotext. Even though Pasolini approaches the English masterpiece via its Italian translation, *I Racconti di Canterbury* succeeds in grasping the essence of the text and of Chaucer's writing as well. However minimalist it is in the film version, the frame-story is retained. The significant number of diegetic discrepancies—narrative concentrations, dilatations, additions, suppressions and metamorphoses of all kinds—does not prevent the spectator who has read Chaucer from recognizing the tales. The pleasure of identifying the original in the film can also be experienced at the structural level. The broken, staccato rhythm of the series of sketches actually restores the paratactic dimension of *The Canterbury Tales*, which amounts to an assemblage of narrative fragments, themselves clustered into several fragments. Lastly the sagacious gaze cast on the hypotext manifests itself through Pasolini's consciousness of a writing in progress in Chaucer's work. We have previously pointed out the cinematic equivalents of an archaic Middle English language, its formulism, and above all its meta-poetic digressions turned into scenes of self-representation of the film *auteur* as Chaucer. Yet the hypertext blends seriousness and play, lucidity and amusement, "intellectual accomplishment and entertainment" (453).

> Ultimately all forms of hypertextuality go hand in hand with some amount of play, consubstantial with the recycling of existent structures. Basically, fixing up, however urgent it may be, always boils down to playing, in that it

deals with and makes use of an object in an unexpected, "undue" fashion. Likewise, treating and using a (hypo)text to serve purposes other than those of the initial programme is a way to play and make light of it.[36]

The exultation found in the film rewriting of a text is probably best sensed at the core of *I Racconti di Canterbury* in the very short sequence added by Pasolini, in which Chaucer, sitting at his desk, laughs as he is reading *Il Decameron*, from which he draws his inspiration to "fix" his own tales, fashioning something new out of pre-existing material. Now this is exactly where medieval literature stands; half-way between tradition and invention.

> Even the undeniably new works like *The Canterbury Tales* claim to be resting upon former texts, entirely or partially fictive, that serve them as a guarantee. The metaphor of the world seen as a book written by God (Hugh of Saint Victor) is more than a mere rhetorical commonplace in the Middle Ages. Therefore the poet does not view himself as a demiurge. He is simply the copist of some *auctoritas*— either God, Nature, Reason, Knowledge, Truth or Love [...]. What is original about medieval literature is that it does not pretend to be original.[37]

Poetic Monstrosity of Film Monstration in Pasolini's Movies Under Study

Out of some well-known models, built upon a certain amount of stereotyped situations and characterized by easily identifiable language registers, Chaucer composed his tales as an experienced "makere," skillful at handling poetic forms from the past, which he reserved and subverted with a meta-literary purpose in mind. The travestied style of the courtly romance in *The Miller's Tale* and *The Reeve's Tale* testify to a literary awareness that sets off the artificiality of the text, which results from subtly assembling various thematic and formal components. The innovation and rich diversity of Chaucer's writing in *The Canterbury Tales* is obtained thanks to the poet's ability to set the audience/readers wondering about the relationship between narrative and discourse. The numerous digressions, stylistic burlesques, and genre parodies that pepper the diegetic progression of the tales point to something at a deeper level. Telling in *The Canterbury Tales* is aware of its limits, with which it plays by way of the mise en abyme of the act of writing. The listener is invited to reconsider his unconditional adherence to the material offered to him in the frequent reminders of the fictionality of the narrative and of its intrinsic character as an artifact. The meta-literariness of the tales cannot but strike the attention of a filmmaker, for whom what matters most is not the story told. The mise en abyme of the cinematographic device in the shots showing Giotto's disciple framing his subjects with his fingers or painting his fresco confirms that the adaptation is far from the traditional genres of the period pieces or historical reconstruction. The spectator's horizon of expectations is deliberately frustrated, so that, on the contrary, an acute sensibility to a self-reflexive form of writing may be highlighted. The literary form of writing is physically designated by the character of the writer in *I Racconti di Canterbury* (a meta-linguistic figure in a movie about cinema), while being mirrored by the form of film writing.

Nevertheless, what mainly motivates the adaptation of the two works of the past, dealing with the pleasurable art of story-telling, is above all the extraordinary resource that Pasolini finds in the film medium. Fascinated by the power of the motion picture to reveal the "dermis of reality," "the visible speech of the bodies," "the animal life of things," he realizes that using a film camera enables him to attain the illusion of a disclosure of reality, the expression of a presence of "the body of the world."[38] Like literary writing, cinema explores, questions, and plays on the borders between *mimesis* (imitation) and *semiosis* (representation). However, the essential difference lies in the fact that whereas the sentence gives only parsimonious indications, the film shot, in a saturation of means of perception, delivers "a virtually endless sum of instantaneous pieces of information."[39] The irreducible otherness of cinema stems from the narrated action being drowned in the empirical world which permeates the whole motion picture. Telling becomes showing. The film director is also a hunter of images/pictures in search of the poetry in the real world he is filming. In Pasolini's movies, when the exhilarating "mystery in some crack of the being" (Vray, 69) is disclosed, the film shot forgets to tell and lets in that essential element that escapes narration and adds the poetry of cinema to the encounter in film "between the line of a regulated dramatic action and the inert incoherent reality" (Vray, 68). Film narration in these particular moments of grace drifts away from saying or writing to description. "As in still lives, where the harmony of life is transfixed in its violent turmoil, beyond time and death,"[40] the tableaux vivants and non-narrative pictures in *Racconti* and *The Decameron* confer on the movies some film monstrosity, if we may say so. They become monsters that exhibit their strangeness in an unusual fashion so that the spectator is kept away from the show and transport him beyond the narrative level. Pasolini's conception of the motion picture can be likened to that of Robert Bresson, who advises us to "pull things out of habit and dechloroform them."[41]

"Tellen Tales" and, "Withouten Moore Speche," "Maken Disport"

How is Pasolini/Chaucer's smile to be interpreted as he puts the finishing touch to his work at the end of *Racconti*? As a hint from the author who takes delight in interspersing his text with marks of enunciation? The final word he traces with his quill, as he utters it, is "amen":

> "Judgment day. Here end the Canterbury tales told only for the pleasure of telling them. — Amen."

Chaucer's Middle Ages is evoked through the picturing of the original manuscript at the end of *I Racconti di Canterbury*. The title is directly mentioned, and an implicit reference to the retraction that follows *The Parson's Tale* is suggested in the reminder of God's supervision as the ultimate judge. His decision to transpose a masterpiece of the past allows the filmmaker to play on the reflection and refraction of the early 1970s in the Middle Ages. The "makere"'s enigmatic smile may signify the sagacious and ironical gaze cast by a medieval mind on the neo-capitalist 20th-century society that Pasolini resented. It is as though Chaucer the writer, a witness of his time, were passing judgment on the modernity of an alienating culture through the filter of a rather disenchanted ideological consciousness. The epilogue addresses a sign of duplicity and complicity on the part of the modern author of a discourse on film discourse itself. The Trilogy of Life comes out right after and in reaction against conventional cinema with a transparent type of narration. Because of its segmentation, its deliberate lack of unity, its abrupt transitions, and the contamination of the narrative by intrusive parasitic visions, Pasolini's two adaptations strike one as singular instances of an uncommon artistic choice for de-narrativization. The joy attained in the art of storytelling sems to derive from the disquieting strangeness, the heresy of a de-narrativizing type of writing. It decomposes and recomposes the source (*The Canterbury Tales*) so as to deconstruct the telling and dismantle and demonstrate its devices. The *artifex* or maker of "the book of the tales of Caunterbury," "enditynge(s) of wordly vanitees" (*The Canterbury Tales*, X(I), 1084), which he has already revoked, adopted this auteur theory six centuries earlier. His writing reached a degree of amused mise en abyme that disconcerts the narratee of "this litel tretys" so much so that it plunges him into doubt. The question of knowing whether the Retraction constitutes an earnest abjuration or on the contrary an ironical awareness of the "vanity" of all artistic works still divides the *The Canterbury Tales* scholars. What conclusion is to be drawn from the experience of telling declined in all its aspects up to the point of self-reflexiveness? Maybe, as Pasolini and Chaucer appear to believe, it could be summed up in a few words: "tellen tales," "withouten moore speche"[42] (*The General Prologue*, 783), and "maken (yow) disport"[43] (*The General Prologue*, 775): telling, falling silent and laughing.

Conclusion

The Film Version of The Canterbury Tales: *An Innovative Vision*

We have tried to demonstrate in what aspects (structural, aesthetic, and ideological) the analysis of *I Racconti di Canterbury* contributes to Chaucerian studies. A similar close critical examining of *The Decameron* is likely to enrich the reading of *The Centovelle*. Our approach, treatment, and assessment of the screening of *The Canterbury Tales,* carried out as objectively as possible, betrays an undeniable bias for Pasolini's movie, which cannot be fully appreciated unless studied in the light of the first part of the *Trilogy of Life*. Our research responds to the intimate feeling that, despite the whiff of scandal about it that persists today, this most personal visual reading of *The Canterbury Tales* deserves consideration. As an autonomous work independent from its source, *I Racconti di Canterbury* legitimately exists beside the revered masterpiece it is inspired by. Through the filter of Pasolini's sensibility as an artist belonging to the post-industrial society, the author of the film fulfills the dream of a work that consists of a true visualization rather than a mere cinematic version. Its genius lies in its originality and poetic expressiveness, and it manages to erase the temporal, cultural, national, and linguistic distance that separates Pasolini from Chaucer. Paradoxically *Racconti* sometimes drifts far away from his source but seizes the gist of it: the apparent de-construction or rather loose, sketchy, disjointed architecture, as well as the acute awareness of the writing process. *I Racconti di Canterbury* also grasps the strong medieval connection between the sublime and the grotesque. Although the film chooses to avoid scrupulous historical reconstruction, the perception of the Middle Ages grants the spectator familiar with Chaucer the exultation of re-capturing the magic of the tales. The danger sensed by Pasolini is that of the (re)semblance which misleads and distracts from the hidden meaning. The sight of the world is likely to be veiled by too great a concern for realism. This is why the maker of the Trilogy of Life defends a non-realistic cinema.

The "De-figuration" Operated by the Motion Picture

He adopts and adapts the medieval idea of the revealing function of the mysterious picture, behind which hides the truth to be disclosed. In his analysis of *The Annunciation* by Fra Angelico, Georges Didi-Huberman[1] demonstrates the non-figurativeness of the *figura*, dissimilar to its referent or signified object. Fra Angelico's painting epitomizes the typically medieval notion of the picture as a mystery. To some extent, the filmmaker shares the conception according to which the picture revives the memory of a riddle in the viewer's mind. An illustration of this theory is supplied by the representations of the Incarnation, to which the Annunciation especially pertains. Beyond the depicted story (*storia*), what is implicitly described is the embodiment of the Word. Actually, figuration should suspend the picture, expose an unusual imageity and convert the gaze to make an opaque signification visible. In his pictorial pastiches that contaminate the telling in both movies, Pasolini hints at the preeminence in the medieval thought of the icon as the best tool of memory, knowledge, and intellection. As a consequence, he frequently resorts to "salient" pictures with a pure visual intensity. Christ in Heaven is replaced by the Madonna in the Last judgment that brings *The Decameron* to a close (before the epilogue), probably because she symbolizes the very *locus* of the Incarnation. She is a figure. Still, her noticeable absence in *I Racconti di Canterbury*, which reaches its visual climax in the evocation of Hell, orientates the interpretation toward a substitution of the divine mystery (God's Word) for that of the insignificant human poetic creation (the writer's word). In *I Racconti di Canterbury*, the motion picture undergoes a de-figuration. It strikes one as odd, for it is unusually visible and visual. The figurative evidence becomes the instrument of a valorization of the iconic visuality. Pasolini's cinema probably answers the dream to incarnate, or rather incorporate, Chaucer's words in the motion picture.

Following the Source Accurately or Creating an Original Work?

The experience of an aesthetic incorporation is what the filmmaker longs to achieve. The cinematic readings of *Il Decameron* and *The Canter-*

bury Tales are actually concerned with what cinema itself (rather than the world) signifies and how it does so. At the beginning of the 1970s, the otherness of *Racconti* exploded on the screen, and like an alien astounded the viewer unaccustomed to this kind of film. We have spoken of "an encounter of the third kind" to describe the semiotic trans**mutation** of the tales that begets a mutant. We could apply the metaphor to the very nature of Pasolini's film practice (intimately linked to his film theory). However baffling its personal perception of the literary masterpiece, the movie claims to be a work of its own more than a mere adaptation, an excrescence or emanation from Chaucer's text. It matters less for a filmmaker to follow the original as closely as possible than to be creative. The inventive stamp of the author of *I Racconti di Canterbury* stems from his quest of the extreme limits of representation (best exemplified in the tableaux vivants), of the infiltration of the discourse by non-narrative intrusions, the choice of a bewildering arrangement of the diegetic sequences, and the presence of non-professional actors sounding out of tune. Our perspective is not relevant to a strict comparative study between Pasolini's movie and Chaucer's tales posed as the reference — which, in the opinion of most critics, is spoiled by the allegedly deviant, transgressive cinematic transposition. On the contrary, by stressing the full novelty of *The Canterbury Tales*, we have attempted to show that, six centuries after its composition in a totally different cultural and intellectual situation, a medieval text brings about, via another medium, a certain reflection of itself, though distorted as in a dream. The second panel of the triptych thwarts the viewer's horizon of expectations— whether or not he has read Chaucer — and evinces a refusal to be subjected to the diktat of the ultimate authority of the source. The shockwave caused by *The Decameron* and especially *I Racconti di Canterbury*, accused of mutilating Boccaccio's and Chaucer's works, appears to us extraordinarily salutary.

Rediscovering Literature through the Universal Language of Film

Not only are *Il Decameron* and *The Canterbury Tales* made accessible to a large audience, but their respective film versions also revive interest in such major literary compositions. They demythologize them by minimizing their sacredness as masterpieces meant for an educated elite. Film language is used to produce the quintessential narrativity of the texts and the pleasure of story-telling. The narrative is reflected in a mise en abyme up to a meta-narrative point, which places two different forms of telling in perspective. Why is it necessary to rise above the clichés relating to the scandalous nature of Pasolini's movies, exaggerately branded as obscene, even pornographic denaturations of their sources? Probably because the best comments upon a work of art emanate not so much from critics as from other works of art that they inspire. *Racconti* questions and sheds new light on a text so well-known, studied in depth that one might lose sight of its meaning. Besides, the multiple interpretations derived from its reading eventually make its reception more delicate. As he is not a Chaucer specialist — he is not a Boccaccio specialist either though he shares the latter's language and culture —, Pasolini fails to cast a scholarly medievalist's look on the tales. It is precisely this lack of erudition that keeps the movie from sinking into heavy academism. Thanks to its fresh, innovative power, the cinematic vision of the work wrenches the viewer from his passivity as a consumer of fiction. Because it is not subordinated to the sacred aura of a medieval literary masterpiece, *I Racconti di Canterbury* abrogates the prerogative of Chaucerians concerning the reading of the text. A great work belongs to all. The universal language of film is particularly apt to diffuse it as widely as possible. Even a non British viewer is likely to sense the spirit of Chaucer's stories. Cinema is not only an art that duplicates life and the real world; it also suffuses it with poetry. Several shots of Pasolini as Chaucer writing his work are inserted between some of the episodes. If we take the example of *La règle du jeu*, we can notice that Jean Renoir carries out a derisive self-mise en scene. He plays Octave, an actor who happens to be a failure and cuts a clownish figure with his bearskin on. When it came out in 1939, the film disconcerted the audience because of the absence of focalization on a central protagonist. The only tenuous mainthread is personified by the figure of the artist behaving like a fool. He somewhat prefigures Pasolini/Chaucer who bumps his nose against the Cook's in the introductory sequence or dozes off with his feet on his desk when he is supposed to be working at his tale, and is brutally awoken by his austere wife.

A Bewildering Form of Writing in Progress

The paradox of the first two episodes of the Trilogy of Life can be explained by the fact that its maker draws his material from two major works of the past the better to "un-read" (*"dé-lire"*) and "des-cribe" them (*"dé-crire"*) in the sense of "un-write" (*"dé-crire"*) to "rewrite" (*"ré-écrire"*) them. To do so, he substitutes his own style, which shifts from telling to describing in these climactic moments of visual bliss, during which the narration is temporarily suspended or impaired by external interferences. He does not intend to cling to the world in a realistic film rendering, but rather seeks to distance himself from it in a totally poetic approach. His aim is to apprehend the world in a new light while being aware of the way this reality is signaled. As an object of contemplative meditation, art is symbolically exposed in the personification of the artist in *The Decameron* and the poet in *Racconti*. The style plays a preeminent part in both movies. These have nothing to do with a sound-and-light-display big-budget blockbuster, churned out standardized products seen by masses of viewers in today's multiplex movie theaters. Pasolini's films belong to a cinema of poetry that reflects (upon) its own art. The film of *The Canterbury Tales*, as we have already remarked, materializes the itinerary or route of a form of writing, but actually puts to rout (out of countenance) and eventually misdirects. In a more conspicuous fashion than in *The Decameron*, *I Racconti di Canterbury* misguides the spectator with its bewildering editing, and gives the feeling that the filmmaker is exploring the various possible directions of his movie. Chaucer himself experiments with diverse aspects of speech as well as the digressive overtures offered by the meanders of the narrative. The form of *I Racconti di Canterbury* consequently seems to translate the actual purpose of the adventure of the *Canterbury Tales*: namely the countless (semantic, thematic, and stylistic) possibilities of storytelling and the impossibility of deciding which way and which voice to follow. Such confounding yet stimulating indecision also tinges the film text, which is basically more like a dream than a movie. (The author himself admits the editing was a bit of a problem.)

A Non-realistic Rendering of the Quintessence of the Original: The Paradox of the Filmmaker

We are now dealing with the issue of the unfinished work. It happens to be the ruling principle in *The Canterbury Tales* as much at the extradiegetic level of the frame-story as at the intra-diegetic one — in *The Cook's Tale*, *The Squire's Tale*, *The Tale of Sir Topas*, and *The Monk's Tale*. *Racconti* reproduces the incompleteness of the source in another shape. The epilogues are either curtailed or obliterated. The effect reinforces the disjointedness or disunity of a film with an oddly erratic rhythm unwonted for a 1972 viewer. Pasolini creates a cultural object: the metamorphosis into film of a text of the past, to which the present offers its advanced technique of the cinematographic device in order to make it visible. In the early 1970s in the literary field, the concept of the open work prevailed. It relegated to secondary importance both the plot and the constraints of dramatic coherence in favor of the numerous resources of a discourse intent on destabilizing the reader the better to sensibilize him to the very making of the textual artifact. Pasolini's film pertains to this aesthetic view and evinces a singular creativeness in resorting to defamiliarization effects intended to make the spectator wonder about the mechanisms of representation. This is why the Middle Ages he depicts does not aim at being realistic, but instead strikes us as a fantasy, delightfully approximative and parallel to the literary source so to say. The costumes, for example, just look medieval, as if loosely based on pictorial models with no concern for historical accuracy whatsoever. This deliberate anachronism and most of the actors' unnatural diction fulfill a heuristic function. They constitute a means to conjure up a past that eventually looks and sounds authentic, strangely enough, in spite of the deliberately artificial style. Unexpected and sometimes saturated because of a contamination of some Old Masters' paintings, Pasolini's shots attain some degree of poetic expressiveness that unveils another possible Middle Ages. The imagined medieval period is a visualization of Chaucer's words, which turns away from the standards of conventional film representation.

The Otherness of a Cinema of Human Animality

The image of *The Canterbury Tales* and the late English medieval period projected by *I Racconti di Canterbury* is located on the edge[2] on account of its picturing of the human body and especially sex. As pointed out previously, the emphasis on corporeity partly plans to subvert the medieval exegetical reflex, which deciphers the empirical world as the signifier of some superior reality. The nakedness of the bodies exhibited collapses into the derisive grotesque, reminiscent of carnivalesque excesses. Nevertheless, the fact is that the bawdiness of Chaucer's farcical, even scatological tales retained by Pasolini should not be ascribed to the bad taste and vulgar complacency, which the Italian filmmaker is still too often reproached for. His heretical gaze appreciates the rich transgressive potential of the explicit celebration of a corporeity that culminates in the crude expression of sexuality.

> As a "celebration" of a kind of prelapsarian sexuality Pasolini never went further: nearly every conceivable form of sexual act is either suggested or shown directly, whether it is flagellation in a brothel, sundry homosexual couplings spied on by cloistered voyeurs, or even a friar in bed with a very large watermelon and a host of alarmed chickens.[3]

The deliberate exhibition of genitals — which claim the liberation of the body in the pursuit of all forms of pleasure — intends to denounce what Pasolini views as the actual pornography, that of a modern society that "confesses sex," as Michel Foucault puts it. The bodies that crowd the screen stand for an ideological protest against the general attempt at reducing the individual subject to a mere object. The exploitation of sex (or sexploitation) by the system is in fact what pornography is all about. Pasolini descries in the Middle Ages the capacity of the body to resist as an instrument of transgression. Sexual identities had not yet appeared in the 14 century. Heteronormative constructs had not been established. Still, the medieval man took a decisive step towards a social model dominated by bourgeois ethics and values. He did not depart from his animality, though, unlike today's man, who lives in an increasingly virtual world ruled by high technology. In the early 1970s, sex was already represented in a conspicuous yet abstract, unreal manner. Man seemed to have lost his primitive animal nature in the reign of hygienic sex mechanically performed by smooth, flawless bodies in many contemporary film productions. After *The Decameron, I Racconti di Canterbury* seeks to refute this exclusive conception of sexuality. The film auteur is eager to assert the existence of another cinema, consisting not so much of a realistic picture as a reflection of *The Canterbury Tales*, a poetic emanation of the text from the magic of cinema.

Bringing Together I Racconti di Canterbury *and* The Decameron

The film device shapes the gaze, the central role of which in *I Racconti di Canterbury* we have already underlined. Staged in a clever mise en abyme, it sheds new light on a text that it wishes to bring back to life. To do so, it resorts to light, in its most expressive effect, as if it were a developer (in the photographic sense of the word) aimed at exposing reality on the film. Yet, we must bear in mind that the real world recorded by the camera is disclosed from a certain angle or vision, which transforms it into a certain reality. This betrays the artist's consciousness at work. One cannot fully appreciate the reflexiveness of the shots of Pasolini/Chaucer in *I Racconti di Canterbury* without a "depth-of-field" consideration of those of the filmmaker as Giotto's disciple in *The Decameron*. The outcome is "a certain realism,"[4] that of a cinema characterized by the unwonted poeticity of its shots—which speak for themselves, expressing nothing but their imageity—and makes The trilogy of life so singular as early as its first part.

> Pasolini's *Decameron* captures both the bawdy spirit of the medieval original and perhaps something of the director's most joyful sense of himself as an artist. It is revealing that he casts himself as a jobbing painter and "disciple of Giotto" in the film — his only major appearance in one of his own features. Never mind that he looks rather more like a defrocked samurai warrior than some genteel Renaissance figure — the character personifies a potent Pasolini mix of raw politics, poetical delicacy and muscular passion.[5]

The study of the second panel of the triptych therefore cannot disregard that of *The Decameron* that opens the visual hymn to the vital force of mankind, and starts reflecting upon the reflexive dimension of the art of storytelling.

Why There Is More to I Racconti di Canterbury *Than a Mere Film Adaptation*

There are two reasons why Pasolini chooses to screen Boccaccio's and Chaucer's works. First, he perceives the extraordinary power and authenticity of the vernacular, a flexible, vivid language perfectly suited to bring to life new protagonists. The heroes, sometimes elevated to a divine or supernatural status in epics, or the noble ladies and true, righteous, valiant knights in courtly romances are gradually replaced by a wider range of medieval social types from the mendicant friar to the miller, summoner or pardoner. The other motivation behind the first two episodes of the trilogy is that both literary compositions share a subtle narrative structure resting upon the frame-story technique, which allows the narration to signal itself indirectly. Pasolini finds in them the enjoyable opportunity to tell stories in his turn while also exploring all the possibilities of the art of telling down to its refutation in the de-narrativization process. Pasolini retains the essential part of the plots in the film versions, while making substantial the loss or at least the fading of the diegetic cohesion by means of narrative ellipses or noticeable dilatations and intrusions of parasitic elements. So it appears that *I Racconti di Canterbury* as well as *The Decameron* cannot possibly be described as film adpatations in the strict sense of the word. We have consequently banished the term from our title. They are works that exist for themselves, independent of their sources. They express the filmmaker's strong affirmation of authorship. He puts two semiotic systems in translation with each other, not so much to transmit Boccaccio's and Chaucer's texts to a 20th-century audience as to offer the latter a refraction of the masterpieces, altered by the filter of his own fantasy. Yet the unexpected, unconventional vision turns out to be innovative. It is animated with a playful spirit — the delight of the storytelling game is proclaimed in the final shot. At the same time, it obliquely passes a sagacious ideological comment on Italy in the early 1970s — even if *Racconti* was shot in England — in a detour via the remote medieval period. *I Racconti di Canterbury* ends with a close-up on the manuscript that the English 14th-century poet is finishing, by reminding us that the tales he has just made up have been told only for the pleasure of telling them. Both structurally complex texts, in which the narrative is artfully reflected in a mise en abyme, *Il Decameron* and *The Can-*

terbury Tales enable a 20th-century poet who employs the film language of reality to enjoy an exhilarating artistic experience. This consists of the author's telling recreational stories, while relishing his own discourse and exposing himself to the danger of the temporary vanishing of the plot in its dramatic progression. The film shot threatens to de-narrativize the narrative in those specific moments when it ceases to tell and becomes the *locus ameonus* of a poetic epiphany. The spectator recognizes the spirit of the visualized originals, though, and senses that the narration matters less than the silent motion picture that succeeds to words. Such pictures, highly evocative of the early years of cinema, are singularly eloquent. The reason why they infiltrate the plot may be found in the epilogue of *I Racconti di Canterbury*. Pasolini/Chaucer utters a conclusive "amen," then falls silent and smiles. After giving thanks to the Lord in Heaven, Chaucer's Retraction hushes the pilgrims' plethoric flow of words voiced throughout the 25 performances. The filmmaker's smile may be construed as the logical conclusion of a game in which speech, however sentential and wise, inevitably leads to its denial and the sudden awareness of the insignificance of any human act of creation, whether text or film. Is the enigmatic grin to be read as a sign of the modesty of Pasolini, who like Chaucer, does not take himself seriously, and considers his work with detached amusement? Like the Host in *The General Prologue*, his "entente" is as follows:

> Fayn wolde I doon yow myrthe, wiste I how. / And of a myrthe I am right now bythoght, / To doon yow ese, and it shal coste noght [*The General Prologue*, 766–68]. /.../ And therfore wol I maken yow disport, / As I seyde erst, and doon yow som confort. [775–76].

Appendix 1: Chart Showing Narrative Structure of *I Racconti di Canterbury* in Text and Film

Order of the Adapted Tales in Chaucer's Text	Order of the Adapted Tales as Originally Planned in the Filmscript	Order of the Adapted Tales in the Final Version of the Film
The General Prologue	Prologue: Chaucer at his desk The Southwark Inn, Chaucer (at desk). Exchange Miller/Host. Angered Reeve.	Prologue: The Southwark marketplace
The Miller's Tale *Angered Reeve determined to get even*	The Miller's Tale *Chaucer writes last words* The Miller's Tale, *reads* Decameron, *resumes work. Exchange Reeve/Host.*	The Merchant's Tale
The Reeve's Tale *The Cook's Prologue: Host teases Cook ("A man may seye ful sooth in game and pley.")*	The Reeve's Tale *Pilgrims on their way. Exchange Cook/ Host.*	The Friar's Tale *Night, silence, pilgrims asleep. Chaucer taking "notes for a book about the pilgrims' tales. The Cook's Tale."*
The Cook's Tale	The Cook's Tale *Host begs Chaucer to tell a tale.*	The Cook's Tale *Chaucer at home reading* Decameron. *Falls asleep. Woken up by authoritarian wife exclaiming: "Geoffrey Chaucer!"*

APPENDIX 1

Order of the Adapted Tales in Chaucer's Text	Order of the Adapted Tales as Originally Planned in the Filmscript	Order of the Adapted Tales in the Final Version of the Film
The Wife of Bath's Prologue FriP: *Friar announces story of a summoner, about whom one cannot speak in flattering terms.*	Chaucer's Tale of Sir Thopas *The Host intervenes.*	The Miller's Tale
The Friar's Tale *Summoner will pay him back in his own coin.*	The Wife of Bath's Prologue *Stormy exchange Summoner/Friar interrupted by Host. Merchant starts speaking.*	The Wife of Bath's Prologue *Chaucer at desk takes his quill.*
The Summoner's Prologue (vision of Hell: 20,000 friars expulsed from Satan's backside) and Tale MerP: *Merchant wishes he had not married a shrew.*	The Merchant's Tale *2nd argument Summoner/Friar.*	The Reeve's Tale
The Merchant's Tale Intro PardT: *Before telling tale, Pardoner stops at a tavern.*	The Friar's Tale	The Pardoner's Prologue/Tale *Chaucer at home writing.*
The Pardoner's Prologue *(Exposes mechanisms of his art of persuasion)* and Tale *Argument with the Host who refuses sham relics the pedlar tries to sell him.*	The Summoner's Prologue and Tale	The Summoner's Tale and Prologue *Vision of Hell, then pilgrims outside Canterbury cathedral. Frontal shot of Chaucer finishing his work. Smile. "Amen" said and written simultaneously. Poet's last words: "Here end the Canterbury tales told only for the pleasure of telling them."*
	The Pardoner's Tale *Quarrel Host/Pardoner. Calmed down by Miller and Wife of Bath.*	
	Epilogue: *(Pilgrims' "Amen" outside cathedral).*	

Appendix 2: Chart Showing Narrative Structure of *The Decameron* in Text and Film

Roman type indicates the first version of the filmscript.
Italics indicates the second.

Order of the adapted tales in Boccaccio's text	Order of the adapted tales as originally planned in the filmscript (2 versions)	Order of the adapted tales in the final version of the film
	I-Ciappelletto	I-Ciappelletto Ciappelletto kills man in sack, and throws corpse into pit.
I, 1 (Ciappelletto)	II, 1 (Martellino) *II, 5 (Andreuccio)*	II, 5 (Andreuccio) *Ciappelletto buys charms of young boy while old Neapolitani s telling tale: IX, 2.*
II, 5 (Andreuccio da Perugia)	II, 5 *III, 1 (Masetto)*	III, 1 (Masetto)
III, 1 (Masetto da Lamperocchio)	II, 7 (Alatiel) *I, 1 (Ciappelletto)*	VII, 2 (Peronella)
IV, 5 (Lisabetta da Messina and Lorenzo ; basil)	III, 1	I, 1 (Ciappelletto). *Episode interrupted premonition of death (pastiches of Bruegel).*
V, 4 (Caterina da Valbona and Ricciardo Manardì, the nightingale)	I, 1	*II- Giotto's disciple* VI, 5 (Forese and the artist)

APPENDIX 2

Order of the adapted tales in Boccaccio's text	Order of the adapted tales as originally planned in the filmscript (2 versions)	Order of the adapted tales in the final version of the film
		Artist's arrival at Santa Chiara, Naples. Preparation of wall by assistants: large blank panel on which the artist begins to paint. Ext. Street: artist observes onlookers, forming frame with fingers. Int. Church: preparation of colors, then artist paints.
VI, 5 (Messer Forese da Rabatta and maestro Giotto)	II-Chichibio	V, 4 ("the nightingale") Convent: meal interrupted by artist's inspiration. Painting sky (Giotto's blue).
VII, 2 (Peronella)	III, 2 (Agilulf and the groom) IV, 8 (Girolamo and Salvestra)	IV, 5 (the basil) Ext. Cattle fair. Artist observes crowd and sees peasant kissing mare.
VII, 10 (Tingoccio Mini and Meuccio di Tura)	III, 10 (Alibech and Rustico) III, 10	IX, 10 (the mare) Pastiche of some paintings by Bruegel. Artist working on scaffolding, then Ext. Shot of marketplace Santa Chiara.
IX, 2 (Isabetta and abbess; the sinful nuns)	IV, 4 (Gerbino) IV, 5 (Lisabetta da Messina)	VII, 10 (Tingoccio and Meuccio) Episode interrupted by vision of Meuccio/artist: pastiche of 2 frescoes by Giotto: Madonna and Last Judgment. Int. Church: scaffolding removed: first two panels completed, celebration of artist and assistants. Artist's last words: "Perché realizzare un'opera, quando è così bello sognarla soltanto?"
IX, 10 (Donno Gianni di Barolo, Pietro da Tresanti and his wife, Gemmata, the mare)	IV, 5 V, 4 (Caterina and Ricciardo)	

Appendix 2

Order of the adapted tales in Boccaccio's text	Order of the adapted tales as originally planned in the filmscript (2 versions)	Order of the adapted tales in the final version of the film
	V, 4 *VI, 4 (Chichibio)*	
	VI, 4	
	III-Giotto VI, 5 (Forese and Giotto) *VII, 2 (Peronella)*	
	VII, 2 VII, 10 (Tingoccio and Meuccio)	
	X, 3 (Natan and Mitridanes) *IX, 10 (the mare)*	
	IX, 10 (the mare)	
	Epilogue: Giotto and his fresco.	

Appendix 3: Chart Showing Echoes and Correspondences Between *I Racconti di Canterbury* and *The Decameron*

	Racconti di Canterbury	The Decameron
Types and characters	Actress Proserpina (naked) and actor Pluto (naked) in *The Merchant's Tale*.	Actress Caterina (naked) (V, 4) and actor Lorenzo (IV, 5).
	Januarie chooses wife by catching glimpse of her backside (*The Merchant's Tale*).	When he sees Gemmata's low-necked gown, Don Gianni decides to reveal secret magic trick (IX, 10).
	Franco Citti/demon in FriT (grave and somber).	Franco Citti/Ciappelletto (iniquitous and somber in I, 1).
	Nino Davoli/Perkyn/Chaplin (tracked down by cops: race in speeded-up motion) (*The Cook's Tale*).	Nino Davoli/Andreuccio smells red flower (echo to Chaplin's mustache) and tracked down by hoodlums of Naples: scene in speeded-up motion and race of bitten sexton in speeded-up motion (II, 5).
	Richly dressed archdeacon in FriT.	Bishop with fine attributes in I, 1 (funeral of "saint") and Ciappelletto's vision (pastiche

Appendix 3

	Racconti di Canterbury	The Decameron
		of Bruegel) and dead bishop in grave (II, 5).
	Bride and wedding party, dancing, music (*The Cook's Tale*).	Bride (Zita, Gemmata's neighbor) and wedding party, dancing, music (IX, 10).
	Effeminate Friar John (*The Summoner's Tale*).	The two *fraticelli* gaping at artist at work in Santa Chiara and thieving sexton's womanly voice (II, 5).
Actions, attitudes	Hops and comic dance of Januarie after (pathetic) sexual performance (*The Merchant's Tale*).	Hops and comic dance in church of Andreuccio covered in excreta but rich (ruby).
	Wife of Bath bites Jankyn's nose (*The Wife of Bath's Prologue*).	Andreuccio bites sexton's leg (II, 5).
	Wife of Bath and fourth husband on top of her, exhausted (opening scene in conjugal bed) (*The Wife of Bath's Prologue*).	Abbess and Masetto, exhausted, in same position (frontal shot) (III, 1).
	Funeral 4th husband and wedding with Jankyn quickened (*The Wife of Bath's Prologue*).	Wedding Ricciardo (good match) and Caterina quickened by girl's parents (V, 4).
	The Flood stratagem: Nicholas, Alisoun, John in kneading-troughs (*The Miller's Tale*).	Andreuccio in cesspit then barrel (II, 5) and Gennaio then Peronella's husband in jar (VII, 2).
	Sinner/preacher (Rufo) urinates on customers in tavern (PardP/T).	Lisabetta's three brothers invite Lorenzo to urinate with them in garden (IV, 5).
Songs, music	Neapolitan complaint ("Fenest' ca luciv'è") sung by Pardoner (prologue).	Same complaint sung by Ciappelletto and usurers in Germany (nostalgia of Naples) (I, 1).
	Religious song in background during conversation demon/summoner (FriT).	Religious song (different) during Ciappelletto's vision (Bruegel) (I, 1)
	Hymn sung by Nicholas (*The Miller's Tale*), then by Aleyn and John (*The Reeve's Tale*) (announces earthly delights to come: "Make pliable that which is rigid for everlasting pleasure").	Hymn sung (differently) by choir of angels around Madonna in artist's vision (pastiche of Giotto) (VII, 10).
	Bells ringing in Canterbury cathedral (epilogue).	Bells ringing at sunrise when Caterina's married to her dear "nightingale" (V, 4) and bells

	Racconti di Canterbury	The Decameron
		rung by abbess who exclaims "Miracle!" (III, 1) / by the two *fraticelli* celebrating completion of second fresco panel.
Figure of the artist	Between FrT and *The Cook's Tale*, pilgrims asleep. Chaucer writes: "Notes for a book about the pilgrims' tales. The cook's tale." By his side, naked boy lying stroking cat.	Artist working with young and good-looking assistants (complicity). Comical scene in speeded-up motion in which artist eats hurriedly to resume work (exalted). Puts some blue paint on a boy's nose for fun.
	Chaucer at his desk surrounded by books: derisive representation of artist fast asleep instead of working. Woken up by bossy wife ("Geoffrey Chaucer!"). Bumps head (as he bumped his nose against Cook's nose in prologue).	Giotto's disciple receives inspiration (during meal at Santa Chiara convent) and vision (fast asleep in dormitory). Paints frenetically, then wonders about purpose of art ("Perché realizzare un'opera quando è così bello sognarla soltanto?").
Tableaux vivants	*Netherlandish Proverbs* by Bruegel (*The Reeve's Tale*).	Pastiche of four paintings by Bruegel:*Children's Games, Triumph of Death, Battle of Carnival and Lent, Land of Cockaigne* in Ciappelletto's vision (I, 1).
	Hell in *Seven Deadly Sins* by Bosch (*The Summoner's Prologue*).	Pastiche of two frescoes by Giotto: *Last Judgment* (choir of angels) and *Ognissanti Madonna* (marial sublime rendered by Silvana Mangano's diaphanous beauty).
Motifs	Januarie's garden (*The Merchant's Tale*) (cold, damp) and flute played by divinity that heralds presence Pluto and Proserpina.	Sunny and lush Mediterranean gardens (III, 1, V, 4, IV, 5) and cicadas singing (III, 1).
	Januarie to Placebo and Justinius: "Get stuffed!" (*The Merchant's Tale*).	Thief to Andreuccio inside grave, when the latter refuses to hand him ruby: "Get stuffed!," and closes lid (II, 5).
	Students' horse (*The Reeve's Tale*) let loose by Symkyn (unbridled sexual desire).	Pietro sells mare at market (animal desire for Gemmata felt by Don Gianni when sees her) (IX, 10).
	Frontal shots of beds (with diamond-shaped motifs on blankets in the	Frontal shots of beds (with same motifs on blankets) in

Racconti di Canterbury	The Decameron
Vasarely style) in *The Merchant's Tale*, *The Cook's Tale*, *The Miller's Tale*, *The Wife of Bath's Prologue*, *Pardoner's Prologue and Tale*, *The Summoner's Tale*.	II, 5, I, 1, V, 4, IV, 5, IX, 10, VII, 10.

Notes

Introduction

1. We refer to Boccacio's work as *Il Decameron* to distinguish it from Pasolini's adaptation, which will be called *The Decameron*.
2. Claude Perrus, "*Le Décaméron* de Boccace," *La nouvelle: Boccace, Marguerite de Navarre, Cervantès*. Etudes recueillies par J. Bessière et Ph. Daros (Coll. Unichamp, 54), 1996, p. 50. Claude Perrus points out that the term *Centovelle* is commonly used to refer to Boccaccio's *Decameron*.
3. This Italian word means "frame." Here it refers to the frame story.
4. André Bazin, "*Le journal d'un curé de campagne* et la stylistique de Robert Bresson" (1951), *Qu'est-ce que le cinéma?* (1958) 1994, p. 126. Writing about adaptations, Bazin defines the film version as "un être esthétique nouveau qui est comme le roman multiplié par le cinéma"—"a new aesthetic being which, in a way, finds itself multiplied by cinema."
5. R.W. Hanning, "'And countrefete the speche of every man / He koude, whan he sholde telle a tale': Toward a Lapsarian Poetics for *The Canterbury Tales*," *Studies in the Age of Chaucer*, vol. 21, 1999, pp. 29–30.
6. *The Middle English Dictionary*, ed. Hans Kurath et al. (Ann Arbor: University of Michigan Press, 1954–), vol. F3, pp. 687–88. Quoted by R.W. Hanning, *ibid*, p. 32.
7. Derek Pearsall, *The Canterbury Tales* (1983), 1995, introduction, p. xii.
8. Pasolini in "Io e Boccaccio," interview with Dario Bellezza, published in *L'Espresso colore* 47 (November 24, 1970). Quoted in *Pier Paolo Pasolini: La Trilogia della vita. Le sceneggiature originali de* Il Decameron, I Racconti di Canterbury, Il Fiore delle mille e una notte, Garzanti: 1995, p. 27.
9. The notion of "commodification," conceived by Karl Marx, refers to the exploitation of the human body by the capitalist system, which reduces it to a consumer good.
10. Diego Rodriguez de Silva y Velázquez. He was a 17th century painter, famous for his *Meninas* (1656). Three centuries later, in 1957, Pablo Picasso humorously questioned this masterpiece of the past.

Chapter 1

1. Pasolini in *Had* 11, 1972, quoted by Jean Sémolué, in "Après *Le Décameron* et *Les Contes de Canterbury*: réflexions sur le récit chez Pasolini, "*Etudes cinématographiques II. Pasolini: un "cinéma de poésie*," 112/114, 1977, p. 50: "C'est le mystère passionnant de ce film. J'aimerais consacrer une étude à ce sujet parce que le montage des *Canterbury Tales* a vraiment été une chose folle. Il y a eu mille combinaisons avant de trouver celle qui me satisfaisait sur le plan rythmique."
2. Gianni Canova, preface to *Pier Paolo Pasolini: la Trilogia della vita. Le sceneggiature originali de* Il Decameron, I Racconti di Canterbury, Il Fiore delle mille e una notte, Garzanti: 1995, p. 30.
3. Laura Mulvey, "Visual Pleasure and

Narrative Cinema" (1975), *Film Theory and Criticism*, 1992 (4th ed.), p. 748. Scopophilia, she explains, is defined by Freud (in *Three Essays on Sexuality*) as: "...one of the component instincts of sexuality which exist as drives quite independently of the erotogenic zones. At this point, he associated scopophilia with taking other people as objects, subjecting them to a controlling and curious gaze.... At the extreme, it can become fixated into a perversion, producing obsessive voyeurs and Peeping Toms, whose only sexual satisfaction can come from watching ... an objectified other." According to Laura Mulvey, while satisfying the basic desire to see, cinema amplifies the scopophilic phenomenon in its most narcissistic aspect. Among "the pleasurable structures of looking in the conventional cinematic situation, the first, scopophilic, arises from pleasures using another person as an object of sexual stimulation through sight," she writes (p. 750).

4. Jill M. Ricketts, *Visualizing Boccaccio: Studies of* The Decameron, *from Giotto to Pasolini*, 1997, p. 120. About the modes of vision adopted by Pasolini in his *Decameron*, Ricketts writes: "In order to make this point, we need to explore how vision and the scopic drive, two fundamental elements of the homosexual "cruising" gaze, relate to the "eye" of the camera and viewership in Pasolini's cinema." The scopic drive is also noticeable in *Racconti di Canterbury*.

5. Gianni Canova, *op. cit.*, 1995, p. 15. He uses the word *spettacolarità*.

6. Pasolini, *op. cit.*, p. 244. He writes: "Il grande quadro realistico medioevale, che preannuncia i Fiamminghi, rappresenta ora il cortile interno della Locanda di Southwark."

7. Mikhail Bakhtin, *Rabelais and his World* (trans. Helene Islowsky), Cambridge: Massachusetts Institute of Technology, 1965, foreword, p. x.

8. Jean Sémolué, *op. cit.*, 1977, pp. 150–51.

9. In the DVD version, the modern–English subtitles read as follows: "Between a jest and a joke many a truth can be told."

10. Claude Perrus, *op. cit.*, p. 50. He explains that Boccaccio uses the word *novella* in the sense of a short fiction narrative. "Originally, *novella* describes both a new event and the oral account of it. The meaning extends to written telling/narration (like the "Occitan" *novas* in verse), then in Italy to a short prose narrative distinct from verse." Moreover, the Author of *Il Decameron* uses four different words in his *Proemio* to refer to the 100 stories, characterized by a stunning variety of narrative forms: "...intendo di raccontare cento novelle, o favole o parabole o istorie...."

11. Pasolini, *Le Monde* (December 5, 1972). Interview with Colette Godard. Quoted by Jean Sémolué, *op. cit.*, 1977, p. 154.

12. It is a hymn translated into English in the DVD version as: "Make pliable that which is rigid for everlasting pleasure." The pleasure Aleyn and John have in mind is carnal pleasure, of course. The same hymn is sung by the choir of angels surrounding the Virgin in the vision inspired from Giotto's *Last Judgment* at the end of *The Decameron*.

13. *The Friar's Tale*, 1321–74 (53 lines!)

14. The homosexual burns on the stake before the crowd as well as the church dignitaries, especially the Archdeacon, the summoner's "employer." Significantly, the scene takes place in the courtyard of Canterbury cathedral.

15. *The Friar's Tale*, 1656–64: "Herketh this word! Beth war, as in this case: / "The leoun sit in his awayt alway / To sle the innocent, if that he may." / Disposeth ay youre hertes to withstonde / The feend, that yow wolde make thral and bonde. / He may nat tempte yow over youre myght, / For Crist wol be youre champion and knyght. / And prayeth that thise somonours hem repente / Of hir mysdedes, er that the feend hem hente!"

16. *The Summoner's Tale*, 1873–1947 (74 lines!).

17. Seneca/Senek speaks of an infuriated judge (« an irous potestat," 2017), of Cambises the drunkard, king of Persia, and of Cyrus his son. See 2017–84.

18. *The Summoner's Tale*, 2152–2294. This constitutes one-quarter of the text, which amounts to 142 lines out of the 585 that make up the whole tale.

19. Hieronymus Bosch (c. 1450–1516), *Tabletop of The Seven Deadly Sins and the Four Last Things* (oil on panel, 120 × 150, Prado, Madrid). Among the four stages in human life, Pasolini pastiches one particular scene, *The Damned Punished in Hell*, that depicts the abominable fate of the damned in the netherworld. The topic recurs in a different fashion in some of the artist's other paintings, such as in the right wing of *The Last Judgment* (oil on panel, 163.7 × 60, Akademie der bildenden Künste, Vienna), *The Fall of the Damned* and *Hell* (oil on panel, 86.5 × 13.3, Palace of the Doges, Venice), a fragment of another *Last Judgment* (oil on panel, 60 × 114, Alte Pinakothek, Munich), or the famous infernal vision, the central image of which, some believe, is a self-portrait of the artist (*The Treeman and Buildings Burning in Hell*), right wing (220 × 97) of *The Garden of Earthly Delights* triptych (oil on panel, 220 × 195, Prado, Madrid).

20. Gianni Canova, preface to *Pier Paolo Pasolini: la Trilogia della vita. Le sceneggiature*

originali de Il Decameron, I Racconti di Canterbury, Il Fiore delle mille e una notte, 1995, p. 30. "Put together in this fashion, the Canterbury Tales outline something like a parable on the theme of seeing and failing to see."

21. Michel Foucault, *Histoire de la sexualité III. Le souci de soi*, 1984, p. 186: "...le plus sûr véhicule de la passion."

22. Pasolini, *Le Sceneggiature...*, 1995, p. 334. He pictures his character as follows: "... fitto come quello di un orso: è anche grosso e goffo come un orso: con l'occhio matto e sanguigno che gli scintilla sul naso rosso."

23. Danièle Régnier-Bohler, "L'amour courtois a-t-il existé?," *L'Histoire (Dossier: Le sexe et le plaisir en Occident)*, 180, Septembre 1994, p. 47.

24. Jacques Le Goff, "le refus du plaisir," *Collections de l'histoire (Dossier: l'amour et la sexualité)* H.S. 5, Juin 1999, pp. 36–37.

25. Michel Foucault, *op. cit.*, 1984, p. 284. This kind of appetite is called "pothos" in ancient Greek, meaning "need, want."

27. Michel Foucault, *Histoire de la sexualité I. La volonté de savoir*, 1976, p. 52. "Dans l'ordre civil, comme dans l'ordre religieux, ce qui était pris en compte, c'était un illégalisme d'ensemble."

28. Jacques Rossiaud, "Comment l'Eglise a mis les sodomites hors la loi," *L'Histoire (Dossier: Enquête sur un tabou: les homosexuels en Occident)*, 221, Mai 1998, p. 38. He writes: "Ce qui compte et ce qui est condamné, ce sont des actes."

29. *Ibid*, p. 42.

30. A film by Charles Chaplin made in 1925. United Artists, U.S.A. (Black and white, silent movie).

31. Although it has been censored over the centuries, sex is not systematically nor blindly repressed. "The law is a component of desire," states Foucault, *HS I*, p. 108. He examines the relationship between power and sex, and writes a history of the discourse on sex since the late 16th century. Instead of repression, which is a far too generally accepted surmise, his argument rests upon an endeavor to figure out what produces discourse, power and knowledge. Sexual intercourse is the target aimed at by power in its attempt to control people's lives. By means of a complex sexuality device, it has submitted individuals to the stern monarchy of sex since the 19th century, hence the want for a different theory of power. The body and pleasures are monopolized, the subject's social life is overrun. Consequently sex is thought as a law and an interdict. Yet, Foucault claims, it should be considered "without the law, and power without the king" (120). Nevertheless, in the Middle Ages, power is viewed in terms of a death menace much more than a way to perpetuate human life.

32. Jacques Le Goff, *op. cit.*, Juin 1999, p. 36. "...justifier la répression de la plus grande partie des pratiques sexuelles."

33. Michel Foucault, *HS III. Le souci de soi*, 1984, p. 183.

34. *Ibid*, pp. 186–87. The rejection of sensual pleasure represents the keystone of Christian ethics which, since Saint Augustine, has reduced original sin to lust, a most comprehensive term describing all forms of the sin of the flesh. Despite the indissociable link between sex and lechery, marriage constitutes a last resort, inasmuch as it is the spiritualization of carnal relationship. It redeems the body for it epitomizes God's love. For its sacramental nature, marriage in fact revives the essential question of the place of sexuality within the limits of law and theology. Foucault writes: "Il y a toute une technique de l'image à organiser pour et contre l'amour."

35. In the ancient Greek conception, desire is kindled by the sight of a beautiful human being, either male or female, according to a vision of love that is not bisexual. Plutarch introduces noticeable changes in ancient erotics in defining one single Eros, which takes into account attraction for male youths and women alike. In addition, he integrates the *aphrodisia* in this new "monistic" stylistics of love (Foucault, *HS II*, 279). The erotics of youths, which gave birth to a subtle cultural construct in Greece, inspires a general form of love, both homosexual and heterosexual. Throughout the centuries, the moral reflection on the use of pleasures gradually focuses on women until it reaches a special degree of the stylization of love in the *fin'amor* conception.

36. Jacques Le Goff, "Le refus du plaisir," *Collections de l'Histoire (Dossier: L'amour et la sexualité)*, H.S. 5, Juin 1999, p. 37: "Diabolisation, au Moyen Age, de la chair et du corps, assimilés à un lieu de débauche, au centre de production du péché, qui enlèvera au contraire toute dignité au corps."

37. In this perspective then, the heterosexuality/homosexuality antinomy is no longer valid. Michel Foucault refers to ancient Greek ethics characterized by a stylistics of the love of youths. The specific type of amorous relationships implies the presence of a full-grown man or *éraste* and his young lover or *éromène* (Foucault, *HS II*, 252). Their relationship is ritualized by a whole set of conventional conducts that determine their respective roles. The male adult is to exert mastery and authority over his partner and himself, in accordance with being the lord of the house (which goes hand in hand with his more or less prominent position in the

life of the city). On the contrary, the passivity of the slave or prostitute, used as a material good, is viewed as degrading and loses any moral and aesthetic legitimacy. The diverse portrayals of medieval sexuality sketched by Pasolini seem to mirror the Greek assimilation of the pattern of sexual practises with that of "the field of social conflicts and hierarchies" (Foucault, HS II, 279).

38. "E uno di quelli che hanno il coito veloce e impaziente come galli. Infatti eiacula subito," which means "He is one of those with a coitus that comes too quickly just like roosters. Therefore he ejaculates in no time."

39. In Histoire de la sexualité III (Le souci de soi), 1984, 156–57, Foucault mentions the phenomenon of "gonorrhea" or "seminis effusion," which refers to the principle of life "wasting away through sex." He quotes the Greek authorities that describe coitus as a mechanical violence, "the giving up of a whole part of what contains a human being. This is how Aristotle explains the *patent* exhaustion that follows sex" ("abandon de toute une part de ce qui contient un être même. C'est ainsi qu'Aristote explique l'abattement *patent* qui suit le rapport sexuel," HS II, 175–76).

40. "Amore mio, mia tenera colombella, fiorellino mio profumato" (*Sceneggiature*, 390).

41. Jacques Le Goff, "Le refus du plaisir," *Collections de l'Histoire* (Dossier: *L'amour et la sexualité*), H.S. 5 Juin 1999, p. 39: "La notion de péché contre-nature (qui) va se dilater au Moyen Age avec l'extension du concept de sodomie (homosexualité, sodomisation de la femme, coït par derrière, ou la femme se tenant au-dessus de l'homme seront proscrits)."

42. Michel Foucault, HS III, p. 183: "Une subordination aussi stricte que possible du désir de l'âme aux besoins du corps, une éthique du désir qui se modèle sur une physique des excrétions."

43. Michel Foucault, HS III, 140: "De là la possibilité d'équivalence entre la possession d'un corps et la possession des richesses."

44. In the filmscript, the dialogue kept in the final version of the movie remains very close to that of *The Miller's Tale*, 3277–81: "And seyde, 'Ywis, but if ich have my wille, / For derne love of thee, lemman, I spille.' / ...Lemman, love al me atones, / Or I wol dyen, also God me save!." ... In modern English, the DVD translation says: "Alison, if I can't love you now, my passion for you will kill me."

45. The DVD English translation for: "Che siamo peggio dei fratei! Sempre col coso dritto!" (279).

46. Rose-Marie and Rainer Hagen, *Pieter Bruegel l'Ancien vers 1529-1569: Paysans, fous,* *et démons*, Cologne: Taschen, 1994, p. 37: "deux qui chient par le même trou."

47. Pieter Bruegel the Elder, *The Netherlandish Proverbs*, 1559. Oil panel, 117 × 163 cm. Berlin, Staatliche Museum zu Berlin — Preussischer Kulturbesitz, Gemäldegalerie. This famous painting is also known as *The Blue Cloak*.

48. As Aleyn asks John in the modern English version (DVD): "Te la faresti una bella chiavata...," *Sceneggiature*, p. 279.

49. Geoffrey Chaucer, *The Reeve's Tale*, 3973–976: "This wenche thikke and wel ygrowen was, / With kamus nose and eyen greye as glas, / With buttokes brode and brestes rounde and hye. / But right fair was hire heer; I wol nat lye."

50. "Se dovunque vada, a piedi o a cavallo, sarò sempre il tuo studente" (*Sceneggiature*, 288). "But evermo, wher so I go or ryde, / I is thyn awen clerk, swa have I seel!" (*The Reeve's Tale*, 4238–239). The DVD translation is as follows: "Farewell, Molly, it's dawn and I must go, but I'll always be your student."

51. *The Reeve's Tale*, 4220: "Now, deere lemman," quod she, "go, far weel!" The Italian cue in the filmscript and the DVD is: "Amore mio caro, va, adio!" (*Sceneggiature*, 288).

52. *The Reeve's Tale*, 4241–246.

53. "...Mia dolce Alison? Mio vago uccellino, mio dolce fiore..." (*Sceneggiature*, p. 269). This corresponds to *The Miller's Tale*, 3698–700: "...honey-comb, sweete Alisoun, / My faire bryd, my sweete cynamome? / ... lemman myn...."

54. *The Miller's Tale*, 3337–338: "...He was somdeel squaymous / Of fartyng and of speche daungerous."

55. Jacques Rossiaud, "La sexualité de l'homme médiéval," in *L'Histoire* (Dossier: *Le sexe et le plaisir en Occident*), 180, Septembre 1994, p. 32: "Une représentation de l'amour et des relations sexuelles incarnée par les fées, les châtelaines qui séduisent le chevalier en quête d'aventures, ou encore les 'pucelles' que les seigneurs offrent à leur visiteur."

56. "Che bel' culetto!" in the script and the movie. This cheeky remark echoes the words uttered by the man in the stocks as he is watching the Wife of Bath walk past in a hurry. He says exactly the same thing.

57. The Italian version of the DVD says: "Tieni, prendi questo, donna mandata dal diavolo ad accendere il fuoco della lussuria. ... Viziosa cosa è il vino, e l'ubriachezza è causa di travagli e di sventure" (*Sceneggiature*, 391). Then, turning to the gamblers, he goes on: "E adesso che vi ho detto della crapula, vi metterò in guardia contro il giocco. Il giocco è il padre della menzogna e dell'inganno, del

maledetto turpiloquio e della bestemmia di Cristo!" (392).

58. Georges Bataille, *L'érotisme,* (1957) 1987, p. 238.

59. "Ainsi l'avachissement d'une immense dérision envahit-il le coeur sans plus d'angoisse, librement. Il suffit pour cela de voler, s'il le faut de tuer, paresseusement de conserver sa vie en ménageant ses forces, en tout cas de vivre aux dépens d'autrui" (Bataille, 238).

60. "Même la morale n'éleva les humbles que pour l'accabler (la classe déchue) davantage. La malédiction de l'Eglise s'appesantit plus lourdement sur l'humanité affaissée" (Bataille, 137).

61. Gianni Canova, preface to *Pier Paolo Pasolini: La Trilogia della vita. Le sceneggiature originali de* Il Decameron, I Racconti di Canterbury, Il Fiore delle Mille e una notte, 1995, p. 18.

62. Michel Leiris, *le ruban au cou d'Olympia,* collection l'Imaginaire, Gallimard, 1981, p. 248.

63. Georges Bataille, *L'érotisme,* p. 215: "Qui exclut radicalement le désordre des sens, ... nie son principe naturel, ... élève ses valeurs à l'abri de la violence et de la saleté des passions."

64. Gianni Canova, *op. cit.,* p. 18: "...la tragedia del nostro essere borghesi è sempre la stessa: *siamo tutti qui.* Piccoli, piccoli, avidi, immemori. Cacciati dall'Eden di Eros da una gigantesca flatulenza infernale."

65. The filmscript says: "Che son così pratica nel tessere stoffe da vincere quelle di Ypres e di Gand" (*Sceneggiature,* 245).

66. To some extent, the Wife could be said to prefigure Bruegel the Elder's famous Dulle Griet. Armed to the teeth, she is on her way to the conquest of Hell. She is usually considered as the embodiment of avidity because she is shown taking loot away with her. She is the well-known fearsome figure of a painting by Bruegel: *Dulle Griet,* c. 1562 (oil on panel, 117, 4 × 162 cm. Anvers, Museum Mayer van den Bergh).

67. The character of the beggar in *Accattone* (1961) already strikes up this very couplet. An amazing continuity can be traced throughout Pasolini's film work. Actually it is a Neapolitan folk song that says: "Fenest'ca luci'e mmo' nu' luce / sign'è ca nenna mia starrà malata. / S'affaccia la surella e mme lu dice: / Nennella toi' è mmorta e s'è atterrata. / Piagneva sempe ca dormeva sola, / Mo' dorme cu' li morti accumpagnata." The English translation found in the DVD goes as follows: "The window that once glowed with light is now darkened / Her sister comes to the window and tells me: 'Your beloved is dead and buried.' / She always lamented that she slept alone. Now she sleeps in the arms of death."

68. Pasolini, *Ecrits sur le cinéma: Pier Paolo Pasolini* (preceded by *Genèse d'un penseur hérétique* by Hervé Joubert-Laurencin), P.U. de Lyon, 1987, pp. 134–35. Pasolini wrote this text as a presentation of a record by Ennio Morricone. (Taken up by Bertini in *Teoria e tecnica del film in Pasolini,* Bulzoni, 1979): "(au) caractère essentiellement poétique, c'est-à-dire empirique."

Chapter 2

1. Gianni Canova, preface to *Pier Paolo Pasolini: Trilogia della vita. Le sceneggiature originali de* Il Decameron, I Racconti di Canterbury, Il Fiore delle Mille e una notte, 1995, p. 12: "Una musica visiva."

2. Pasolini in "Le regole di un' illusione," Associazione "Fondo Pier Paolo Pasolini," Roma, 1991, p. 252. Quoted by Gianni Canova, *ibid,* p. 26: "Si tratta di un film corale, che si è rifiutato decisamente di essere un film "a episodi...."

3. "...in tanto che molte volte nelle cose da lui fatte si truova che il visovo senso degli uomini vi prese errore, quello credendo esser vero che era dipinto."

4. Patrick Rumble, *Allegories of Contamination: Pier Paolo Pasolini's Trilogy of Life,* 1996, p. 35.

5. Pasolini in *Empirismo eretico* (Milano: Garzanti, 1972), 128–29; *Heretical Empiricism,* trans. L.K. Barnett and B. Lawton (Bloomington and Indianapolis: Indiana University Press, 1988), 123–24. Quoted by Patrick Rumble, *ibid.* The Italian original text reads as follows, p. 10: "La riproduzione audiovisiva della realtà è una lingua o un linguaggio identico in Italia o in Francia, nel Ghana o negli Stati Uniti. ... le stuture della lingua del cinema si presentano dunque più che come internazionali e interclassiste, come transnazionali e transclassiste...."

6. For Pasolini, Naples represents an oasis of pure sensuality, very close to man's religious roots. In *Canzione italiano,* Bologna, Guanda, 1955, p. xci, he expresses his passion for a people unable to live without the sun and the hubbub in the alleys and shops, a rough world in which they try to survive through petty larceny in a constant atmosphere of sensuous, almost religious excitement. Pasolini refers to Neapolitans, whose musicality of the language he is very receptive to, as a "tribe" (in the noble sense of the word) that refuses the New Power, what is called History, modernity. He finds this negation of History sound and fair. Therefore, one understands the significance of Naples as a topos with a specific meaning in Pasolini's

mind. The South, symbolized by Naples as well as the people, the archaic and the sacred constitute one of the major poles in Pasolini's film and poetic work.

7. Salman Rushdie quoted by Patrick Rumble, *op. cit.*, p. 13.

8. Pasolini in *EE*, 129; *HE*, 124 quoted by Rumble, *ibid*, p. 11. Here is the Italian original, p. 10: "...una possibile situazione sociolinguistica di un mondo reso tendenzialmente unitario dalla completa industrializzazione e dal conseguente livellamento implicante la scomparsa delle tradizioni particolaristiche e nazionali."

9. "...si simile a quella, che non simile, anzi piu tosto dessa paresse...," (*Decameron*, vol. 2, 737).

10. The first draft of the script of *Il Decameron* meant, in addition to the 10 *novelle* of the final version, to adapt the comic adventures of Martellino (II, 1), Chichibio (VI, 4), Agilulfo (III, 2), and the young monk Rustico who teaches the pretty, artless Alibech how "to put the devil back into Hell" (III, 10). However, Pasolini also intended to screen another three narratives belonging to a much nobler genre: those of Alatiel (II, 7), Gerbino (IV, 4), and Natan and Mitridanes (X, 3). Then a second shorter version of the movie planned to suppress the following episodes: II, 1; II, 7; III, 2; IV, 4; and X, and add an extra tragic-sounding story on the thwarted love of Girolamo and Salvestra (IV, 8). Eventually II, 10, IV, 4, and VI, 4 are dropped. Pasolini instead chooses VII, 10 (Tingoccio and Meuccio), and moves the story of Peronella (VII, 2) from Part II to Part I of the movie.

11. Jacques Aumont, *L'œil interminable: cinéma et peinture*, 1989, p. 220: "Jusqu'à la fin de la Renaissance au moins, on croit à une action magique, à une influence vivante de l'image."

12. Jill M. Ricketts, *Visualizing Boccaccio: Studies on Illustrations of* The Decameron *from Giotto to Pasolini*, 1997, chapter 5: "Living Pictures. High Art Pastiche and the Cruising Gaze in Pasolini's *Decameron*," pp. 118–64.

13. Pasolini in *EE*, 85; *HE*, 79, quoted by Patrick Rumble, *op. cit.*, 1996, p. 15.

14. Pasolini, *Sceneggiature*, p. 773: "L'Italia cioè non sta vivendo altro che un processo di addatamento alla propria degradazione, da cui cerca di liberarsi solo nominalmente."

15. "Ma se pur prosuppor si volesse che io fossi stato di quelle e lo 'nventore e lo scrittore, che non fui...."

16. "...Estimai che quegli medesimi non stesser male nelle mie novelle, scritte per cacciar la malincolia delle femine" (1260).

17. "Confesso nondimeno le cose di questo mondo non avere stabilità alcuna ma sempre essere in mutamento, e cosi potrebbe della mia lingua essere intervenuto; la quale, non credendo io al mio giudizio, il quale a mio potere io fuggo nelle mie cose..." (1261).

18. Pasolini, "l'Abiura," *Sceneggiature*, p. 773: "Tutti si sono adattati o attraverso il non voler accorgersi di niente o attroverso la più inerte sdrammatizzazione."

19. *Ibid*, p. 773: "Ma devo ammettere che anche l'essersi accorti o l'aver drammatizzato non preserva affatto dall'adattamento o dall'accettazione. Dunque io mi sto adattando alla degradazione e sto accetando l'inaccettibile."

20. *Ibid*, p. 773–74: "Manovro per risistemare la mia vita. Sto dimenticando com'erano *prima* le cose. Le amate facce di ieri cominciano a ingiallire. Mi è davanti — pian piano senza più alternative — il presente. Riadatto il mio impegno ad una maggiore leggibilità (*Salò?*)."

21. Pieter Bruegel the Elder, *The Parable of the Blind*, 1568. Naples, Museo Nazionale di Capodimonte. (Oil, 86 × 156 cm).

22. This cue does not appear in the film script, in which the story is narrated in greater detail with no dialogues at all (Pasolini, *Sceneggiature*, pp. 114–15).

23. The equation with the comic figure of Chaplin in his silent movies is also suggested in the scene, where facing his so-called stepsister at the table, Andreuccio inhales the fragrance of a scarlet carnation, which he holds just beneath his nose in place of the famous actor's small mustache.

24. The abbess says: "...so you can stay and satisfy us all without killing yourself" (English subtitles in the DVD version).

25. Pieter Bruegel the Elder, *The Peasant Wedding Dance*, 1566. Oil on panel, 119 × 157 cm. Detroit (MI), The Detroit Institute of Arts, City of Detroit Purchase.

26. He does the same just before V, 4, IV, 5, and IX, 10.

27. Pasolini, *Sceneggiature*, p. 216: "Chi bruccia nel fuoco, chi è messo nell'acqua bollente, chi nel ghiaccio e chi nella merda."

28. *Ibid*, p. 217: "Non tenere paura, stronzo: che qua non si tiene nessun conto delle comari!"

29. Patrick Rumble, *Allegories of Contamination: Pier Paolo Pasolini's* Trilogy of Life, 1996, p. 108.

30. Boccaccio, *Il Decameron*, vol. 1, p. 7–8: "...e oltre a ciò, ristrette da'voleri, da'piaceri, da'commandamenti de'padri, delle madri, de'fratelli e de'mariti, il più del tempo nel piccolo circuito delle loro camere racchiuse dimorano...."

31. Luiz Costa-Lima, *Control of the Imagi-*

nary: Reason and Imagination in Modern Times (Minneapolis: University of Minnesota Press), 1988: 3–34. Cité en note 45 in P. Rumble, *ibid*, p. 116.

32. *Il Decameron*, vol. 2, p. 1259: "...che a voi donne, alle quali tanto del tempo avanza quanto negli amorosi piaceri non ispendete. E oltre a questo, per ciò che né a Atene né a Bologna o a Parigi alcuna di voi non va a studiare più distesamente parlar vi si conviene che a quegli che hanno negli studii gl'ingegni assottigliatti."

33. Pasolini in "Cinema e Literature," *Antaeus* (Winter 1976), 133, quoted by Patrick Rumble, *op. cit.*, p. 107.

34. Patrick Rumble, *op. cit.*, p. 108. He draws from Millicent Marcus, "*The Decameron*: Pasolini as a Reader of Boccacio," *The Italian Quarterly*, 82, as well as from his recent study of *The Decameron* and *Il Vangelo secondo Matteo* in the context of a theoretical debate on the screening of literary work in *Filmmaking by the Book* (Baltimore: Johns Hopkins University Press, 1993).

35. Caterina da Valbona lies to her parents in order to spend the night with Ricciardo on the terrace (V, 4). Lisabetta hides to kiss Lorenzo so as not to be seen by her brothers after their night of passion (IV, 5). The nuns in III, 1 hire Masetto so that he will satisfy each one of them sexually without the others being aware of it at first. Sister Isabetta and the abbess (IX, 2) receive their respective lovers in the secret of their respective cells.

36. Carolyn Dinshaw, "Getting Medieval: Pulp Fiction, Gawain, Foucault," *The Book and the Body*, 1997, p. 147.

37. Carolyn Dinshaw refers to Michel Foucault, especially to the first volume of *Histoire de la sexualité*.

38. Maurizio Viano, *A Certain Realism: Making Use of Pasolini's Film Theory and Practice*, Berkeley: University of California Press, 1993, p. 368.

39. Pasolini as Giotto's disciple playfully puts a touch of blue paint on a young assistant's nose.

40. Pieter Bruegel, *Battle Between Carnival and Lent*, 1559. Oil on panel, 118 × 164.5 cm. Vienna, Kunsthistorisches Museum Wien.

41. Pieter Bruegel, *The Allegory of Hope*, 1559. Drawing, 22 × 29.5. Berlin-Dahlem, Kupferstichkabinet.

42. Pieter Bruegel, *Children's Games*, 1560. Oil panel, 118 × 161, Vienna, Kunsthistorisches Museum.

43. Pieter Breugel, *The Triumph of Death*, c. 1562. Oil on panel, 117 × 162 cm. Madrid, Museo del Prado.

44. Pieter Bruegel, *The Land of Cockaigne*, 1567. Oil on panel, 52 × 78, Munich, Alte Pinakothek.

45. Giotto di Bondone, *Last Judgment*, c. 1305. Scrovegni Chapel, Padova.

46. Giotto di Bondone, *Ognissanti Madonna*, 1310. Uffizi Gallery, Florence.

Chapter 3

1. Pasolini quoted by Patrick Rumble in "Stylistic Contamination in the Trilogy of Life: The Case of Il Fiore," *Pier Paolo Pasolini: Contemporary Perspectives*, 1994, p. 220.

2. René de Ceccatty, "Sur Pier Paolo Pasolini," in *Pier Paolo Pasolini, poète et cinéaste*, 1998, p. 97

3. She is played by the actress Elisabetta Vito Genovese, who is also naked when she is Caterina da Valbona in *The Decameron* (V, 4) and Proserpina in *The Merchant's Tale* sequence of *I Racconti di Canterbury*.

4. The first one explains to the boy that what she is pointing at under the surface of the water is "l'erba aromatica dei ponti" (*Sceneggiature*, p. 731)—"the fragrant grass of the fields." The second girl says it is "il sesamo sbucciato" (732)—"the split pomegranate." Then Munis breaks in with a third metaphor: "l'albergo di Abu Mansur"—"the inn of the hearty welcome." Nur-ed-Din joins in the game by stating that it is now their turn to find a name for his penis, which appears in anamorphosis in the water. This time he is the one who deprives the girls of the power of double entendre. He disarms them by answering: "Si chiama il mulo che pascola l'erba dei ponti, mangia per pranzo il sesamo sbucciato, e passa la notte all' albergo di Abu Mansur" (733)—"It is the colt that grazes the fragrant grass in the fields, eats the pomegranate with a slit in it, and spends the night at the inn of the hearty welcome." The clever boy gets plenty of fond kisses from the three amused girls.

5. Maurizio Viano, *A Certain Realism: Making Use of Pasolini's Film Theory and Practice*, 1993, p. 289.

6. *Il Fiore* is contaminated by an old, unfamiliar figurative model. Pasolini indeed borrows from oriental miniatures of the past that have nothing in common with Western painting. The architecture, settings, costumes and characters' postures are inspired from the exotic and enigmatic Eastern visual arts. Even the "ars erotica" defamiliarizes the spectator. The underlying Eastern iconic references are aimed at shaking, even thwarting "the bourgeois visual angle." "This alien space in the film is embedded within what Stephen Heath (*Questions of Cinema*, Bloomington: Indiana

University Press, 1981) identifies as the "Quattrocento space" in the humanist codification of perspective. This code, which provides the ideological conditions and subjective dispositions for the technical development of the camera, is the perceptual rule that underpins what Pasolini calls the bourgeois *angolo visuale* that continues to establish its hegemony" (Pasolini quoted by Rumble, *op. cit.*, 1994, p. 220). The Western viewer is destabilized by a figural disorientation caused by "the mutilation of certain visual codes" (Gian Pietro Brunetta, *Storia del cinema* (2 vol), Rome: ed. Riuniti, 1979, p. 662, quoted by P. Rumble, *ibid*, p. 216).

7. Pasolini in *Il Tempo*, 1974 (interview), cited by Paul Willemen, "Pasolini on Film," in *Pier Paolo Pasolini*, ed. Paul Willemen (BFI), 1977, p. 74–75.

Chapter 4

1. Gianni Canova, "Prefazione," *Pier Paolo Pasolini: Trilogia della vita. Le sceneggiature originali de* Il Decameron, I Racconti di Canterbury, and Il Fiore delle mille e una notte, 1995, p. 39.

2. Pier Paolo Pasolini in a self-interview published on March 25, 1975, in *Il Corriere della Sera*, quoted by Nico Naldini, *Pier Paolo Pasolini*, 1989. Trans. René de Ceccatty (1991), p. 388: "Un sexe dont la jovialité est une compensation—comme ça l'était en effet—à la répression: phénomène qui allait désormais s'achever à jamais."

3. Pasolini at a congress in Bologna on: "Erotisme, subversion, marchandise," quoted by Nico Naldini, 1989 (Ceccatty, 1991), *ibid*, p. 364: "En refoulant le sexe dans (m)es films, ont refoulé leur contenu et les ont donc trouvés vides, ne comprenant pas que l'idéologie s'y trouvait...."

4. A definition of the word "scandale" found in *Le Petit Robert 1: Dictionnaire de la langue française*, 1990, p. 1773–74: "Incitation à se détourner de Dieu."

5. Pasolini quoted by Naldini, *op. cit.*, 1989 (trans R. de Ceccatty, 1991), p. 364: "Et comme tout aveu est également un défi, une provocation est également contenue dans mon dernier cinéma."

6. Gianni Canova, *op. cit.*, p. 15: "un progetto di *spettacolarità* totalmente agli antipodi rispetto al linguaggio iconico che sarebbe risultato egemone nell'Italia degli anni immediatamente successivi e che avrebbe trovato nella frivola mediocrità del piccolo schermo domestico la sua più piena ed emblematica espressione."

7. Adelio Ferrero, *Il cinema di Pasolini*, Marsilio, Venezia, 1977, p. 126. Quoted by Gianni Canova, *ibid*, p. 14.

8. Lino Micciché, *Cinema italiano: gli anni '60 e oltre*, Marsilio, Venezia, 1995, p. 363. Quoted by Gianni Canova, *ibid*, p. 14–15.

9. E. Jattarelli, "Pornografia a dispense con Il Decamerone," *Il Tempo*, June 30, 1971. Quoted by Canova, ibid, p. 14.

10. Angelina Briosci, quoted by Barth David Schwartz in *Pasolini Requiem*,1992, p. 607.

11. Maurizio Viano, *A Certain Realism: Making Use of Pasolini's Film Theory and Practice*, 1993, p. 271.

12. Jill M. Ricketts, *Visualizing Boccacio: Studies on Illustrations of* The Decameron, *from Giotto to Pasolini*, 1997, p. 130.

13. C. Laurenzi, "*Il Fiore delle mille e una notte*," in *Il Giornale nuovo* of August 30, 1974, p. 16. Quoted by Maurizio Viano, *op. cit.*, p. 286.

14. René Girard, *Je vois tomber Satan comme l'éclair*, 1999, p. 297.

15. *Ibid*, p. 37: "Comme son ombre un obstacle invisible sur lequel il ne cesse de broncher."

16. Ibid, p. 151: "...plongent les communautés dans des crises qui s'exaspèrent de plus en plus jusqu'à l'instant paroxystique où la polarisation unanime contre une victime unique fournit le scandale universel, "l'abscès de fixation," qui apaise la violence et recompose l'ensemble décomposé."

17. Pasolini quoted by Nico Naldini, *op. cit.*, 1989. (Translated by R. de Ceccatty, 1991), p. 402: "Je pense que scandaliser est un droit, être scandalisé un plaisir et que quiconque refuse le plaisir d'être scandalisé est un moraliste."

18. Kevin J. Harty, *The Reel Middle Ages: Films about Medieval Europe*, 1999, p. 125.

19. "Rien de ce qui est osé n'est obscène ici" dans cette "leçon de fidélité à la saveur d'un grand texte."

20. Kevin Harty, about *Novelle galeotte d'amore dal Decamerone* by Antonio Margheriti (1972), *ibid*, p. 198.

21. Thomas Quinn Curtiss, "A Fancy-Free Flight in *Decamerone*," in *The International Herald Tribune* of June 26, 1971.

22. Ibid.

23. Barthélémy Amengual, "Du cinéma porno comme rédemption de la réalité physique » (in *Cinéma d'aujourd'hui*, nouvelle série 4, hiver 1975, pp. 25–32), *Du réalisme au cinéma* (Anthologie établie par Suzanne Liandrat-Guigues), 1997, p. 848: "du côté du sexe" pour "transgresser les tabous culturels," "approcher tout le réel sans contraintes ni barrières, réfuter les mystifications et les leurres de l'idéologie."

24. Amengual, *ibid*, p. 850: "Le porno vérifie la définition que Pier Paolo Pasolini donne du cinéma comme reproduction du langage de l'action."
25. Amengual points out that the uniformity of this kind of cinema is due to the pseudo-diversity of television.
26. Amengual, *op. cit.*, p. 853: "un cinéma du discours, de la déconstruction, de l'*ébranlement*...."
27. Amengual speaks of "actions plus ou moins révolutionnaires qui l'assaillent aussi sur le front culturel."
28. Amengual, *ibid*, p. 848: "entre celui du film scientifique et celui des actualités."
29. In Pasolini's conception, the film camera is laid down facing the world, picking up only bits and pieces of it, already isolated before they are framed by the objective.
30. Alain Bergala, "Pasolini cinéaste," *Cahiers du Cinéma (Hors-série)*, 1981, p. 65: "un cinéma de la révélation au sens rossellinien ou bazinien mais un cinéma condamné à buter sur la sacralité du gros plan, du visage, du détail dilaté."
31. Hervé Joubert-Laurencin, *Pasolini: portrait du poète en cinéaste*, 1995, p. 238: "l'institutionnalisation de l'érotisme et de la transgression de la morale judéo-chrétienne" par le porno et "le marchandage des corps de la société industrielle."

Chapter 5

1. André Gardies, *Le récit filmique*, 1993, p. 55.
2. Francis Vanoye, *Récit écrit, récit filmique*, 1989, p. 137.
3. Vanoye, *ibid*, p. 136: "En fait, personnage littéraire et personnage filmique sont deux signes qui diffèrent par le signifiant (par la substance et la forme de l'expression), et par la forme du contenu."
4. Gardies, *op. cit.*, p. 66: "...participe (alors) de l'activité textuelle et d'un processus complexe de sémiotisation grâce auxquels elle s'enrichit de sens multiples. Dans cette perspective, on voit combien il serait erroné d'analyser le personnage du film comme un simple personnage...."
5. Michel Serceau, *op. cit.*, 1999, p. 98: "La caractérisation, et ... la psychologisation, ... le cède(nt) à l'actantialisation...."
6. Pier Paolo Pasolini, *Accatone, Mamma Roma, Ostia*, Garzanti ed. Gli elefanti (1st edition): 1993, p. 329: "What? have you just seen the devil?"
7. Lillian M. Bisson, *Chaucer and the Late Medieval World*, 1999, p. 99.

8. Johan Huizinga, (*Herfsttij der Middeleeuwen*, Harlem, 1919. Trad. J. Bastin: *Le déclin du Moyen Age*, 1932.) *L'automne du Moyen Age*, 1975, pp. 167–68: "(C)eux qui accomplissent souvent ces voyages deviennent rarement des saints."
9. Pierre d'Ailly, *De Reformatione* in Gerson, opera II, p. 911, quoted by Johan Huizinga, *ibid*, 1975, p. 157–58: "que l'on banisse de l'Eglise les quêteurs d'indulgences qui la souillent de leurs mensonges et la rendent ridicule."
10. Donald R. Howard, *The Idea of the Canterbury Tales*, 1976, p. 403.
11. *Ibid*, p. 99.
12. Marcel Pacaut, *Les ordres monastiques et religieux au Moyen Age*, 1993, p. 160: "l'agencement et le fonctionnement de la vie monastique et religieuse."
13. This film is known in English-speaking countries as *The Flowers of St. Francis*. (Italy, 1950.) *Francis, God's Fool* and *Francis, God's Jester* are alternative titles, as Kevin J. Harty specifies in *The Reel Middle Ages: Films About Medieval Europe*, 1999, p.100.
14. Donald Howard, *op. cit.*, 1976, p. 100.
15. Johan Huizinga, *op. cit.*, 1975, p. 183: "De toutes les contradictions que présente la vie religieuse de cette période, la plus insoluble est peut-être le mépris avoué pour le clergé, mépris qui se concilie, on ne sait comment, avec le très grand respect qu'inspire la sainteté du sacerdoce."
16. In the Wife's allusion in the opening of her tale to the threat posed by friars to girls' chastity, as well as in the somewhat scatological satire of *The Summoner's Prologue* and *The Summoner's Tale*.
17. Pier Paolo Pasolini, *Trilogia della vita: Le sceneggiature originali de* Il Decameron, I Racconti di Canterbury, Il Fiore delle mille e una notte, 1995, p. 393: "the best fucker in Fish Street."
18. Huizinga, *op. cit.*, 1975, p. 87: "une contradiction qui est devenue presque incompréhensible."
19. *Ibid:* "Dans la conscience du moyen âge, se forment, pour ainsi dire l'une à côté de l'autre, deux conceptions de la vie: la conception pieuse, ascétique, attire à elle tous les sentiments moraux; la sensualité, abandonnée au diable, se venge terriblement. Que l'un ou l'autre de ces penchants prédomine, nous avons ou le saint ou le pécheur; mais ils se tiennent en équilibre instable avec d'énormes écarts de la balance."
20. Nicole Gonthier, *Education et cultures dans l'Europe occidentale chrétienne (du XIIe au milieu du XIVe siècles)*, 1998, p. 51 (Note 3): "In 1418 a special police force is set in Venice, the *collegium sodomitarum*, to watch the shady

places and track down the denounced sodomites. In 1432 its Florentine equivalent is created. It is referred to as the night watch or office." Nicole Gonthier draws from Jacques Rossiaud, *La prostitution médiévale*, Paris, Flammarion: 1988, p. 99.

Chapter 6

1. Michel Serceau, *L'adaptation cinématographique des textes littéraires: théories et lectures*, 1999, p. 41: "créer des homologues de l'écriture à partir des possibilités du langage cinématographique."
2. Donald R. Howard, *The Idea of* The Canterbury Tales, 1976, p. 331.
3. Paul Zumthor, *La lettre et la voix: De la "littérature" médiévale*, 1987, p. 347. Editor's note: La "littérature" médiévale fut l'oeuvre de la voix, non de la lettre: ce n'était donc pas une "littérature," encore moins une "écriture" ou un "texte."
4. A manuscript (Cambridge, Corpus Christi 61) mentioned by Donald R. Howard, *op. cit.*, 1976, p. 63: "This quality *voiceness* is what people want to illustrate when they reproduce the famous frontispiece from an early fifteenth-century manuscript of *Troilus* (Cambridge, Corpus Christi 61) showing Chaucer reading aloud to the court."
5. Leo Carruthers, Jacob's Well: *Etudes d'un sermonnaire penitential anglais du XIVe siècle*, 1987, p. 113: "Les *artes praedicandi* recommandent l'emploi d'histoires et de similitudes destinées à alléger un sermon trop lourd, à égayer l'enseignement doctrinal et à pimenter un récit trop banal.... Les anecdotes rendent le texte plus intéressant et lui donnent parfois une certaine drôlerie, mettant en relief les faiblesses humaines."
6. The speech delivered by the old knight in *The Merchant's Tale* actually parodies the verbal sparrings improvised on a specific theme in 12th-century rhetorics.
7. *The Miller's Tale*, 3346–47: "I dar wel seyn, if she hadde been a mous, / and he a cat, he wolde hire hente anon."
8. Lawrence D. Kritzman, *The Rhetoric of Sexuality and the Literature of the French Renaissance*, Cambridge University Press: 1991, pp. 97–111. Quoted by Seth Lerer, "The Courtly Body and Late Medieval Literary Culture," in *The Book and the Body*, 1997, p. 88.
9. Seth Lerer, *ibid.*
10. Lawrence D. Kritzman, *op. cit.*, quoted by Seth Lerer, *ibid*, p. 88.
11. "Why sholde men elles in hir bookes sette / That man shal yelde to his wyf hire dette? / Now wherwith sholde he make his paiement, / If he ne used his sely instrument?" (*The Wife of Bath's Prologue*, 129–31, as well as 198–203, 411, 415, 521–24).
12. "Thou swynes-heed" (*The Reeve's Tale*, 4262), "false harlot," "false traitour" (4268–69), "for goddes banes" (4073), "thou is a fonne! (4089), "A wide fyr / Upon thair bodyes falle!" (4172).
13. "Man sal taa of twa thynges: / Slyk as he fyndes, or taa slyk as he brynges" (4129–30) or "The gretteste clerkes been noght wisest men" (4054).
14. "That as an hors he (the miller) fnorteth in his sleep, / Ne of his tayl bihynde he took no keep" (*The Reeve's Tale*, 4163–64) or "She was as digne as water in a ditch" (3964).
15. *Pier Paolo Pasolini: Trilogia della vita. Le sceneggiature originali de* Il Decameron, I Racconti di Canterbury, Il Fiore delle mille e una notte, 1995, p. 286: "...E chi ci ha voglia di dormire sta notte? Mi venga un colpo se io non riesco a fare la festa a questa ragazza! (E non c'è una legge che dice: "Se uno è stato danneggiato in una cosa si rifarà in un'altra?" Insomma il grano ci è stato rubato, non c'è niente da fare, oggi ci è andate male.) E io voglio un compenso...." In Chaucer's text, this corresponds to *The Reeve's Tale*, 4178–86: "...yon wenche wil I swyve. / Som esement has lawe yshapen us, / For, John, ther is no lawe that says thus: / That gif a man in a point be agreved, / That in another he sal be releved. / ... And syn I sal have neen amendement / Agayn my los, I will have esement."
16. "For he had swonken al the longe nyght" (*The Reeve's Tale*, 4235). "Myn heed is toty of my swynk to-nyght" (*The Reeve's Tale*, 4253). In Middle English, "swynke(n)" means "to work," "to labor." See the definition in the glossary of *The Riverside Chaucer*, 1987, p. 1296. In this particular context, it alludes to the sexual act.
17. "Swyve" means "to copulate with," "to fornicate" (*The Riverside Chaucer*, p. 1296).
18. Interview with Pier Paolo Pasolini in *Jeune cinéma*, reproduced in *Pier Paolo Pasolini*, ed. Paul Willemen, (British Film Institute), 1977, p. 70.
19. Paul Zumthor, *La lettre et la voix. De la "littérature" médiévale*, 1987, p. 232: He speaks of a "familiarité savoureuse contribuant à l'impression de conversation ou confidence."
20. Paul Zumthor, *ibid*, p. 217: A proverb, he writes, "met en lumière les racines que plonge toute diction formulaire dans les traditions d'un univers oral."
21. As already specified, line 4355 is the aphorism ascribed to the Cook at the beginning of the film, when he hits Pasolini/Chaucer's nose.

22. Pieter Bruegel the Elder, *Flemish Proverbs*, 1559. Oil panel (117 × 163 cm). Berlin-Dahlem, Staatliche Museen.
23. *The Cook's Tale*, 4367–69: "Broun as a berye, a propre short felawe, / With lokkes blake, ykembd ful festisly."
24. Vittore Branca, Introduction, p. xxiii of *Il Decameron*, vol. 1.
25. Vittorio Branca, *ibid*, p. xxiv: "…varietà dialettali o regionalistiche, … suggestioni delle diverse culture antiche e moderne. Egli aveva desta la coscienza di una diversificazione sociale in senso linguistico non meno profonda e significativa di quelle geografiche o cronologiche o culturali."
26. Jacques Aumont, *L'œil interminable: cinéma et peinture*, 1989, p. 123: "un effet archaïsant."
27. Larry D. Benson, *The Riverside Chaucer*, introduction, 1987, p. 5.
28. Jean Boccace, *Le Décaméron* (illustré par l'auteur et les peintres de son époque). Translated by Marthe Dozon, Catherine Guimbard, Marc Scialom, reviewed by Christian Bec, edited by Diane de Selliers, Paris: 1999, p. 662.
29. Larry D. Benson, *op. cit.*, p. 5.
30. Vittorio Branca, Introduction to Jean Boccace, *Le Décaméron, op. cit.*, p. 24.
31. Ciardi-Dupré quoted by Vittore Branca, *op. cit.*, p. 27: "méthode narrative continue pour des petits cycles de trois ou quatre épisodes … annonçant la nouvelle tendance qui se développera dans les cycles de fresques et dans les retables d'autel du gothique tardif."
32. Vittore Branca, *ibid*: "le style giottesque tardif des paysages citadins et rustiques."
33. Johan Huizinga, *L'automne du Moyen Age*, 1975, p. 144: "…vers 1400, en effet, la sculpture et la peinture acquièrent les moyens d'expression réaliste nécessaires au traitement de ce sujet (les horreurs de la décomposition et de la mort). … les tombes seront ornées des images hideuses de cadavres nus et pourris, pieds et poings rigides, bouche béante."
34. Pieter Bruegel the Elder, *Dulle Griet*, 1562/1563. Oil panel 117.4 × 162 cm. Anvers, Mayer Van den Bergh Museum. Colette Hellings specifies that the painting illustrates a proverb published in 1550 in *Gemeene Duytsche Spreckwoorden: Adagia oft Proverbia ghenoemt* 21, by P. Warnersen. "Sie solde wel een roof voer die Helle halen / ende coemen ongeschondet weder," which in English means: "She would go and fetch her spoils before Hell / and would come back safe and sound," in *Pieter Bruegel l'Ancien: les tableaux racontent des histoires*, Paris, L'école des loisirs (Archimède): 1994, p. 11.
35. Vittorio, Introduction, *Le Décaméron*, 1999, p. 34: "capturer ce qui n'est pas toujours donné à l'autre de représenter par leur intégration respective."
36. *The Merchant's Tale*, 1582–83: "As whoso tooke a mirour, polisshed bryght, / And sette it in a commune market-place."
37. *The Friar's Tale*, 1458–60: "Ye han a mannes shap as wel as I; / Han ye a figure thanne determinat / In helle, ther ye been in youre estat?"
38. Pasolini, *Sceneggiature*, 1995, p. 372: "Perciò vivo di estorsioni e di ricatti." The modern English DVD version reads as follows: "So I live by extorsion and blackmail."
39. As the theological treatises and medieval works on demonology used to classify them. Two examples can be quoted, *The Speculum Naturale* by Vincent of Beauvais and *The Summa Theologica* by Thomas Aquinas.
40. *The Friar's Tale*, 1482–85: "And somtyme we been Goddes instrumentz / And meenes to doon his comandementz, / Whan that hym list, upon his creatures, / In divers art and in diverse figures."
41. Pier Paolo Pasolini in an interview with André Cormand and Dominique Maillet in *La revue du cinéma*, 267, January 1973, Paris, p. 90: "C'est toujours de la musique populaire que j'ai choisie en Angleterre même, quand j'y suis allé pour tourner le film. J'ai acheté beaucoup de disques et j'ai écouté beaucoup de musique, de chants populaires anglais, écossais … Morricone a simplement adapté cette musique pour certains instruments, il n'a fait qu'une transcription technique pour des instruments particuliers. Dans certains cas seulement, il a composé à partir de thèmes de musique populaire. Le principe a été le même pour le *Decameron*, où toute la musique venait du folklore napolitain."
42. Author's transcription of the English couplet, which does not appear in the filmscript and has no subtitles in the DVD version.
43. Author's transcription.
44. Jacques Aumont, *L'œil interminable. Cinéma et peinture*, 1989, p. 224. He speaks of Jean-Luc Godard as a painter. He writes that the filmmaker: "…refait des toiles célèbres, les explore, les démonte et les monte, les pousse à leur limite et essaie des variantes, les combine entre elles et les simplifie. Bref il les met au travail, et à la question."
45. *Ibid*: "devenir-cinéma de la peinture … et non simplement un vague devenir-mouvement."
46. Pieter Bruegel the Elder, *The Land of Cockaigne*, 1567. Oil panel, 52 × 78. Munich, Alte Pinakothek.
47. Jérôme Bosch, *The Seven Deadly Sins (and the Four Last Things)*. Tabletop, c. 1485–1500. Oil, 120 × 150 cm. Madrid, Museo del Prado.

48. Pier Paolo Pasolini spoke in an interview in *La revue du cinéma*, 267, January 1973, p. 88, about *The Decameron* and *Racconti*: "La conscience métalinguistique est plus forte dans ces deux derniers films que dans mes précédents."

49. Rogier Van der Weyden, *Saint Luke Painting the Virgin*, c. 1435–40. Oil, 140 × 110 cm. Boston, Museum of Fine Arts.

50. Hans Holbein the Younger, *Portrait of Erasmus Writing*, 1523. Oil, 42 × 32 cm. Paris, Musée du Louvre.

51. Quentin Massys, *Erasmus of Rotterdam*, 1517. Rome, Galleria Corsini.

52. We think of a portrait of Saint Jerome in his study by Antonello da Massina. Albrecht Dürer also represented Jerome. We may also read the shot as a hint at various portraits of northern Renaissance authors and artists.

53. Nicole de Mourgues, "Le nom propre, la signature en peinture et au cinéma," *Cinéma et peinture: approches*, 1990, p. 138.

54. François Jost, "Le picto-film," *ibid*, 1990, p. 119. The movie he examines in particular is Godard's *Passion*, made in 1982.

55. Walter Benjamin, quoted by Patrice Rollet in "Le mage et le chirurgien. Walter Benjamin, de la peinture au cinéma," *ibid*, 1990, p. 41.

56. François Albera, "Le retour à la peinture de Vladimir Nilsen: le cinéma comme art graphique," *ibid*, 1990, p. 50.

57. Frank Kessler, "La métaphore picturale: note sur une esthétique du cinéma expressionniste," *ibid*, 1990, p. 86.

58. Bart Van de Leck, "Sur la peinture et l'architecture," *De Stijl*, 1918. Quoted by Patrick de Haas, "Dimensions," *ibid*, p. 60: "...chaque art doit rechercher par ses moyens spécifiques l'expression de son essence plastique et ce n'est que lorsque la 'pureté' aura été atteinte qu'une 'imbrication sera possible dans laquelle se manifestera l'unité des différents arts par la mise en évidence de leurs éléments communs.'"

59. Pietro Montani, "Le seuil infranchissable de la représentation. Du rapport peinture-cinéma chez Eisenstein," *ibid*, 1990, p. 78: "vers cet irreprésentable qui ne peut jamais être atteint, qui est, perpétuellement, à la fois *signalé* et *différé*."

60. João Mario Grilo, *op. cit.*, 1990, p. 97: "produit une réalité plus inconnue, moins structurée de l'événement cinématographique."

61. *Ibid*, p. 98: "le poids discontinu et inoubliable d'images difficilement traduisibles qui persistent au-delà des récits."

62. Eric de Kuyper, "Caméra-stylo, caméra-crayon, caméra-pinceau. Notes sur le visuel et le tactile," *ibid*, 1990, p. 171: "la double affirmation de trop plein et de vide total."

63. Jacques Le Goff, "Les Moyen Age de Michelet" (in *Pour un autre moyen âge. Temps, travail et culture en Occident: dix-huit essais*, 1977), *Un autre moyen âge*, 1999, pp. 23–47.

64. *Ibid*, 1999, p. 44: "...que le médiéviste sache donc enlever les échafaudages de chiffres et retrouver un Moyen Age 'tel qu'en lui-même,' approximatif, massif, craignant d'offenser Dieu en trop comptant...."

65. *Ibid*, 1999, p. 45: "une époque qui sut, par l'imagination, ériger sur ses manques et ses faiblesses une si grande civilisation du rêve. ... Les croisades s'ébranlent à l'appel d'une Jérusalem imaginaire...."

66. Kevin J. Harty, *The Reel Middle Ages: Films About Medieval Europe*, 1999, pp. 152–53: "Those responsible for knights claimed Sir Thomas Malory's 15th-century *Le Morte D'arthur* as their source, but the film's real debt is to the American Western and the *Classics Illustrated* series. The film's significance lies in its being MGM's first Cinemascope production, not in any new light it sheds on the legend of Arthur and the Knights of the Round Table."

67. Giuseppe Sergi, *L'idée du Moyen Age: Entre sens commun et pratique historique*, 1998, translated by C. Paul-Maïer and P. Michon, 2000, p. 7.

68. Jacques Le Goff (*La naissance du Purgatoire*, 1981), *Un autre Moyen Age*, p. 781. He speaks of "cet entre-deux du destin eschatologique de l'homme."

69. Lillian M. Bisson, *Chaucer and the Late Medieval World*, 1999, p. 243.

70. Jacques Le Goff ("L'Occident médiéval et le temps, 1999), *Un autre Moyen Age*, 1999, p. 437: The different times distinguished by medieval men "finissent par déraper, s'envoler, s'écraser vers le temps eschatologique, des 'derniers' temps et du Jugement dernier, débouchant sur la fin du temps lui-même, sur l'éternité."

71. Jacques Le Goff, *Un autre Moyen Age*, p. 46. He quotes Jules Michelet: "Michelet a découvert un Moyen Age des marges, de la périphérie, de l'excentricité ... 'C'est le fait du Moyen Age de mettre toujours en face le très haut et le très bas,' s'est-il écrié ... 'Dieu et Satan, la sorcière et la sainte, l'ogive et la lèpre.'"

72. Jacques Le Goff (*L'imaginaire médiéval*, 1985), *ibid*, 1999, p. 534. He speaks of "un aspect de la promotion du temps du récit ... successif..., segment de temps narratif, historique, linéaire et sécable."

73. *Ibid*, p. 536: Le Goff writes that the historical time of the exemplum tends toward a present of man's conversion that heralds future access to blissful eternity.

74. Carl Lindhall, *Earnest Games: Folkloric Patterns in the Canterbury Tales*. Bloomington

and Indianapolis: Indiana University Press, 1987, p. 533. Quoted by Lillian M. Bisson, *op. cit.*, 1999, pp. 249–50.

75. Pier Paolo Pasolini in an interview with André Cormand and Dominique Maillet in *La revue du cinéma*, 267 (January 1973), p. 84: "Peut-être, dans Boccace, n'y a-t-il pas le problème du sexe alors qu'il existe chez Chaucer qui, à mon sens, préfigure la petite bourgeoisie."

76. Carolyn Dinshaw, "Getting Medieval: Pulp Fiction, Gawain, Foucault," *The Book and the Body*, 1997, pp. 116–55.

77. Carolyn Dinshaw, *op. cit.*, 1997, p. 143. She refers to the French philosopher.

78. An allusion to Foucault's famous work entitled *Surveiller et punir*, Paris: Gallimard, 1975.

79. Jacques Le Goff (*L'imaginaire médiéval*, 1985, 1991), *op. cit.*, 1999, p. 549: "le chaotique l'emporte sur un dessin rationnel."

80. Piero Camporesi in *Le pain sauvage: l'imaginaire de la faim de la Renaissance au 18e siècle*, Paris, 1981, 87. Quoted by Jacques Le Goff, *ibid.*

81. Jacques Le Goff, *ibid*, p. 462: "C'est l'idée d'un paradis terrestre et de l'âge d'or, qui ne sont pas en avant, mais en arrière, et, si l'on cherche à les retrouver dans un *millenium* optique c'est non pas un horizon futur mais comme un retour aux origines."

Chapter 7

1. André Gardies, "La littérature comme banque de données," *Littérature et cinéma. Ecrire l'image.* C.I.E.R.E.C. (travaux xcvii), Université de Saint-Etienne, 1999, p. 104.

2. *Pier Paolo Pasolini*, ed. Paul Willemen (British Film Institute), 1977, p. 72.

3. Millicent Marcus, "The Decameron: Pasolini as a Reader of Boccaccio," *The Italian Quarterly*, 82/83 (Fall 1980/Winter 1981), p. 180.

4. André Bazin, "*Le journal d'un curé de campagne* et la stylistique de Robert Bresson," *Qu'est-ce que le cinéma ?* (1958, 1985), 1994, p. 119.

5. Keith Cohen, *Film and Fiction: The Dynamics of Exchange* (New Haven: Yale University Press, 1979). Quoted by Dudley Andrew in "Adaptation (from *Concepts in Film Theory*, 1984)," *Film Theory and Criticism*, ed. G. Mast, M. Cohen, L. Braudy, 1992, p. 427.

6. André Bazin, "Pour un cinéma impur: défense de l'adaptation," *op. cit.*, 1994, p. 95.

7. Alain Garcia, *L'adaptation du roman au film*, 1990 , p. 202.

8. *Ibid*, p. 255: "Le sujet est repensé, revisité par le cinéaste. Il n'y a pas de traduction, il n'y a pas d'équivalence ou de métamorphose; Il y a allusion au contenu, transcodage des procédés de narration et réincarnation de la même oeuvre ... il y a eu un acte unique en soi du point de vue de la création, une sorte de réincarnation, de seconde naissance du récit initial."

9. George Bluestone, *Novels into Films* (Berkeley: University of California Press, 1957). Quoted by Dudley Andrew, *op. cit.*, 1992, p. 424.

10. Jean Mitry, "Remarks on the Problem of Cinematic Adaptation," *Bulletin of the Midwest Modern Association* 1 (Spring 1971): 1–9. Quoted by Dudley Andrew, *ibid.*

11. Nelson Goodman, *Languages of Art* (Indianapolis: Bobbs-Merill, 1968). Quoted by Dudley Andrew, *ibid*, p. 425.

12. Pasolini quoted by Hervé Joubert-Laurencin, *Pasolini: portrait du poète en cinéaste*, 1995, p.172: "retrouver l'esprit en passant par la lettre, et retomber sur la lettre en développant et se servant pour son propre compte de l'esprit."

13. Dudley Andrew, *op. cit.*, 1992, p. 423: "...the original artwork can be likened to a crystal chandelier whose formal beauty is a product of its intricate but fully artificial arrangement of parts while the cinema would be a crude flashlight interesting not for its own shape or the quality of its light but for what it makes appear in this or that dark corner."

14. Hervé Joubert-Laurencin, *Pier Paolo Pasolini: Ecrits sur la peinture* (coll. "Arts et esthétique"), ed. Le Carré, 1997. Présentation, p. 7.

15. Fabien S. Gérard, "La toile et l'écran," *L'univers esthétique de Pasolini*, 1984, p. 65.

16. Hervé Joubert-Laurencin, *op. cit.*, 1997, p. 7. The phrase is drawn from the dedication in the incipit of *Mamma Roma* to Roberto Longhi. Pasolini writes: "cui sono debitore della mia *fulgurazione figurativa*."

17. Fabien S. Gérard, *op. cit.*, p. 82.

18. Hervé Joubert-Laurencin, *op. cit.*, 1997, p. 32–33. Pasolini, "Recorded diary," May 3–4, 1962, Rome: "Et je ne parviens pas à concevoir des images, des paysages, la composition de figures, en dehors de ma première passion picturale, médiévale, qui n'a d'autre perspective que l'homme. Par conséquent, quand mes images sont en mouvement, elles sont en mouvement un peu comme si la caméra s'approchait d'elles sur un tableau; je conçois toujours le fond d'un tableau comme un décor, et c'est pour cette raison que je l'attaque toujours frontalement ... Cela explique que ma caméra se déplace sur des fonds et des figures ressenties principalement comme immobiles et nettement mises en relief par un traitement en clair obscur."

19. Millicent Marcus, *op. cit.*, 1980–81, p. 179.

20. Danièle Berton, "Images en perspectives," *Littérature et cinéma. Ecrire l'image*, 1999, p. 197: "donne corps illusoire à l'illusion linguistique."

21. Patrick Drevet, "Le papillon et la fleur," *ibid*, 1999, p. 53: "La quête d'image résulte, devant le réel, d'un état intérieur qui dispose à être ouvert à tout ce qui serait susceptible d'éveiller l'intuition d'une image."

22. *Ibid*, p. 65: "A terme, l'espace intérieur, qui est le domaine de l'écriture, rejoint l'espace infini de l'image cinématographique, **mais** techniquement leur processus et leurs effets ne sont pas compatibles."

23. Jean-Claude Séguin, "Un cas de transmutation: *The Shanghai Gesture/ El embrujo de Shanghai*," *Littérature et cinéma. Ecrire l'image*, C.I.E.R.E.C. (travaux xcvii), Université de Saint-Etienne, 1999, p. 182.

24. Nicole Dusi, "De l'adaptation comme traduction: Le mépris de Godard et Il disprezzo de Moravia," *Cinéma et littérature*, dir. F. Vanoye, C.R.I T.M. (ritm 19), Paris X, 1999, p. 90.

25. Cornelius Crowley, "Jane Campion and the Requirements of Adaptation," *The Portrait of a Lady*: Henry James, Jane Campion, 1998, p. 141.

26. Siegfried Kracauer, "Basic Concepts (from *Theory of Film*, 1960)," *Film Theory and Criticism*, (1974, 1992), pp. 9–20.

27. Christian Metz, *Essais sur la signification au cinéma (tome 2)*, (1972) 1986, p.191.

28. Gerald Mast, Marshal Cohen, Leo Braudy, eds., *Film Theory and Criticism*, 1992, p. 580.

29. Erwin Panofsky, "Style and Medium in the Motion Pictures" (1934, 1947), *Film Theory and Criticism*, 1992, p. 224. He resorts to a metaphor that assimilates the making of a film with the building of a cathedral in the Middle Ages. In both cases the completion of the final product presupposes the collaboration of several people.

30. Peter Wollen, "The Auteur Theory" (from *Signs and Meanings in Cinema*, 1969), *ibid*, 1992, pp. 589–605.

31. Geoffrey Nowell-Smith quoted by Peter Wollen, *ibid*, (1974) 1992, p. 591.

32. Millicent Marcus, "*The Decameron*:Pasolini as a Reader of Boccaccio," *The Italian Quarterly* (82–83), Fall 1980/Winter 81, p. 178.

33. Gérard Genette, *Palimpsestes: La littérature au second degré*, 1982, p. 450.

34. *Ibid*, p. 451.

35. *Ibid:* "...des objets plus complexes et plus savoureux ... : une fonction nouvelle se superpose et s'enchevêtre à une structure ancienne, et la dissonance entre ces deux éléments coprésents donne sa saveur à l'ensemble."

36. *Ibid*, p. 452: "A la limite, aucune forme d'hypertextualité ne va sans une part de jeu, consubstantielle à la pratique du remploi de structures existantes: au fond, le **bricolage**, quelle qu'en soit l'urgence, est toujours un **jeu**, en ce sens au moins qu'il traite et utilise un objet d'une manière imprévue, non programmée, et donc "indue"—le vrai jeu comporte toujours une part de perversion. De même, traiter et utiliser un (hypo)texte à des fins extérieures à son programme initial est une façon d'en jouer et de s'en jouer."

37. Michel Stanesco, *Lire le Moyen Age*, 1998, pp. 186–87: "Même les oeuvres d'une indéniable nouveauté (*The Canterbury Tales* en l'occurrence) se réclament d'un texte antérieur, complètement ou partiellement fictif, qui lui sert de *garant*. La métaphore du monde vu comme un livre écrit de la main de dieu (Hugues de Saint-Victor) est tout pour le Moyen Age plus qu'un lieu commun rhétorique; aussi le poète ne se prend-il pas pour un démiurge, il est simplement le copiste d'une *auctoritas*—Dieu, mais aussi le Nature, la Raison, le Savoir, la Vérité, l'Amour. ... L'originalité de la littérature médiévale est de prétendre ne pas être originale."

38. Jean-Bernard Vray, "Patrick Drevet: le cinéma et le corps du monde," *Littérature et cinéma. Ecrire l'image*, 1999, p. 72. These are metaphors that Vray borrows from Antonin Artaud.

39. Julien Gracq, "En lisant, en écrivant" (Œuvres complètes, tome 2, 1995, pp. 719–29), quoted by Jean-Bernard Vray, *ibid*, p. 69.

40. Patrick Drevet, *Petites études sur le désir de voir*, tome 2, 1996, p. 49. Quoted by Jean-Bernard Vray, *ibid*, p. 74.

41. Robert Bresson in *Notes sur le cinématographe*, 1975, p. 136. Quoted by Jean-Bernard Vray, *ibid*, p. 71: "Tirer les choses de l'habitude, les déchloroformer."

42. We could also quote *The Manciple's Tale*, 333: "to restreyne and kep wel thy tonge" or *The Parsons Prologue*, 45: "I wol nat glose" (*The Parsons Prologue*, 45).

43. Or "(Maken) greet chiere" (GP, 747) or "speken of myrthe" (759).

Conclusion

1. Georges Didi-Huberman, *Fra Angelico: dissemblance et figuration* (1990) 1995, p. 446.

2. We are alluding to Michael Camille, *Image on the Edge: The Margins of Medieval Art* (1992). Translated by Béatrice Bonne and Jean-

Claude Bonne. *Images dans les marges*. Paris, Gallimard: 1997, p. 247.

3. Notes by Roger Clarke accompanying the DVD. of Pasolini's *The Canterbury Tales*. British Film Institute Video Publishing. London. 2001.

4. Reference to the title of the book written by Maurizio Viano, *A Certain Realism: Making Use of Pasolini's Film Theory and Practice*, 1993, p. 368

5. Notes by Roger Clarke accompanying the DVD of *Pasolini's Decameron*. British Film Institute Video Publishing. 2001.

Bibliography

Geoffrey Chaucer: The Canterbury Tales

Manuscripts

San Marino, California
Huntington Library El. 26 C. 9.
(The Ellesmere MS).
Ellesmere: *The Ellesmere Manuscript Reproduced in Facsimile* (2 vols, Manchester, 1911), reprinted as *The Ellesmere Manuscript of Chaucer's Canterbury Tales: A Working Facsimile*, Introduction by Ralph Hanna (Cambridge, 1989).
Aberystwyth, National Library of Wales
Peniarth 392 *The Decameron*
(The Hengwrt MS)
Hengwrt: *The Canterbury Tales: A Facsimile and Transcription of the Hengwrt Manuscript*, ed. Paul G. Ruggiers (Variorum I, Norman, Okla., 1979).

Printed Editions

Skeat, Walter W., ed. *The Complete Works of Geoffrey Chaucer*, 6 vols. Oxford: Clarendon Press, 1894.
Manly, John M., and E.M. Rickert, eds. *The Text of the Canterbury Tales*, 8 vols. Chicago: University Chicago Press, 1940.
Robinson, F.N., ed. *The Works of Geoffrey Chaucer*. Boston: Houghton Mifflin; London: Oxford U.P., 1957.
Cawley, A.C., ed. *Chaucer: The Canterbury Tales*. London: Everyman's Library, 1991 (1958) (reprinted with revisions).
Pratt, Robert A., ed. *The Tales of Canterbury, Geoffrey Chaucer*. Boston: Houghton Mifflin, 1974.
Pearsall, Derek, ed. *A Variorum Edition of the Works of Geoffrey Chaucer*. Norman: University of Oklahoma Press, 1984.
Benson, Larry, gen. ed. *The Decameron. The Riverside Chaucer* (3rd ed.). Oxford: O.U.P., 1987.

Modern English Translations

Coghill, Neville, trans. and ed. *Geoffrey Chaucer: The Canterbury Tales*. Harmondsworth, Penguin Classics, 1977 (1951) (verse).
Lumianski, Robert M., trans. and ed. *The Canterbury Tales by Geoffrey Chaucer*. New York, 1948 (prose).
Wright, David, trans. and ed. *Geoffrey Chaucer: The Canterbury Tales. A Verse Translation*, Oxford: O.U.P., 1985.

French Translations

Crépin, André, trans. *Chaucer: Les Contes de Canterbury*. Paris: Gallimard ("Folio Classiques"), 2000.
De Caluwé-Dor, Juliette, trans. *Les Contes de Cantorbéry*. Vol.1, Gand: Story-Scientia, 1977, 147p., and vol.2., Louvain: Peeters, 1986.
De Caluwé-Dor, Juliette, trans. *Les Contes de Cantorbéry*. Paris: Christian Bourgois ("10/18: Bibliothèque médiévale"), 1991 (les principaux contes dans un ordre remanié).

Biographies and Bibliographies

Allen, Mark and John H. Fisher. *The Essential Chaucer: An Annotated Bibliography of Major Modern Studies*. London: Mansell, 1987.
Brewer, Derek. *Chaucer and His World*. London: Methuen, 1978.
Howard, Donald, R. *Chaucer: His Life, His Works, His World*. New York: Dutton, 1987.
Rooney, Anne. *Geoffrey Chaucer: A Guide Through the Critical Maze*. Bristol: Bristol Press, 1989.

Giovanni Boccaccio: Il Decameron

Manuscripts

The work was written between 1349 and 1351. There are three major manuscripts:

Italian Ms 482, B.N.F. ("the Parisian manuscript").
Ms Hamilton 90, Staatsbibliothek, Berlin ("the Berlin manuscript").
Italian Ms 63, B.N.F. (1427).

Printed Editions

Ceva Valla, Elena, a cura di. *Decameròn*, (Bibl. Universale Rizzoli 220–27), 2 vols. Milano, 1950.
Quaglio, A.E., a cura di. *Decameròn*. Milano, 1974.
Branca, Vittore, a cura di. *Giovanni Boccaccio: Decameron*, nuova edizione (3d ed.). Torino: Giulio Einaudi editore ("Einaudi Tascabili Classici"), 1992 (1980).

French Translations

Bourciez, Jean, trans. *Boccace: Le Décaméron*. Paris: Bordas ("Classiques Garnier"), 1988 (1952).
Dozon, Marthe, Catherine Guimbard, Marc Scialom, trans., (revue par Christian BEC). *Boccace: Le Décaméron (illustré par l'auteur et les peintres de son époque)*, (Introduction de Vittore Branca, translated by de l'italien par Frédérique Verrier.) Paris: Ed. Diane de Selliers, 1999

Bibliographies and Biographies

Branca, Vittore. a cura di, "La vita e le opere di Giovanni Boccaccio," in *Giovanni Boccaccio: Decameron*, nuova edizione (3d ed.). Torino: Giulio Einaudi ("Einaudi Tascabili Classici"), 1992 (1980), vol. 1.

Branca, Vittore. *Boccaccio: The Man and His Works*, trans. by R. Mongers and co-trans. and edited by Dennis McAuliffe. New York University Press, 1976.

Pasolini's Films

La Trilogia della vita

Il Decamerone. Italian color film produced by Alberto Grimaldi, 107 min, 1971 (Silver Bear Prize at Berlin Festival, 1971). Distributed by Metro-Goldwyn-Mayer. Co-production PEA Produzioni Europee Associate S.A.S./Rome. Les Productions Artistes Associés/Paris—Artemis Films/Berlin. Video cassette, collection "Cinéma fnac," Italian version with French subtitles, M.G.M./U.A. Home Entertainment, Inc., 1995.

The Decameron (Il Decameron). *The Decameron*. V. *The Decameron*. Italian version with English subtitles, distributed by M.G.M. Distribution Company, 1998, London: BFI films, 2001.

I Racconti di Canterbury. Italian color film produced by Alberto Grimaldi, 107 min, 1972 (Golden Bear Prize at Berlin Festival, 1972). Distributed by Metro-Goldwyn-Mayer. Co-production PEA Produzioni Europee Associate S.A.S./ Rome. Les Productions Artistes Associés/Paris—Artemis Films/Berlin. Video cassette, collection "Cinéma fnac," Italian version with French subtitles, M.G.M./U.A. Home Entertainment, Inc., 1993.

The Canterbury Tales (I Racconti di Canterbury). *The Decameron*. V. *The Decameron*. Italian version with English subtitles, distributed by M.G.M., 1998, London: BFI films, 2001.

Il Fiore delle mille e una notte, Italian color film produced by Alberto Grimaldi, 129 min/148 min, 1974 (Grand Prix Spécial du Jury at the Cannes Festival, 1974). Co-production PEA Produzioni Europee Associate S.A.S./ Rome. Les Productions Artistes Associés /Paris.

Other Films by Pasolini

Accattone, Italian black-and-white film produced by Alfredo Bini, Arco Film (Rome) / Cino Del Luca (Rome): 116 min, 1961.

Mamma Roma, Italian black-and-white film produced by Alfredo Bini, Arco Film (Rome): 105 min/114 min, 1962.

Il Vangelo secondo Matteo, Italian black-and-white film produced by Alfredo Bini, Arco Film (Rome) / Lux Compagnie Cinématographique de France (Paris): 137 min/142 min, 1964.

Uccellacci e uccellini, Italian black-and-white film produced by Alfredo Bini, Arco Film (Rome): 86 min, 1966.

Edipo Re, Italian color film produced by Alfredo Bini, Arco Film (Rome) / la Sofamis (Casablanca): 104 min/110 min, 1966.

Teorema, Italian color film produced by Franco Rossellini and Manolo Bolognini, Aetos Film (Rome): 98 min, 1968.

Porcile, Italian color film produced by Gianni Barcelloni Corte BBG cin. Srl (1st épisode), and Gian Vittorio Baldi / IDI Cinemaatografica (Rome) / I Film dell'Orso / CAPAC Filmédis (Paris) (2nd episode): 98 min, 1968–69.

Medea, Italian color film produced by Franco Rossellini and Marina Cicogna, San Marco SPA (Rome) / Les Films Number One (Paris) / Janus Film und Fernsehen (Frankfort): 110min/118 min, 1969–70.

Salò o le 120 giornate di Sodoma, Italian color film produced by Alberto Grimaldi, PEA (Rome) / Les Productions Artistes Associés (Paris), 116 mn, 1975.

The Canterbury Tales

Critical Studies

BOOKS AND COLLECTIONS OF ESSAYS

Bishop, Ian. *The Narrative Art of* The Canterbury Tales. London: Dent ("Everyman's University Library"), 1988.

Bisson, Lillian M. *Chaucer and the Late Medieval World*. London: Macmillan, 1999.
Boitani, P., and J. Mann, eds. *The Cambridge Chaucer Companion*. Cambridge U.P., 1988 (1986).
Brewer, Derek, ed. *An Introduction to Chaucer*. London: Longman, 1984.
Cooper, Helen. *Oxford Guides to Chaucer: The Canterbury Tales*. Oxford: O.U.P., 1989.
Davenport, W.A. *Chaucer and His English Contemporaries (Prologue and Tale in* The Canterbury Tales*)*. London: Macmillan Press, 1998.
Dinshaw, Carolyn Louise. *Chaucer's Sexual Politics*. University of Wisconsin, 1989.
Ganim, John, M. *Chaucerian Theatricality*. Princeton U.P., 1990.
Howard, Donald, R. *The Idea of* The Canterbury Tales. University of California Press, 1976.
Hussey, Maurice. *Chaucer's World: A Pictorial Companion*. Cambridge University Press, 1967.
Kendrick, Laura. *Chaucerian Play: Comedy and Control in* The Canterbury Tales. Berkeley: University of California Press, 1988.
Koff, Leonard Michael, and Brenda Deen Schildgen, eds. *The* Decameron *and the* Canterbury Tales: *New Essays on an Old Question*. London: Associated University Presses, 2000.
Kolve, V.A. *Chaucer and the Imagery of Narrative: The First Five Canterbury Tales*. London, 1995 (1984).
Mehl, Dieter. *Geoffrey Chaucer: An Introduction to His Narrative Poetry*. Cambridge: C.U.P., 1990 (1986).
Pearsall, Derek. *The Canterbury Tales*. London: Routledge, 1993 (1985).
Rigby, S.H. *Chaucer in Context (Society, Allegory and Gender)*. Manchester U.P. ("Medieval Manchester Studies"), 2000 (1996).
Robertson, *The Decameron*.W., Jr., *A Preface to Chaucer: Studies in Medieval Perspectives*. (3rd ed.) Princeton University Press, 1973 (1962).

Articles

Brewer, Derek. "From the Many to the One: Prologue and Epilogue in Chaucer's *Canterbury Tales*," *Prologues et Epilogues dans la littérature anglaise du moyen âge*, textes réunis et présentés par Leo Carruthers et Adrian Papahagi, publication A.M.A.E.S. (24). Paris: a.m.A.E.S., 2001, pp. 55–72.
Cook, James, W. "'That she was out of alle charitee': Point-Counterpoint in *The Wife of Bath's Prologue* and *Tale*," *The Chaucer Review*, vol. 13. Pennsylvania State University, 1978–79, pp. 51–65.
Cooper, Helen. "Sources and Analogues of Chaucer's *Canterbury Tales*: Reviewing the Work," *Studies in the Age of Chaucer*, vol.19, ed. The New Chaucer Society. Ohio State University, Columbus, 1997, pp. 183–210.
Ganim, John. "Chaucer, Boccaccio, Confession and Subjectivity," *The* Decameron *and the* Canterbury Tales: *New Essays on an Old Question*, eds. Leonard M. Koff and Brenda *The Decameron*. Schildgen. London: Associated University Presses, 2000, pp. 128–47.
Georgianna, Linda. "Anticlericalism in Boccaccio and Chaucer: the Bark and the Bite," *The* Decameron *and the* Canterbury Tales: *New Essays on an Old Question*, eds. Leonard M. Koff and Brenda *The Decameron*. Schildgen London: Associated University Presses, 2000, pp. 148–73.
Hanning, Robert W., "And 'countrefete the speche of every man / He koude, whan he sholde telle a tale': Toward a Lapsarian Poetics for *The Canterbury Tales*," *Studies in the Age of Chaucer*, vol. 20, ed. New Chaucer Society, Columbus: Ohio State University, 1999, pp. 27–58.
Hussey, S.S. "Chaucer: The Minor Poems and the Prose," *The Middle Ages*, ed. W.F. BOLTON, Penguin Books ("The Penguin History of Literature"), vol. 1, (1970) 1993 (3rd ed.), pp. 172–203.
Jacobs, Kathryn. "Rewriting the Marital Contract: Adultery in *The Canterbury Tales*," *The Chaucer Review*, vol. 29, 4. The Pennsylvania State University, 1995, pp. 337–47.
Lindley, Arthur. "Vanysshed Was This Daunce, He Nyste Where: Alisoun's Absence in *The Wife of Bath's Prologue* and *Tale*," *E.L.H.* 59, 1992, pp. 1–21.

Manning, Stephen. "Rhetoric, Game, Morality, and Geoffrey Chaucer," *Studies in the Age of Chaucer* 1, 1979, pp. 105-8.
Payne, Robert O. "Chaucer's Realization of himself as Rhetor," *Medieval Eloquence*, ed. James J. Murphy. University of California Press, 1978.
Reiss, Edmund. "Chaucer and Medieval Irony," *Studies in the Age of Chaucer* 1, 1979, pp. 67-82.
Schildgen, Brenda Deen. "Boethius and Consolation of Literature in Boccaccio's *Decameron* and Chaucer's *Canterbury Tales*," *The* Decameron *and the* Canterbury Tales: *New Essays on an Old Question*, ed. Leonard M. Koff and Brenda *The Decameron*. Schildgen. London: Associated University Presses, 2000, pp. 102-27.
Schuman, Samuel. "The Mechanism in *The Canterbury Tales*," *The Chaucer Review* 20, 1986, pp. 201-06.
Taavitsainen, Irma. "Narrative Patterns of Affect in Four Genres of *The Canterbury Tales*," *The Chaucer Review* , vol. 30, 2, 1995, pp. 191-208.
Taylor, Karla. "Chaucer's Uncommon Voice: Some Contexts for Influence," *The* Decameron *and the* Canterbury Tales: *New Essays on an Old Question*, eds. Leonard Michael Koff and Brenda Deen Schildgen. London: Associated University Presses, 2000, pp. 47-82.
Woods, William F. "Private and Public Space in *The Miller's Tale*," *The Chaucer Review*, vol. 29, 2, Pennsylvania State University, 1994, pp. 166-78.
Woods, William F. "The Logic of Deprivation in *The Reeve's Tale*," *The Chaucer Review*, vol. 30, 2, Pennsylvania State University, 1995, pp. 150-63.

Il Decameron

Critical Studies

BOOKS

Almansi, Guido. *The Writer as Liar: Narrative Technique in* The Decameron. London and Boston: Routledge & Kegan Paul, 1975.
Marino, Lucia. The Decameron's *"Cornice": Allusion, Allegory, and Iconology*. Ravenna: Longo Editore, 1979.
Potter, Joy Hambuechen. *Five Frames for* The Decameron: *Communication and Social Systems in the* Cornice. Princeton University Press, 1982.

ARTICLES

Cottino-Jones, Marga. "The City/Country Conflict in *The Decameron*," *Studi Sul Boccaccio*, vol. 8, dir. Vittore BRANCA, redattore Giorgio Padoan, Firenze: Sansoni Editore, 1974.
Goursonnet, André. "Amour et stratégie narrative dans *Le Décaméron* de Jean Boccace," *Sémiologie de l'amour dans les civilisations méditerranéennes*, publ. Faculté des Lettres et Sciences Humaines de Nice, 29 (1ère série), Paris: Les Belles Lettres, 1985, pp. 69-86.
Mazzotta, Giuseppe. "*The Decameron:* The Marginality of Literature," *University of Toronto Press*, vol. 42, 1, Fall 1972, pp. 64-81.

Il Decameron, I Racconti di Canterbury (and Il Fiore delle Mille e una Notte)

Biographies of Pasolini

Naldini, Nico. *Pier Paolo Pasolini*, trans. by René de Céccaty (*Pasolini, una vita*, G. Einaudi Editore, 1989). Paris: Gallimard, 1991.
Siciliano, Enzo. *Pasolini, une vie*, trans. by Jacques Joly and Emmanuelle Genevois (Milano: Rizzoli, 1978). Paris: Editions de la différence ("Essais"), 1983.

Brief Bibliography of Pasolini

Pasolini, Pier Paolo. *Accattone, Mamma Roma, Ostia* (filmscripts). Milano:Garzanti Editore, 1993.

Pasolini, Pier Paolo. *Trilogia della vita. Le sceneggiature originali de* Il Decameron, I Racconti di Canterbury, Il Fiore delle Mille e una Notte (Prefazione di Gianni Canova, Milano: Garzanti Editore, 1995, 775 p. (Filmscripts).

Pasolini, Pier Paolo. *La Divine Mimesis*, trans. by Danièle Sallenave. Paris: Flammarion, 1980 (1975, actually started in 1963 then reviewed several times and published unfinished) 111 p.

Pasolini, Pier Paolo. *Ecrits corsaires*, trans. by René de Céccatty (*Scritti corsari*, Milano: Garzanti, 1975). Paris: Flammarion ("Champs Contre-champs"), 1976, 281 p.

Pasolini, Pier Paolo. *Ecrits sur le cinéma*, textes écrits entre 1957 et 1974, réunis et présentés par et précédé de "Genèse *Decameron*'un penseur hérétique" de Hervé Joubert-Laurencin. Presses Universitaires de Lyon / Institut Louis Lumière, 1987.

Pasolini, Pier Paolo. *Heretical Empiricism*, trans. L.K. Barnett and Ben Lawton. Bloomington and Indianapolis: Indiana University Press, 1988.

Critical Studies

BOOKS

Ceccatty, René de. *Sur Pier Paolo Pasolini*. Ed. Scorff, 1998.

Greene, Naomi. *Pier Paolo Pasolini: Cinema as Heresy*. New Jersey: Princeton University Press, 1990.

Joubert-Laurencin, Hervé. *Pasolini: portrait du poète en cinéaste*. Paris: Cahiers du Cinéma, 1995.

Macciocchi, Maria Antonietta, dir. *Pier Paolo Pasolini: séminaire*. Paris: Grasset ("Figures"), 1980.

Ricketts, Jill M. *Visualizing Boccaccio: Studies on Illustrations of* The Decameron *from Giotto to Pasolini*. Cambridge U.P., 1997.

Rumble, Patrick, and Bart Testa, ed. *Pier Paolo Pasolini: Contemporary Perspectives*. University of Toronto Press ("Major Italian Authors"), 1994.

Rumble, Patrick. *Allegories of Contamination: Pasolini's* Trilogy of Life. University of Toronto Press, 1996.

Schwartz, Barth David. *Pasolini Requiem*. New York: Pantheon Books, 1992.

Viano, Maurizio. *A Certain Realism: Making Use of Pasolini's Film Theory and Practice*. University of California Press, 1993.

REVIEWS

Bergala, Alain, and Jean Narboni. *Les Cahiers du cinéma: Pasolini cinéaste*. Hors-Série. Paris: Ed. de l'Etoile, 1984.

Estève, Michel, collectif sous la direction de. *Pier Paolo Pasolini I. Le mythe et le sacré*, Etudes cinématographiques 109/111. Paris: Minard ("Lettres Modernes"), 1976.

Estève, Michel. collectif sous la direction de. *Pier Paolo Pasolini II. Un "cinéma de poésie,"* Etudes cinématographiques 112/114. Paris: Minard ("Lettres Modernes"), 1977.

Revue du Cinéma. Paris, 267: Janvier 1973.

Willemen, Paul, ed. *Pier Paolo Pasolini*. London: British Film Institute, 1977.

ARTICLES

"Entretien avec Pier Paolo Pasolini. *Le Decameron, Les Contes de Canterbury, Les Mille et une Nuits,*" propos recueillis par André Cornand and Dominique Maillet, pp. 83–92, in *La Revue du Cinéma*. Paris, 267: Janvier 1973, p. 144.

Amengual, Barthélémy. "*Les Mille et une nuits* ou les nourritures terrestres," *Etudes cinématographiques: Pasolini (2. un "cinéma de poésie")*, 112/114. Paris: éd. Minard, "Lettres Modernes," 1977.

Buci-Glucksmann, Christine. "Pasolini, Gramsci: lecture d'une marginalité," *Pier Paolo Pasolini: séminaire*, dir., Maria Antonietta Macciocchi. Paris: Grasset ("Figures"), 1980, pp. 245–64.
Ceccaty, René de. "Le langage de la réalité," *L'univers esthétique de Pasolini* (album de l'exposition: "L'univers esthétique de Pasolini," chapelle de la Sorbonne, du 27–11 au 31-12-1984). Paris: Persona, 1984, pp. 41–50.
Costa, Antonio. "Pasolini's Semiological Heresy," *Pier Paolo Pasolini*, ed., Paul Willemen. London: British Film Institute, 1977, pp. 32–42.
Dyer, Richard. "Pasolini and Homosexuality," *Pier Paolo Pasolini*, ed. Paul Willemen. London: British Film Institute, 1977, pp. 57–63.
Gerard, Fabien. "La toile et l'écran," *L'univers esthétique de Pasolini* (album de l'exposition: "L'univers esthétique de Pasolini," chapelle de la Sorbonne, du 27–11 au 31-12-1984). Paris: Persona, 1984, pp. 65–88.
Harty, Kevin. "*The Decameron* on Film," *Approaches to Teaching Boccaccio's* Decameron, ed. James H. McGregor. New York: Modern Language Associations, 2000, pp. 164–71.
Lauretis, Teresa de. "Re-reading Pasolini's Essays on Cinema." *The Italian Quarterly* (82 Fall 1980 / 83 Winter 1981), pp. 159–165.
Lawton, Ben. "The Evolving Rejection of Homosexuality, the Sub-proletariat, and the Third World in the Films of Pier Paolo Pasolini," *The Italian Quarterly* (82 Fall 1980 / 83 Winter 1981), pp. 167–173.
Lawton, Ben. "The Storyteller's Art in Pasolini's *Decameron*," *Modern European Filmmakers and the Art of Adaptation*, eds. Andrew S. Horton and John Magretta. New York: Fred Ungar Publishing Company, 1981, pp. 203–221.
Macciocchi, Maria Antonietta. "Quatre hérésies cardinales pour Pasolini," *Pier Paolo Pasolini: séminaire*, dir., Maria Antonietta Macciocchi. Paris: Grasset ("Figures"), 1980, pp. 127–58.
Marcus, Millicent. "*The Decameron*: Pasolini as a Reader of Boccacio." *The Italian Quarterly* (82 Fall 1980 / 83 Winter 1981), pp. 175–180.
Marcus, Millicent. "Screening *The Decameron*," *Studi sul Boccaccio*, vol. 20, Firenze, 1991–92, pp. 345–53.
Nowell-Smith, Geoffrey. "Pasolini's Originality," *Pier Paolo Pasolini*, ed., Paul Willemen. London: British Film Institute, 1977, pp. 4–20.
Rumble, Patrick. "Stylistic Contamination in the *Trilogia della vita*," *Pier Paolo Pasolini: Contemporary Perspectives*, ed., Patrick Rumble and Bart Testa. University of Toronto Press ("Major Italian Authors"), 1994, pp. 210–31.
Semolué, Jean. "Après *Le Décaméron* et *Les Contes de Canterbury*: réflexions sur le récit chez Pasolini," *Etudes cinématographiques: Pasolini (2. un "cinéma de poésie")*, 112/114. Paris: éd. Minard, "Lettres Modernes," 1977, pp. 127–71.
Ward, David. "A Genial Analytic Mind: Film and Cinema in Pasolini's Film Theory," *Pier Paolo Pasolini: Contemporary Perspectives*, ed., Patrick Rumble and Bart Testa. University of Toronto Press ("Major Italian Authors"), 1994, pp. 127–51.
Willemen, Paul, ed., "Pasolini on Film" (extracts of interviews and statements by the filmmaker in the appendix to *Pasolini on Pasolini* by Oswald Stack), *Pier Paolo Pasolini*. London: British Film Institute, 1977, pp. 67–77.

Medieval Context

Literature

BOOKS AND COLLECTIONS OF ARTICLES

Boitani, Piero, ed. *Chaucer and the Italian Trecento*. Cambridge: C.U.P., 1983.
Carruthers, Leo, and Adrian Papahagi, eds. *Prologues et Epilogues dans la littérature anglaise du moyen âge*. A.M.A.E.S. 24. Paris: A.M.A.E.S., 2001.

Carruthers, Leo. *L'anglais médiéval (introduction, textes commentés et traduits)*. Turnhout and Paris: Brepols ("L'atelier du médiéviste 4"), 1997.
Crepin, André, and Hélène Taurinya-Dauby, *Histoire de la littérature anglaise du moyen âge*. Paris: Nathan, 1993.
Ford, Boris, ed., *I: Medieval Literature: The European Inheritance*. (3rd ed.) Penguin Books (Part II of the New Pelican Guide to English Literature), 1995 (1984).
Lewis, C.S. *The Discarded Image: An Introduction to Medieval and Renaissance Literature*. Cambridge: C.U.P., 1988 (1964).
Zumthor, Paul. *Essai de poétique médiévale*. Paris: Seuil ("Poétique"), 1972.
Zumthor, Paul. *La lettre et la voix (De la "littéraure" médiévale)*. Paris: Seuil ("Poétique"), 1987, 347 p.
Zumthor, Paul. *Langue, texte, énigme*. Paris: Seuil ("Poétique"), 1975, 267p.

ARTICLES

Bolton, W.F. "The Conditions of Literary Composition in Medieval England," *The Middle Ages*, ed. W.F. Bolton. (3rd ed.) Penguin Books ("The Penguin History of Literature"), vol. 1, 1993 (1970), pp. 1–27.
Brewer, Derek. "Medieval European Literature," *I: Medieval Literature: The European Inheritance*, ed. Boris Ford. (3rd ed.) Penguin Books (Part II of the New Pelican Guide to English Literature), 1995 (1984), pp. 41–81.
Camille, Michael. "The Book as Flesh and Fetish in Richard de Bury's *Philobiblion*," *The Book and the Body*, ed. Dolores Frese Warwick and Katherine O'Brien O'Keeffe. University of Notre Dame Press, 1997, pp. 34–77.
Dinshaw, Carolyn. "Getting Medieval: *Pulp Fiction*, Gawain, Foucault," *The Book and the Body*, ed. Dolores Frese Warwick and Katherine O' Brien O' Keeffe, University of Notre Dame Press, 1997, pp. 116–63.
Lerer, Seth. "The Courtly Body and Late Medieval Literary Culture," *The Book and the Body*, ed. Dolores Frese Warwick and Katherine O' Brien O' Keeffe. University of Notre Dame Press, 1997, pp. 78–115.
Sheperd, G.T. "Early Middle English Literature," *The Middle Ages*, ed. W.F. Bolton. (3rd ed.) Penguin Books ("The Penguin History of Literature"), vol. 1, 1993 (1970), pp. 81–117.

Culture, Aesthetics, History

BOOKS AND COLLECTIONS OF ARTICLES

Bolton, W.F., ed. *The Middle Ages*. (3rd ed.) Penguin Books ("The Penguin History of Literature"), vol. 1, 1993 (1970).
Bruyne, Edgar de. *Etudes d'esthétique médiévale*. Paris: Albin Michel ("Bibliothèque de l'Evolution de l'Humanité"), 2 vols., 1998 (1946).
Frese, Dolores Warwick, and Katherine O'Brien O'Keeffe, eds. *The Book and the Body*. University of Notre Dame Press, 1997.
Gonthier, Nicole. *Education et cultures dans l'Europe occidentale chrétienne (du XIIe au milieu du Xve siècles)*. Paris: Ellipses ("C.A.P.E.S./Agrégation"), 1998.
Huizinga, Johan. *L'automne du Moyen Age*, 1919, trad. du néerlandais par J. Bastin. Paris: Payot ("Petite Bibliothèque Payot"), 1975.
Pacaut, Marcel. *Les ordres monastiques et religieux au Moyen Age*. Paris: Nathan ("Fac. Histoire"), 1993.
Power, Eileen. *Medieval Women*. Cambridge University Press ("Canto Ed."), 1997 (1975).
Sergi, Giuseppe. *L'idée du moyen âge (Entre sens commun et pratique historique*, 1988), trans. by Corinne Paul-Maïer and Pascal Michon. Paris: Flammarion ("Champs"), 2000.

ARTICLES AND THESES

Carruthers, Leo. *Jacob's Well: Etudes d'un sermonnaire pénitentiel anglais du Xve siècle*, thèse de Doctorat d'Etat. Université de Paris IV-Sorbonne, Juin 1987.

Génicot, Léopold "L'Occident médiéval," *Dictionnaire du Moyen Age: histoire et société*. Paris: Albin Michel ("Encyclopaedia Universalis"), 1997, pp. 644–64.
Holt, J.C. "Medieval Europe," *I: Medieval Literature: The European Inheritance*, ed. Boris Ford. (3rd ed.) Penguin Books (Part II of the New Pelican Guide to English Literature), 1995 (1984), pp. 13–37.

Literary Theory and Aesthetics: Narrative and Discourse

Books

Auerbach, Erich. *Mimesis: la représentation du réel dans la littérature occidentale*, trans. Cornelius Heim. Paris: Gallimard ("Tel"), 1968 (1946).
Barthes, Roland. *Essais critiques*. Paris: Seuil ("Points Essais"), 1964.
Barthes, Roland. *Leçon (inaugurale de la chaire de sémiologie littéraire du Collège de France, prononcée le 7-1-1977)*. Paris: Seuil ("Points Essais"), 1978, p. 46
Barthes, Roland, Léo Bersani, Philippe Hamon, Michel Riffaterre, Ian Watt. *Littérature et réalité*. Paris: Seuil, 1982, 181 p.
Daros, Philippe, Claude Perrus, Nicole Cazauran, Jean-Marie Lasperas. *La nouvelle: Boccace, Marguerite de Navarre, Cervantès*, études recueillies par Jean Bessiere et Philippe DAROS. Paris: H. Champion ("Collection Unichamp"), 1996.
Genette, Gérard. *Nouveau discours du récit*, Paris: Seuil ("Poétique"), 1983, 119 p.
Genette, Gérard. *Palimpsestes (La littérature au second degré)*, Paris: Seuil ("Poétique"), 1982.
Jauss, Hans Robert. *Pour une esthétique de la réception* (préface de Jean Starobinski). 1972–75, trans. by Claude Maillard. Paris: Gallimard ("Tel"), 1978.
Lecercle, François, C. Perrus, N. Cazauran, J-M. Lasperas, *The Decameron*. Souiller, *La nouvelle: stratégie de la fin. Boccace, Cervantès, Marguerite de Navarre*, dir. B. Didier, *The Decameron*. Levy-Bertherat, G. Ponnau. Paris: SEDES (Cahiers de Littérature Générale et Comparée), 1996.
Propp, Vladimir, *Morphologie du conte* (suivi de Meletinski, E. *Les transformations des contes merveilleux*), trans. M. Derrida, T. Todorov, and C. Kahn. Paris: Seuil ("Poétique"), 1970 (1965).
Todorov, Tzvetan, William Empson, Jean Cohen, Geoffrey Hartman, François Rigolo. *Sémantique de la poésie*. Paris: Seuil, 1979.

Articles and Essays

Gaudreault, Romain. "Renouvellement du modèle actantiel," *Poétique 107*. Paris: Seuil, September 1996, pp. 355–68.
Genette, Gérard. "Introduction à l'architexte," *Théorie des genres*. Paris: Points Seuil, 1986, pp. 89–159.
Grall, Catherine. "Incipit de nouvelles, incipit de recueils," *L'Incipit*, La licorne (U.F.R. Langues et Littératures Poitiers, Hors-série Colloques III), 1er trim. 1990, pp. 271–89.
Husson, Didier. "Logique des possibles narratifs," *Poétique 87*. Paris: Seuil, September 1991, pp. 289–313.
Jauss, Hans Robert. "Littérature et théorie des genres," *Théorie des genres*. Paris: Points Seuil, 1986, pp. 37–76.
Sakai, Anne. "Quand les personnages s'emparent du conteur," *Poétique 80*. Paris: Seuil, November 1989, pp. 405–19.
Schaeffer, Jean-Marie. "Du texte au genre: notes sur la problématique générique," *Théorie des genres*. Paris: Points Seuil, 1986, pp. 179–05.
Scholes, Robert. "Les modes de fiction," *Théorie des genres*. Paris: Points Seuil, 1986, pp. 77–88.

Cinema: Practice, Theory, Criticism

Books and Collections of Essays

Aumont, Jacques, Alain Bergala, Michel Marie, and Marc Vernet. *Esthétique du film*. Paris: Nathan ("Fac. Cinéma"), 1994 (1983).
Aumont, Jacques, *L'œil interminable (cinéma et peinture)*. Paris: Librairie Séguier, 1989.
Bazin, André. *Qu'est-ce que le cinéma?* (1958). (2nd éd.) Paris: Les éditions du Cerf (Collection "7 Art" dirigée par Guy Hennebelle), 1994.
Bellour, Raymond, dir. *Cinéma et peinture (Approches)*. Paris: P.U.F. ("Ecritures et arts contemporains"), 1990.
Bondanella, Peter. *Italian Cinema: From Neorealism to the Present*. New York: Frederick Ungar, 1983.
Branigan, Edward. *Narrative Comprehension and Film*. London & New York: Routledge, 1992.
Deleuze, Gilles. *Cinéma: I. Image-mouvement*. Paris: Editions de Minuit ("Critique"), 1983 (1996).
Deleuze, Gilles. *Cinéma: II. Image-temps*. Paris: Editions de Minuit ("Critique"), 1985 (réimpr. 1999).
Garcia, Alain. *L'adaptation du roman au film*. Paris: I.F. Diffusion-Dujarric, 1990.
Gardies, André. *Le récit filmique*. Paris: Hachette Supérieur, 1993.
Harty, Kevin J. *The Reel Middle Ages (Films About Medieval Europe)*. Jefferson, North Carolina & London: McFarland & Company, Inc., Publishers, 1999.
Hutton, Andrew, and Joan Magretta, eds. *Modern European Film Makers and the Art of Adaptation*, New York: Frederick Ungar, 1981.
Louvel, Liliane. *L'Incipit*, eds. La licorne (U.F.R. Langues et Littératures Poitiers, Hors-série Colloques III), 1er trim. 1990.
Mast, Gerald, Marshall Cohen, and Leo Braudy, eds. *Film Theory and Criticism (Introductory Readings)*. (4th ed.) New York and Oxford: O.U.P., 1992.
Metz, Christian. *Essais sur la signification au cinéma, Tome 1*. Paris: Klincksieck, 1994 (1968).
Metz, Christian. *Essais sur la signification au cinéma, Tome 2*. Paris: Klincksieck, 1986 (1972).
Murcia, Claude, and Gilles Menegaldo, dir. *Les contraintes de la cohérence dans le cinéma de fiction*, La licorne (U.F.R. Langues et Littératures Poitiers, 17), 1er trim. 1990.
Murcia, Claude, and Jean Lelaidier, textes réunis par. *Littérature et cinéma*, La licorne (U.F.R. Langues et Littératures Poitiers), 3e trim, 1993.
Schifano, Laurence. *Le cinéma italien de 1945 à nos jours (crise et création)*. Paris: Nathan Université ("Cinéma 128"), 1995.
Serceau, Michel. *L'adaptation cinématographique des textes littéraires (Théories et lectures)*. Liège: Editions du Cefal ("Grand écran, petit écran. Essais"), 1999.
Vanoye, Francis, dir. *Cinéma et littérature*. Centre de Recherches Interdisciplinaires sur les Textes Modernes. Université de Paris X-Nanterre, 1999.
Vanoye, Francis. *Récit écrit, récit filmique. Cinéma et récit I*. Paris: Nathan ("Fac. Cinéma"), 1989.
Vray, Jean-Bernard, sous la responsabilité de. *Littérature et cinéma: Ecrire l'image*. l'Université de Saint-Etienne (Centre Interdisciplinaire d'Etudes et de Recherches sur l'Expression Contemporaine. Travaux XCVII), 1999.

Articles

Andrew, Dudley. "Adaptation (from *Concepts in Film Theory)*" (1984), *Film Theory and Criticism (Introductory Readings)*, ed. Gerald Mast, Marshall Cohen, and Leo Braudy. (4th ed.) New York and Oxford: O.U.P., 1992, pp. 420–28.
Berton, Danièle. "Images en perspectives," *Littérature et cinéma: Ecrire l'image*, sous la responsabilité de Jean-Bernard Vray. l'Université de Saint-Etienne (Centre Interdisciplinaire d'Etudes et de Recherches sur l'Expression Contemporaine. Travaux XCVII), 1999, pp. 195–208.

Carroll, Noël. "The Specificity Thesis (from *Philosophical Problems of Classical Film Theory*)" (1988), *Film Theory and Criticism (Introductory Readings)*, eds. Gerald Mast, Marshall Cohen, and Leo Braudy. (4th ed.) New York and Oxford: O.U.P., 1992, pp. 278–85.

Cavell, Stanley. "From *The World Viewed: Photograph and Screen*" (1971), *Film Theory and Criticism (Introductory Readings)*, ed. Gerald Mast, Marshall Cohen, and Leo Braudy. (4th ed.) New York and Oxford: O.U.P., 1992, pp. 291–301.

Chatman, Seymour. "What Novels Can Do That Films Can't (and Vice Versa)" (1980), *Film Theory and Criticism (Introductory Readings)*, ed. Gerald Mast, Marshall Cohen, and Leo Braudy. (4th ed.) New York and Oxford: O.U.P., 1992, pp. 403–19.

Crowley, Cornelius. "Jane Campion and the Requirements of Adaptation," *The Portrait of a Lady: Henry James, Jane Campion*, dir. Claudine Verley. Paris: Ellipses ("C.A.P.E.S./Agrégation"), 1998, pp. 131–41.

Drevet, Patrick. "Le papillon et la fleur," *Littérature et cinéma: Ecrire l'image*, sous la responsabilité de Jean-Bernard Vray. l'Université de Saint-Etienne (Centre Interdisciplinaire d'Etudes et de Recherches sur l'Expression Contemporaine. Travaux XCVII), 1999, pp. 51–65.

Dusi, Nicole. "De l'adaptation comme traduction: *Le mépris* de Godard et *Il disprezzo* de Moravia," *Cinéma et littérature*, dir. Francis Vanoye, publ. Centre de Recherches Interdisciplinaires sur les Textes Modernes, (ritm 19), Université de Paris X-Nanterre, 1999, pp. 67–96.

Gardies, André. "La littérature comme banque de données," *Littérature et cinéma: Ecrire l'image*, sous la responsabilité de Jean-Bernard Vray. l'Université de Saint-Etienne (Centre Interdisciplinaire d'Etudes et de Recherches sur l'Expression Contemporaine. Travaux XCVII), 1999, pp. 103–11.

Grilo, João Mario. "Le filmique et le pictural: une lecture à partir de Busby Berkeley," *Cinéma et peinture (Approches)*, dir. Raymond, Bellour. Paris: P.U.F. ("Ecritures et arts contemporains"), 1990, pp. 95–108.

Haas, Patrick de. "Dimensions," *Cinéma et peinture (Approches)*, dir. Raymond, Bellour. Paris: P.U.F. ("Ecritures et arts contemporains"), 1990, pp. 59–66.

Jost, François. "Le picto-film," *Cinéma et peinture (Approches)*, dir. Raymond, Bellour. Paris: P.U.F. ("Ecritures et arts contemporains"), 1990, pp. 109–22.

Jost, François. "L'auteur construit," *Littérature et cinéma*, La licorne (U.F.R. Langues et Littératures Poitiers), 3e trim. 1993, pp. 19–24.

Kessler, Frank. "La métaphore picturale: notes sur une esthétique du cinéma expressionniste," *Cinéma et peinture (Approches)*, dir. Raymond, Bellour. Paris: P.U.F. ("Ecritures et arts contemporains"), 1990, pp. 83–94.

Kracauer, Siegfried. "Basic concepts (from *Theory of Film*)" (1960), *Film Theory and Criticism (Introductory Readings)*, ed. Gerald Mast, Marshall Cohen, and Leo Braudy. (4th ed.) New York and Oxford: O.U.P., 1992, pp. 278–85.

Kuyper, Eric de. "Caméra-stylo, caméra-crayon, caméra-pinceau," *Cinéma et peinture (Approches)*, dir. Raymond, Bellour, Paris: P.U.F. ("Ecritures et arts contemporains"), 1990, pp. 163–73.

Metz, Christian. "From *The Imaginary Signifier*" (1975), *Film Theory and Criticism (Introductory Readings)*, ed. Gerald Mast, Marshall Cohen, and Leo Braudy. (4th ed.) New York and Oxford: O.U.P., 1992, pp. 730–47.

Metz, Christian. "Quelques vues sur le visible," *Littérature et cinéma*, La licorne (U.F.R. Langues et Littératures Poitiers), 3e trim. 1993, pp. 11–18.

Montani, Pietro. "Le seuil infranchissable de la représentation. Du rapport peinture-cinéma chez Eisenstein," *Cinéma et peinture (Approches)*, dir. Raymond, Bellour. Paris: P.U.F. ("Ecritures et arts contemporains"), 1990, pp. 67–82.

Mottet, Annie. "Un film de . . . inspiré de: représentation de l'écrivain dans les génériques de films," *Cinéma et littérature*, dir. Francis Vanoye. Centre de Recherches Interdisciplinaires sur les Textes Modernes, (ritm 19). Université de Paris X-Nanterre, 1999, pp. 11–21.

Mourgues, Nicole de. "Le nom propre, la signature en peinture et au cinéma," *Cinéma et peinture (Approches)*, dir. Raymond, Bellour. Paris: P.U.F. ("Ecritures et arts contemporains"), 1990, pp. 137-54.

Mulvey, Laura. "Visual Pleasure and Narrative Cinema" (1975), *Film Theory and Criticism (Introductory Readings)*, ed. Gerald Mast, Marshall Cohen, and Leo Braudy. (4th ed.) New York and Oxford: O.U.P., 1992, pp. 746-57.

Panofsky, Erwin, "Style and Medium in the Motion Pictures" (1934 ; revised 1947), *Film Theory and Criticism (Introductory Readings)*, ed. Gerald Mast, Marshall Cohen and Leo Braudy. (4th ed.) New York and Oxford: O.U.P., 1992, pp. 233-48.

Rollet, Patrice. "Le mage et le chirurgien: notes sur la "relève" de la peinture dans le cinéma selon Walter Benjamin," *Cinéma et peinture (Approches)*, dir. Raymond, Bellour. Paris: P.U.F. ("Ecritures et arts contemporains"), 1990, pp. 31-46.

Sarris, Andrew. "Notes on the *Auteur* Theory," (1962), *Film Theory and Criticism (Introductory Readings)*, ed. Gerald Mast, Marshall Cohen, and Leo Braudy. (4th ed.) New York and Oxford: O.U.P., 1992, pp. 585-88.

Seguin, Jean-Claude. "Un cas de transmutation: *The Shangai Gesture/El embrujo de Shangai*," *Littérature et cinéma: Ecrire l'image*, sous la responsabilité de Jean-Bernard Vray. l'Université de Saint-Etienne (Centre Interdisciplinaire d'Etudes et de Recherches sur l'Expression Contemporaine. Travaux XCVII), 1999, pp. 181-94.

Vanoye, Francis. "Le scénario comme genre, le scénario comme texte," *Littérature et cinéma*, La licorne (U.F.R. Langues et Littératures Poitiers), 3e trim. 1993, pp. 25-30.

Vray, Jean-Bernard. "Patrick Drevet: le cinéma et le corps du monde," *Littérature et cinéma: Ecrire l'image*, sous la responsabilité de Jean-Bernard Vray. l'Université de Saint-Etienne (Centre Interdisciplinaire d'Etudes et de Recherches sur l'Expression Contemporaine. Travaux XCVII), 1999, pp. 67-75.

Wollen, Peter. "The *Auteur* Theory (from *Signs and Meanings in the Cinema*" (1972), *Film Theory and Criticism (Introductory Readings)*, ed. Gerald Mast, Marshall Cohen, and Leo Braudy. (4th ed.) New York and Oxford: O.U.P., 1992, pp. 589-605.

Other References

Eroticism, Sexuality, Scandal

BOOKS

Bataille, Georges. *Œuvres complètes X: L'érotisme (1957), Le procès de Gilles de Rais (1965), Les larmes d'Eros (1961)*. Paris: Gallimard, 1987, 734 p.

Foucault, Michel. *Histoire de la sexualité I. La volonté de savoir*. Paris: Gallimard ("Tel"), 2000 (1976).

Foucault, Michel, *Histoire de la sexualité II. L'usage des plaisirs*. Paris: Gallimard ("Tel"), 1999 (1984).

Foucault, Michel. *Histoire de la sexualité III. Le souci de soi*. Paris: Gallimard ("Tel"), 2000 (1984).

Girard, René. *Je vois Satan tomber comme l'éclair*. Paris: Grasset et Fasquelle, 1999.

Mircea, Eliade. *Le sacré et le profane*. Paris: Gallimard ("Folio: Essais"), 1965.

Rougemont, Denis de. *L'amour en Occident*. Paris: Plon, 1972 (1956).

Articles

Amengual, Barthélémy. "Du cinéma porno comme rédemption de la réalité physique," tiré de *Cinéma d'aujourd'hui* (nouvelle série), 4, hiver 1975, pp. 25-32, in *Du réalisme au cinéma* (Anthologie établie par Suzanne Liandrat-Guigues, Série "cinéma" dirigée par Michel Marie ("Réf."), 1997, p. 1003.

Le Goff, Jacques. "La vie privée de Saint Louis," *L'Histoire. Le sexe et le plaisir en Occident (dossier)*, 180, Septembre 1994, pp. 48-50.

Le Goff, Jacques. "Le refus du plaisir," *Les Collections de l'Histoire. L'amour et la sexualité: Le couple et le péché (dossier)*, Hors-série 5, Juin 1999, pp. 36–41.
L'Histoire. Enquête sur un tabou: les homosexuels en Occident (dossier), 221, Mai 1998, pp. 38–45, 71–75.
L'Histoire. Le sexe et le plaisir en Occident (dossier: "Le sexe et le plaisir au moyen âge"), 180, Septembre 1994, pp. 32–50.
Les Collections de l'Histoire. L'amour et la sexualité (dossier " Le couple et le péché"), Hors-série 5, Juin 1999, pp. 31–113.
Régnier-Bohler, Danièle. "L'amour courtois a-t-il existé?," *L'Histoire. Le sexe et le plaisir en Occident (dossier)*, 180, Septembre 1994, pp. 45–47.
Rossiaud, Jacques. "Comment l'Eglise a mis les sodomites hors la loi," *L'Histoire. Enquête sur un tabou: les homosexuels en Occident (dossier)*, 221, Mai 1998, pp. 38–45.
Rossiaud, Jacques. "La sexualité de l'homme médiéval," *L'Histoire. Le sexe et le plaisir en Occident (dossier)*, 180, Septembre 1994, pp. 32–41.

The Visual Arts

Books

Bosing, Walter. *Jérôme Bosch (environ 1450–1516: entre le ciel et l'enfer)* (London: Thames & Hudson, 1973). Cologne: Benedikt Taschen, 1990.
Camille, Michael. *Le monde gothique*, trans. by Isabelle Leymarie and Claire Rouyer (*Gothic Art, Visions and Revelations of the Medieval World*). Paris: Flammarion ("Tout l'Art Contexte"), 1996.
Camille, Michael. *Images dans les marges: aux limites de l'art médiéval*, trans. by Béatrice et Jean-Claude Bonne (*Image on the Edge: The Margins of Medieval Art*, 1992). Paris: Gallimard, 1997.
Didi-Huberman, Georges. *Fra Angelico: dissemblance et figuration*. Paris: Flammarion ("Champs"), 1990, (1995).
Gibson, Walter S. *Bruegel*. London: Thames & Hudson ("World of Art"), 1993 (1977).
Gibson, Walter S., *Hieronymus Bosch*, London: Thames & Hudson ("World of Art"), 1995 (1973).
Hagen, Rose-Marie, and Rainer, *Pieter Bruegel (l'Ancien vers 1525–1569: paysans, fous et démons)*, trans. by Thérèse Chatelain-Südkamp. Cologne: Benedikt Taschen, 1994.
Harbison, Craig, *La Renaissance dans les pays du Nord*, trad. de l'anglais par Dennis Collins (*The Art of the Northern Renaissance*). Paris: Flammarion ("Tout l'Art Contexte"), 1995, 175 p.
Panofsky, Erwin, *La Renaissance et ses avant-courriers dans l'art d'Occident*, translated by Laure Meyer (*Renaissance and Renascences in Western Art*). (3e éd.) Paris: Flammarion ("Champs-Art") 1993 (1960), 440 p.

Dictionaries and Encyclopedias

Anthologie du cinéma, Tome 10, entrée: "Les années 1970: à la recherche d'un cinéma populaire. Une trilogie visionnaire." Paris: Ed. de l'Avant-scène, 1979, pp. 20–30.
Cuddon, J.A. *The Penguin Dictionary of Literary Terms and Literary Theory*. (Rev. ed.) Harmondsworth: Penguin, 1991 (1977).
Davis, Norman, Douglas Gray, Patricia Ingham, Anne Wallace-Hadrill, eds. *A Chaucer Glossary*. Oxford: Clarendon Press, 1979.
Dictionnaire du Moyen Age: histoire et société. Paris: Albin Michel, Encyclopaedia Universalis, 1997.
Encyclopaedia Universalis. CD-ROM Mac Version 6 (texte intégral de l'édition papier en 28 vols. and nombreux articles tirés des suppléments annuels *Universalia* et *La Science au Présent* publiés par E.U.), 2000, E.U. France s.a.

Kurath, Hans, et al., eds. *The Middle English Dictionary*. Ann Arbor: University of Michigan Press, 1952–.

Rapp, Bernard, and Jean-Claude LAMY, dir. *Dictionnaire des films (10,000 films du monde entier)*. Paris: Larousse, 1991, 855 p.

Robert, Paul, dir. *Le Robert et Signorelli: Dictionnaire français/italien, italien/français*. Paris: Dictionnaires Le Robert (Milano: Signorelli), 1997 (1981).

Index

abjuration (Abiura) 44, 56, 58, 59, 60, 94, 154
Absolon (*Miller's Tale*) 21, 22, 27, 28, 33, 38, 39, 46, 113, 117, 128
Accattone 102, 145
actantialization 98, 99, 116, 122
adaptation 3, 6, 7, 8, 11, 12, 16, 17, 20, 32, 41, 61, 65, 66, 68, 75, 76, 77, 85, 97, 111, 116, 128, 132, 135, 141, 142, 143, 144, 145, 146, 148, 149, 150, 152, 156, 157, 162
adaptor 8, 50, 73, 76, 143, 144
addition 61
adultery 23, 25, 27, 94, 101
Aleyn and John (*Reeve's Tale*) 27, 37, 38, 46, 114, 119
alien (mutant) 10, 157
Alisoun (*Miller's Tale*) 22, 27, 33, 34, 36, 38, 39, 41, 46, 100, 101, 117, 118, 128
Allegory of Hope 82, 83
alteration 9, 13, 18, 60, 66, 150
Amengal, Barthélémy 95
Andreuccio da Perugia (*Decameron, II, 5*) 29, 54, 66, 67, 70, 90, 99, 115, 135
Andrew, Dudley 144, 145
Annunciation 156
Arabian Nights 87, 90
archaicism 124, 125, 128, 151
Arcite (*Knight's Tale*) 119
Aumont, Jacques 53, 128, 129
auteurs (politique des) 148, 149, 151, 154, 161

Aziz(a) (*Il Fiore*) 88, 90

Bakhtin, Mikhail 134, 136
baroque 93, 95
Barthes, Roland 149
Bataille, Georges 41, 42, 43, 44, 137
Battle Between Carnival and Lent 82, 83, 136
Bazin, André 7, 96, 142, 143, 145
Benjamin, Walter 131
Bernanos, Georges 143
Betti, Laura 22
Bisson, Lillian 102, 103, 107, 135, 136, 137
blasphemy 19, 62, 78, 102, 107
blindness 18, 26, 27, 28, 32, 72
Bluestone, George 143
Boccaccio 1, 2, 29, 49, 50, 51, 52, 55, 56, 58, 59, 60, 64, 67, 71, 74, 75, 76, 93, 94, 102, 109, 124, 125, 129, 134, 149, 150, 162
body 7, 10, 11, 13, 15, 18, 20, 22, 30, 31, 33, 34, 35, 36, 37, 38, 40, 41, 42, 43, 44, 55, 56, 58, 60, 61, 63, 65, 80, 81, 86, 87, 88, 89, 90, 91, 93, 95, 96, 109, 110, 113, 115, 117, 125, 129, 135, 136, 153, 160, 161
Boethius 134
borrowing 144, 145
Bosch, Hieronymus 20, 28, 45, 48, 84, 85, 89, 96, 110, 129, 131
Branca, Vittore 123, 124
Bresson, Robert 143, 145, 153
brigata 14, 57, 61, 68, 150

205

Bruegel the Elder 37, 46, 64, 68, 81, 82, 83, 85, 121, 125, 126, 139
Bruegel the Younger 68
Budur (*Il Fiore*) 88
burlesque 17, 34, 39, 45, 48, 109, 110, 113, 117, 123, 135, 152

camera 18, 19, 20, 22, 23, 24, 29, 30, 31, 33, 34, 45, 47, 48, 54, 66, 68, 71, 76, 77, 81, 84, 87, 91, 95, 96, 100, 115, 125, 126, 127, 130, 131, 146, 147, 148, 153
Canon's Yeoman's Tale 38
Canova, Gianni 15, 44, 50, 90, 91
Canterbury Tales 1, 2, 3, 5, 6, 7, 8, 9, 10, 11, 15, 16, 43, 51, 58, 59, 60, 90, 103, 106, 108, 111, 112, 114, 116, 120, 122, 130, 136, 137, 145, 150, 151, 152, 154, 155, 157, 159, 161, 163
Carmine (*Accattone*) 102
Carnival 7, 135, 136, 137, 160
Carruthers, Leo 114
Caterina da Valbona (*Decameron, V, 4*) 65, 72
Ceccatty, René de 86
Celestial Jerusalem 20, 103, 108, 111
Centovelle 1, 2, 6, 10, 49, 60, 124, 129, 142, 150, 155
Chaplin, Charles 18, 25, 30, 45, 48, 99, 120
character 97, 98, 99, 100, 104, 106, 108, 114, 116, 124, 137, 153
Chaucer 1, 2, 7, 9 10, 11, 15, 22, 32, 37, 39, 43, 49, 51, 58, 59, 92, 93, 99, 102, 104, 105, 106, 107, 108, 109, 111, 112, 113, 118, 120, 123, 124, 128, 129, 134, 136, 137, 141, 149, 151, 152, 154, 157, 159, 161, 163
Chauntecleer (*Nun's Priest's Tale*) 122
Children's Games 82
Christianity 23, 25, 28, 33, 36, 42, 43, 58, 59, 61, 69, 102, 103, 107, 108, 112, 134, 135, 137
church 20, 22, 23, 24, 35, 36, 42, 57, 58, 61, 66, 67, 69, 78, 89, 103, 105, 106, 107, 109, 113, 115, 126, 134
Ciappelletto (*Decameron, I, 1*) 47, 50, 54, 61, 62, 63, 64, 70, 77, 78, 81, 83, 84, 102, 107, 110, 115, 129, 150
cinécriture 111
cinema 13, 19, 30, 45, 49, 51, 52, 53, 55, 58, 75, 76, 79, 84, 87, 90, 91, 93, 94, 95, 128, 130, 131, 132, 142, 143, 144, 145, 146, 147, 148, 149, 150, 151, 152, 153, 154, 155, 156, 157, 158, 159, 161, 163
Citti, Franco 18, 62, 96, 102, 127

Clerk's Tale 15, 115
Cohen, Keith 142, 143
comedy 13, 14, 15, 17, 18, 22, 24, 27, 34, 39, 46, 52, 55, 61, 63, 64, 66, 68, 70, 94, 96, 99, 106, 109, 115, 116, 117, 123, 124, 134
commodification 10, 18, 30, 31, 43, 80, 96
conclusion 19, 20, 52, 56, 57, 58, 59, 61, 74, 77, 81, 112, 163
condensation 16, 17, 151
confession 19, 57, 58, 60, 61, 62, 78, 138, 160
contamination 7, 18, 28, 52, 79, 84, 85, 119, 122, 139, 154, 160
contemptus mundi 104
Cook's Prologue and Tale 12, 14, 17, 24, 25, 29, 31, 45, 46, 47, 48, 66, 99, 119, 120, 121, 122, 123, 129, 158, 159
cornice 5, 6, 50, 73, 76, 77, 150
corporeality 6, 30, 80, 91, 115, 147, 160
courtois 20, 21, 33, 39, 40, 53, 55, 119, 122, 123, 128, 133, 134, 150, 152, 162
Cripples (Parable of the Blind) 64

Damyan (*Merchant's Tale*) 21, 22, 23, 27, 28, 46, 67, 101
Davoli, Nino 18, 29, 66, 88, 96, 99, 100
De Consolatione Philosophiae 134
death 19, 20, 24, 26, 40, 41, 43, 45, 46, 62, 63, 70, 71, 72, 78, 81, 82, 83, 88, 90, 91, 96, 100, 101, 102, 115, 125, 129, 136, 153
Il Decameron (book) 1, 2, 5, 6, 29, 31, 50, 51, 56, 57, 58, 60, 61, 63, 65, 66, 71, 73, 74, 77, 90, 100, 101, 102, 116, 123, 124, 145, 146, 150, 152, 156, 157, 162
The Decameron (film) 1, 6, 9, 10, 11, 12, 16, 18, 29, 33, 44, 45, 47, 49, 50, 52, 53, 54, 56, 60, 62, 70, 72, 73, 75, 77, 78, 79, 80, 81, 84, 86, 87, 88, 89, 90, 92, 93, 94, 95, 97, 98, 115, 128, 130, 131, 133, 135, 137, 138, 139, 140, 142, 146, 147, 148, 153, 154, 156, 157, 159, 161, 162
Decameron (I, 1) 61, 62, 63, 69, 70, 77, 129
Decameron (II, 5) 63, 66, 68, 77, 78, 99
Decameron (II, 7) 75
Decameron (III, 1) 63, 66, 67, 77, 107, 129
Decameron (IV, 4) 75
Decameron (IV, 5) 63, 64, 70, 72
Decameron (V, 4) 63, 65, 72
Decameron (VI, 5) 52, 63, 64
Decameron (VII, 2) 65, 66, 77, 101
Decameron (VII, 10) 68, 69, 70, 84
Decameron (IX, 2) 54, 64, 76, 77

Decameron (*IX, 10*) 63, 68, 69, 107
Decameron (*X, 3*) 75
Deleuze, Gilles 147
Deposition 145
desire 20, 21, 24, 27, 28, 34, 35, 37, 40, 43, 67, 72, 74, 79, 87, 88, 93, 118, 119, 122
devil (Satan) 12, 18, 19, 23, 25, 27, 28, 29, 90, 93, 101, 102, 105, 109, 110, 127, 129, 134, 135, 137
dialect 120, 124
Didi-Huberman, Georges 156
dilatation 10, 16, 17, 61, 69, 71, 96, 151, 162
Dinshaw, Carolyn 138
discourse 2, 7, 8, 10, 15, 17, 21, 23, 45, 53, 54, 55, 60, 80, 85, 88, 93, 95, 101, 106, 112, 114, 116, 118, 120, 121, 122, 134, 137, 152, 154, 157, 159, 163
Dominican Order 104
Don Gianni (*Decameron, IX, 10*) 33, 68, 107, 115
Dracula 148
Drevet, Patrick 147
Dulle Griet 125

Eastern world 92
editing 16, 50, 54, 131, 146, 159
Eisenstein 132
ellipsis 16, 61, 63, 84, 162
Emilye (*Knight's Tale*) 119
England (English) 118, 120, 128, 151, 162
epilogue 12, 16, 17, 18, 19, 20, 28, 40, 44, 53, 65, 67, 71, 76, 84, 113, 154, 156, 159
Erasmus of Rotterdam 130
erection 21, 27, 40, 87, 89, 119
eroticism 28, 30, 33, 37, 39, 41, 42, 43, 44, 48, 73, 80, 81, 87, 91, 96, 117, 118, 135, 137
eschatology 20, 40, 45, 103, 110, 133, 134, 135
excretia 19, 34, 37, 41, 66, 67, 70, 136
exoticism 92

fabliau 39, 53, 135, 136
faithfulness 141
farce 13, 14, 17, 22, 44, 45, 48, 53, 75, 96, 99, 160
figuration 7, 82, 84, 129, 132, 145, 146, 156
filmscript 12, 13, 16, 21, 32, 45, 75, 119, 134, 145
Il Fiore delle mille e una notte 1, 7, 56, 81, 86, 87, 88, 89, 90, 91, 92, 93, 95, 102
flatulence 19, 44, 48, 90, 107, 129
Flemish masters 13, 82

Flemish Proverbs 121
Flowers of Saint Francis (Francesco guillare di Dio) 105
Forese da Rabatta (*Decameron, VI, 5*) 52, 63, 64, 68
Foucault, Michel 23, 32, 35, 36, 43, 45, 78, 80, 138, 160
Fra Angelico 156
frame-story 5, 14, 15, 16, 48, 50, 57, 73, 76, 103, 115, 150, 151, 159, 162
France (French) 92, 93, 96, 111, 113, 132, 148
Franciscan Order 104, 105
Franklin's Tale 134
fraticelli 67, 84, 109
free indirect style 86, 126
fresco 50, 53, 62, 64, 68, 73, 76, 79, 84, 125, 133, 146, 153
Friar John (*Summoner's Tale*) 19, 20, 26, 28, 105, 106, 107, 110, 113
Friar's Prologue and Tale 12, 17, 18, 23, 24, 25, 26, 27, 28, 29, 31, 40, 43, 62, 80, 102, 104, 105, 107, 110, 116, 119, 126, 127

Garcia, Alain 143, 144
Gardies, André 97, 98, 141
gay 24, 84, 87
gaze, glance 10, 12, 18, 20, 21, 22, 23, 24, 48, 49, 68, 77, 82, 84, 85, 86, 93, 102, 115, 146, 151, 160, 161
Gemmata (*Decameron, IX, 10*) 33, 68, 107, 115
General Prologue 14, 15, 22, 35, 103, 104, 105, 108, 111, 113, 125, 126, 134, 154, 163
Genette, Gérard 15, 151
Gennari (*Decameron, VI, 5*) 64, 68
Gérard, Fabien 146
Giannello (*Decameron, VII, 2*) 101
Giotto's disciple 9, 44, 50, 51, 52, 63, 64, 67, 68, 69, 77, 79, 80, 83, 84, 85, 109, 110, 125, 130, 131, 133, 146, 150, 152, 161
Girard, René 93
gluttony 19, 26, 40, 62, 105, 108
God 24, 42, 43, 56, 58, 59, 60, 61, 64, 81, 83, 90, 103, 104, 106, 110, 114, 118, 132, 134, 152, 154, 156
Gothic 125, 130
Gower, John 8, 9
Grand Guignol 48, 135
Greimas, Claude 98
grotesque 10, 14, 15, 20, 22, 24, 44, 45, 46, 48, 64, 66, 68, 96, 108, 110, 123, 134, 135, 155, 160

Hagen, Rainer 37

Hagen, Rose 37
Hanning, R.W. 8
Harty, Kevin 94, 95
Hell 18, 19, 20, 26, 28, 29, 44, 45, 62, 84, 90, 96, 105, 106, 110, 125, 127, 129, 131, 136, 156
heresy (heretic) 8, 24, 52, 60, 109, 110, 138, 139, 154, 160
Hollywood 15, 30, 48
homosexuality 18, 23, 24, 26, 31, 32, 33, 40, 80, 81, 84, 85, 87, 109, 110, 119, 138, 160
Host 14, 20, 103, 108, 121, 163
Howard, Donald 104, 105, 106, 108, 111, 112, 113, 122, 123
Huizinga, Johan 103, 104, 106, 109

ideology 2, 7, 8, 60, 73, 74, 78, 85, 90, 95, 113, 136, 138, 149, 150, 154, 155, 160, 162
image 53, 87, 88, 96, 110, 117, 125, 126, 130, 131, 133, 134, 146, 147, 153
imageity 2, 79, 123, 131, 156, 161
imagery 44, 45, 46, 116, 119
imitation 7, 8, 75, 132, 142
Incarnation 134, 156
Innocent III 104
intersection 144
Isabetta (*Decameron*, IX, 2) 64
Italy 43, 47, 48, 51, 55, 60, 64, 74, 75, 90, 91, 94, 113, 123, 124, 141, 145, 151, 162

Jankyn (*Wife of Bath's Tale*) 17, 22, 34, 35, 36, 66, 118
Januarie (*Merchant's Tale*) 17, 21, 23, 27, 28, 30, 31, 45, 72, 114, 116, 118, 126, 128
John the carpenter (*Miller's Tale*) 16, 21, 34, 36, 38, 39, 45, 100, 114, 117, 135
Jost, François 131
Journal d'un curé de campagne 143, 145
jugglery 114, 115

Kessler, Franck 131
knight 21, 28, 39, 162
Knights of the Round Table 133
Knight's Tale 119, 122, 123, 134, 136
Kracauer, Siegfried 148

Land of Cockaigne 83, 129, 138, 139
Last Judgment 44, 51, 70, 79, 83, 84, 105, 110, 131, 134, 136, 156
Le Goff, Jacques 25, 33, 133, 134, 137
Leiris, Michel 44
Lerer, Seth 117

Lisabetta da Messina (*Decameron*, IV, 5) 71, 72
Longhi, Roberto 145
Lorenzo (*Decameron*, IV, 5) 71, 72
lust 14, 19, 21, 22, 25, 31, 32, 33, 35, 36, 37, 39, 62, 66, 69, 115

Madonna 70, 83, 84, 110, 132, 156
Magnani, Anna (*Mamma Roma*) 102
Malyne (*Reeve's Tale*) 37, 38, 47
Mamma Roma 102, 146
Man of Law's Tale 134
Manciple's Tale 111, 112, 121
marriage 17, 21, 23, 24, 28, 35, 36, 44, 68, 114, 116, 126
Masetto (*Decameron*, III, 1) 66, 67, 129
Maupassant, Guy de 143
May (*Merchant's Tale*) 17, 21, 23, 27, 28, 30, 31, 67, 72, 118, 126
Medea 144
Mendicant Order 104, 105, 106, 107, 114
Merchant's Prologue and Tale 12, 17, 21, 23, 27, 28, 43, 67, 72, 101, 116, 119, 121, 126, 128
Metz, Christian 143, 144, 148
Micciché, Lino 91
Michelet, Jules 132, 134
Middle Ages 3, 7, 14, 21, 23, 24, 31, 33, 42, 49, 56, 74, 76, 79, 80, 91, 96, 107, 109, 112, 128, 129, 132, 133, 134, 135, 138, 146, 152, 154, 155, 160, 161
Middle English 124, 128, 151
Miller's Prologue and Tale 12, 14, 16, 21, 27, 33, 34, 36, 37, 38, 39, 41, 45, 46, 100, 113, 114, 116, 117, 119, 121, 122, 125, 128, 129, 135, 152
Millicent, Marcus 142, 146, 150
Mitry, Jean 143
monachism 104, 135
Monk's Tale 104, 159
monstrosity 39, 44, 60, 152, 153
Montani, Pietro 132
Morricone, Ennio 128
Mourgues, Nicole de 131
Munis (*Il Fiore*) 86
Musciatto (*Decameron*, I, 1) 61, 62, 81
music(al) 46, 47, 48, 49, 114, 117, 128

nakedness 7, 24, 27, 30, 31, 32, 34, 37, 38, 41, 43, 65, 70, 72, 86, 90, 93, 94, 119, 125, 160
Naldini, Nico 91
Neapolitanization 8, 47, 51, 52, 54, 62, 63, 64, 65, 75, 100, 105, 115, 120, 124, 128, 137, 150

Index

Netherlandish Proverbs 37
Nicholas (*Miller's Tale*) 17, 21, 22, 27, 33, 36, 39, 46, 100, 114, 117, 118
nightingale (*Decameron, V, 4*) 65, 72
novella 15, 50, 53, 55, 57, 61, 62, 63, 64, 65, 66, 68, 70, 72, 73, 75, 76, 77, 84, 100, 150
Nuns' Priest's Tale 15, 67
Nur-ed-Din (*Il Fiore*) 87

obscenity 30, 37, 40, 41, 42, 44, 48, 80, 89, 92, 93, 94, 95, 109, 132, 158

Pacaut, Marcel 107
painting 20, 24, 45, 48, 50, 52, 53, 62, 63, 77, 79, 82, 83, 84, 85, 86, 110, 125, 128, 129, 130, 131, 139, 145? 146, 150, 153, 156, 160
Palamon (*Knight's Tale*) 119
paradise 44, 102, 133, 156
Pardoner's Prologue and Tale 12, 13, 15, 18, 19, 20, 26, 31, 32, 34, 37, 39, 40, 41, 42, 43, 46, 47, 101, 103, 104, 105, 107, 108, 109, 110, 111, 113, 114, 116, 120, 129, 135, 137
parody (parodical) 14, 19, 21, 22, 25, 29, 33, 78, 107, 112, 114, 123, 134, 135, 136, 152
Parson's Prologue and Tale 5, 15, 20, 59, 103, 107, 108, 112, 113, 116, 120, 122, 134, 154
Partie de campagne 143
Pasolini 1, 2, 6, 7, 8, 9, 10, 11, 12, 13, 15, 16, 20, 23, 29, 30, 37, 39, 41, 42, 43, 47, 49, 50, 51, 53, 55, 58, 59, 60, 62, 64, 67, 71, 72, 75, 77, 78, 79, 82, 86, 89, 92, 93, 95, 102, 107, 110, 115, 116, 120, 123, 124, 128, 130, 131, 132, 134, 135, 137, 138, 140, 141, 142, 144, 145, 146, 147, 149, 150, 151, 152, 156
Pasolini-Chaucer 14, 15, 16, 20, 25, 119, 129, 130, 132, 136, 149, 153, 154, 155, 157, 158, 159, 160, 161, 163
pastiche 45, 48, 52, 53, 66, 80, 82, 83, 84, 89, 95, 109, 110, 129, 156
Pearsall, Derek 9
Peasant Wedding Dance 68
penis 21, 22, 33, 39, 88, 119
Perkyn the Reveler (*Cook's Tale*) 17, 24, 25, 26, 29, 31, 45, 46, 47, 48, 66, 99, 120, 122, 123
Peronella (*Decameron, VII, 2*) 65, 101, 115
Physician's Tale 134
Picasso 10

pictoriality 131, 136, 145, 146, 149, 156, 160
Piers Plowman 137
Pietro da Tresanti (*Decameron, IX, 10*) 68, 107
pilgrim 14, 15, 20, 48, 102, 103, 111, 113, 115, 124, 137, 163
pilgrimage 14, 67, 102, 103, 111, 133, 137
Pluto (*Merchant's Tale*) 17, 30, 72
polyphony 6
Pontormo 145
pornography 7, 58, 60, 86, 89, 91, 92, 94, 95, 96, 158, 160, 161
Portrait of Erasmus Writing 130
Prioress's Tale 104, 134
Proemio (*Il Decameron*) 73, 74
prologue 12, 13, 14, 15, 16, 18, 19, 47, 71, 76, 112, 113
Propp, Vladimir 98
Proserpina (*Merchant's Tale*) 17, 27, 30, 72
prostitute (prostitution) 12, 18, 25, 31, 32, 34, 39, 42, 43, 44, 95, 115, 123, 137
proverb 18, 37, 112, 120, 121, 122, 123
Pulp Fiction 138
Purgatory 44, 69, 70, 72, 103, 133, 134

I Racconti di Canterbury 1, 2, 6, 7, 8, 9, 10, 11, 12, 13, 15, 16, 18, 20, 30, 36, 37, 40, 42, 44, 45, 47, 51, 52, 53, 55, 56, 60, 62, 63, 66, 67, 72, 78, 80, 81, 84, 88, 89, 90, 92, 94, 96, 97, 105, 110, 114, 115, 125, 126, 130, 131, 133, 135, 136, 137, 140, 142, 144, 146, 147, 148, 151, 152, 153, 154, 155, 156, 157, 159, 161, 162, 163
realism 12, 15, 93, 95, 96, 125, 156, 158, 160, 161
redemption 134
Reeve's Prologue and Tale 12, 14, 16, 17, 27, 36, 37, 45, 46, 47, 114, 116, 118, 121, 122, 125, 126, 129, 152
La Règle du jeu 158
(re)invention 148, 152
religion 23, 25, 34, 43, 57, 58, 59, 82, 83, 85, 90, 95, 102, 103, 104, 106, 107, 110, 118, 137
Renoir, Jean 143, 158
Retraction 9, 56, 58, 59, 60, 110, 154, 163
Ricciardo Manardi (*Decameron, V, 4*) 65
Riccotta 145
Ricketts, Jill 23, 54, 82, 83, 92
Roman de la Rose 72
Rossellini, Roberto 96, 105
Rossiaud, Jacques 24, 39
Rufo il Rosso (*Racconti, Pardoner's Tale*) 107, 108

Rumble, Patrick 50, 51, 52, 54, 55, 58, 59, 60, 73, 74, 75, 77, 78

sacrality 96, 127, 135, 150, 157, 158
Saint Anthony 104
Saint Francis of Assisi 77, 105, 135
Saint Luke Painting the Virgin 129
Salò or the 120 Days of Sodome 45, 56, 60, 91
Santa Chiara (Naples) 67, 69, 77, 79, 84, 109, 146
satire 102, 106, 124, 125, 134
scandal 7, 42, 57, 80, 85, 90, 92, 93, 155, 157
scapegoat 93
scatology 20, 26, 30, 37, 38, 39, 40, 45, 92, 110, 135, 160
Sceneggiature (Il Decameron, I racconti di Canterbury, Il Fiore delle mille e una notte) 13, 14, 28, 32, 33, 35, 36
Schism 107
scopophilia 13, 23, 84
Scrovegni Chapel 132
Second Nun's Tale 134
Sémolué, Jean 14
Serceau, Michel 111
Sergi, Giuseppe 133
sermon 15, 19, 26, 40, 61, 69, 78, 108, 113, 114, 116, 120
Seven Deadly Sins 20, 40, 129
sexuality 7, 17, 19, 21, 22, 23, 24, 25, 27, 28, 30, 31, 32, 33, 34, 36, 37, 38, 39, 40, 41, 42, 43, 44, 45, 55, 57, 58, 60, 62, 64, 67, 69, 70, 80, 86, 87, 90, 91, 92, 93, 94, 95, 96, 107, 110, 116, 117, 118, 119, 126, 128, 136, 137, 138, 139, 160, 161
Shipman's Tale 119
sinfullness 9, 12, 15, 19, 23, 30, 31, 32, 33, 40, 42, 43, 59, 60, 62, 69, 70, 83, 103, 107, 108, 109, 110, 120, 133, 137
Sir Gawain and the Green Knight 138
sodomy (sodomite) 23, 24, 31, 32, 33, 39, 40, 78, 81, 102, 109, 110, 126, 137
Southwark (marketplace) 13, 46, 105, 141
Squire's Tale 159
summoner (character in *The Friar's Tale*) 12, 18, 24, 25, 27, 28, 32, 102, 127
Summoner's Prologue and Tale 12, 14, 18, 19, 25, 26, 28, 46, 48, 84, 103, 105, 106, 107, 113, 116, 121, 129, 135, 136
Symkyn (*Reeve's Tale*) 17, 27, 37, 47, 114, 119

tableau vivant 13, 15, 37, 40, 44, 45, 51, 62, 76, 81, 82, 83, 84, 110, 129, 130, 132, 153, 157
Tale of Melibee 134
Tale of Sir Topas 134, 159
television 90, 91, 93, 95
Teseida 134
Theorem 86
Thomas (*Summoner's Tale*) 19, 26, 46, 106, 107
Tingoccio and Meuccio (*Decameron, VII, 10*) 69, 70, 72
translation 3, 8, 143, 145
(trans)mutation 6, 8, 66, 97, 140, 144, 147, 157
transnational 50, 51
transposition 10, 13, 16, 144, 150, 157
trans-semiotization 2, 10, 97, 111, 144
Trilogy of life 1, 3, 7, 10, 11, 44, 52, 53, 58, 60, 80, 81, 87, 89, 90, 92, 93, 94, 95, 109, 149, 154, 156, 158, 161
triptych 67, 77, 79, 90, 93, 109, 157, 162
Triumph of Death 82
Troilus and Criseyde 8, 58, 112
Truffaut, François 148

Uccellacci e uccellini 18
urine 19, 39, 40, 41, 71, 92, 108, 114, 136
usurer 62, 78, 81, 102

vampirization 148
Vangelo secondo Matteo 144
Vanoye, Francis 97, 98
Vasareli 129
Viano, Maurizio 80, 87, 88, 92
visionary 7, 20, 28, 29, 35, 37, 44, 49, 68, 70, 76, 78, 82, 83, 84, 85, 88, 110, 111, 129, 133, 134, 136, 141, 146, 155, 158, 161, 162
visuality 84, 85, 96, 116, 124, 126, 129, 130, 145, 147, 148, 155, 156, 158, 162
visualization 2, 6, 9, 45, 48, 86, 99, 111, 124, 125, 132, 142, 144, 145, 146, 155, 160, 163
voyeurism 12, 13, 20, 24
Vray, Bernard 153

Welles, Orson 145
Wife of Bath's Prologue and Tale 12, 13, 14, 15, 17, 22, 34, 35, 36, 37, 46, 66, 101, 107, 111, 115, 117, 118, 119, 121
Wollen, Peter 148, 149

Zumthor, Paul 112, 114, 115, 120, 121, 122
Zumurrud (*Il Fiore*) 87

www.ingramcontent.com/pod-product-compliance
Lightning Source LLC
Chambersburg PA
CBHW032056300426
44116CB00007B/758